DUKE UNIVERSITY PUBLICATIONS

Howells
& Italy

A sketch of Howells made by his wife
in Venice during the first year of their
marriage, 1863

JAMES L. WOODRESS, Jr.

Howells
& Italy

DUKE UNIVERSITY PRESS

DURHAM, NORTH CAROLINA · 1952

PRINTED IN THE UNITED STATES OF AMERICA
BY THE SEEMAN PRINTERY, INC., DURHAM, NORTH CAROLINA

To
Clarence Gohdes

Preface

THE READER who knows William Dean Howells only through *The Rise of Silas Lapham* will perhaps be astonished at the breadth, depth, and continuity of his cosmopolitan interests. During sixty-eight years of continuous literary activity, from 1852 until his death in 1920 at the age of eighty-three, he maintained broad horizons, international sympathies, and a catholic literary taste. In his maturity he had a ready grasp of German, Spanish, French, Italian, and Russian literatures and read all but the last in the original. His ten visits to Europe between 1861 and 1913 took him to most of the countries of western Europe, and his literary friends and acquaintances included men of various nationalities; but of all the foreign threads which are woven into the texture of his life, the most prominent and persistent is the Italian.

As American consul at Venice during the Civil War, Howells spent four leisurely and formative years gathering impressions and experiences which were to play a vital part in shaping his long and productive literary career. Italy was the laboratory in which he observed life and first began writing of the contemporary scene about him. Under the influence of Venice and the dramatist Goldoni he laid a foundation for the Howells brand of Realism which in turn left its mark on American literature. On the more personal level, the polish which Howells acquired in Italy made possible his leap from Columbus to Boston, from the *Ohio State Journal* to the *Atlantic Monthly;* and the wealth which he amassed from the riches of Italian culture bought him the intellectual companionship of the Cambridge literati. Viewing his career in retrospect, one cannot see how young Howells could have prepared himself better for his subsequent role as a transitional figure between the older Boston literary tradition and the belles-lettres of the twentieth century.

Howells's frequent and extended use of his Italian experience testifies to the importance of Italy in his life. A cascade of novels, travel books, critical essays, reminiscent sketches, poems, translations, and incidental uses of Italian background provides tangible evidence in his writings of this attraction. In addition to writing, he lectured on Italian poetry, participated in the meetings of the Dante Club and of the Dante Society, corresponded with Italian friends and authors, aided Italian writers and lecturers, and returned to Italy three times to renew the inspiration of his years in Venice.

I have given close attention to the Italian phase of Howells's biography because his literary output is inextricably linked with his life. His vast production, including more than one hundred books and many hundreds of periodical contributions, was accomplished only by an extraordinary economy of effort and the elimination of waste motion; hence few of his experiences escaped literary exploitation. The deeper I have gone into his life, the more light I have been able to throw on the correlation between his creative activity and his personal history.

Howells's biographer faces the problem of sifting the facts from the superabundance of published source material. The two-volume collection of letters edited by Mildred Howells is, of course, of inestimable value. The travel books also are useful if the investigator remembers that Howells on occasion altered actual events for dramatic purposes. Although he never finished his autobiography, he wrote voluminously of his own life, and the older he grew the

more he wrote about himself. Sometimes he wrote with
scrupulous accuracy after consulting letters saved by members of his family, but often in his old age his reminiscences
telescoped dates, transposed events, or confused his own
fiction with reality. Of immense help in tracking down
these many sources is the bibliography of Howells's writings
compiled by George Arms and William M. Gibson.

Fortunately there is much available manuscript material
from which the student may work. The Howells Collection
at Harvard contains perhaps three thousand letters, mostly
unpublished, written to Howells by more than five hundred correspondents over a period of nearly sixty-five years.
In addition, there are perhaps two thousand of Howells's
own letters in various libraries throughout the country.
Approximately three-quarters of these are held by Harvard,
but of these some one thousand are restricted.

As a general principle in the preparation of this study, I
have been wary of taking at face value uncorroborated
statements which Howells made about his experiences or
impressions many years after they took place. Where un-
confirmed incidents are suspiciously like Howells's fiction
or first reported in his old age, I have been inclined to reject
their authenticity or at least to view them with a jaundiced
eye. On some occasions, where Howells supplied plausible
details for known biographical facts, even though furnished
at a late date, I have accepted them. No doubt additional
research will admit details now rejected and force the ex-
clusion of facts I have accepted.

I wish to acknowledge my indebtedness to Professor
Clarence Gohdes of Duke University, who first encouraged
me to undertake this study and subsequently directed my
research and read my manuscript; to Professor Napoleone
Orsini of the University of Wisconsin, who gave expert
criticism of my discussion of Italian literature; to Professors
Jay B. Hubbell, Paull F. Baum, William H. Irving, Ernest

W. Nelson, and Lewis Leary, also of Duke University, who
read my manuscript and offered many valuable suggestions;
to Professor George Arms of the University of New Mexico,
with whom I have had much correspondence since beginning this work; and to my wife, whose aid in preparing
copy and compiling bibliography has been indispensable.
Special acknowledgment also is due Miss Frances Lauman
of the Cornell University Library and the late H. W. L.
Dana of Cambridge, Massachusetts, whose specific contributions have been noted elsewhere; to Mr. Almon R. Wright
of the National Archives, Washington, D. C., who went
to considerable effort to supply me with data pertaining to
Howells's official relationship with the State Department;
and to the staffs of the Houghton Library and the Huntington Library, who extended many courtesies when I was
working with their Howells collections. In addition, I wish
to thank the photoreproduction departments of the many
libraries and historical societies which supplied me with
microfilm and photostatic copies of manuscript material and
the several members of the Duke University Library staff
who gave me generous assistance.

For permission to quote or to cite unpublished sources,
location of which is indicated in the notes, I am indebted to
the following owners of manuscript material: for letters and
miscellaneous documents, the Harvard University Library;
for letters, the Columbia University Library, the Yale University Library, the Cornell University Library, the Boston
Public Library, the Henry W. and Albert A. Berg Collection of the New York Public Library, the Ohio State Archaeological and Historical Society, the Historical Society of
Pennsylvania, and the Longfellow Estate.

For financial assistance in making publication of this
study possible, I wish to thank the Graduate School of
Duke University; for a reduced teaching load while the
manuscript was in preparation, I wish to thank President

M. O. Ross, Dr. Paul A. Cundiff, and members of the Faculty Fellowship Committee of Butler University.

No book could be published without the expert assistance of professional editors, and for skilful and sympathetic handling of my manuscript I wish to thank Mr. Ashbel Brice and Mr. Norman Knox of the Duke University Press. Other debts are due to F. C. Marston, Jr., whose dissertation, "The Early Life of William Dean Howells," (Brown University, 1944) was of great help at the start of this study and to E. H. Cady of Syracuse University, whose interest in *Howells and Italy* was an inspiration while I was preparing my book for publication.

My final acknowledgment is to Miss Mildred Howells, who has generously allowed me to reproduce as my frontispiece the sketch of her father which her mother made in Venice in 1863.

J. L. W., Jr.

Indianapolis
February, 1952

NOTES

Unless otherwise indicated, Howells is the author of all works cited. In the Notes and Bibliography the following works by Howells have been represented by these symbols:

AFR—*A Fearful Responsibility and Other Stories.*
LinL—*Life in Letters of William Dean Howells.*
LF&A—*Literary Friends and Acquaintance.*
AFC—*A Foregone Conclusion.*
IJs—*Italian Journeys.*
VL—*Venetian Life;* 1892 ed.
MLP—*My Literary Passions.*
MIP—*Modern Italian Poets.*
C&F—*Criticism and Fiction.*
LofA—*The Lady of the Aroostook.*
IS—*Indian Summer.*
TCs—*Tuscan Cities.*

Where the source is a manuscript letter, the following information (if not indicated clearly in the text) is given: writer and recipient, date, and location of MS. The place and date of publication of books cited may be found in the bibliography.

Contents

FRONTISPIECE ii

PREFACE vii

I. Venice, 1861-65

BY SEA AND LAND TO VENICE 3

EARLY MONTHS IN ITALY 8

FRIENDSHIPS, VISITORS, AND MARRIAGE 17

1863 26

1864: "THE TURNING POINT OF MY LIFE" 34

RETURN TO AMERICA 45

II. Literary Apprentice

VENETIAN LIFE 50

ITALIAN JOURNEYS 66

POETRY 78

ESSAYS AND CRITICAL BEGINNINGS 91

III. Italian Literature

DANTE AND LONGFELLOW 98

MODERN POETRY: ESSAYS, LECTURES, TRANSLATIONS 112

GOLDONI AND REALISM 131

THE ITALIAN NOVEL 147

IV. Italian Life

FICTION: 1868-81 151

ITALY REVISITED 171

INVETERATE ITALOPHILE 186

CONCLUSION 199

BIBLIOGRAPHY 202

INDEX 215

Howells
& Italy

. . . the citizen of every free country loves Italy next to his own land, and feels her prosperous fortune to be the advantage of civilization.

—W. D. Howells, *The Unity of Italy*

I. Venice: 1861-65

BY SEA AND LAND TO VENICE

A COLD, disheartening drizzle was falling in New York on the morning of November 9, 1861, when the one-screw steamship *City of Glasgow* slipped her cable from a Manhattan pier to begin a stormy autumnal voyage to Liverpool. Among the passengers waving good-by to their friends from the slippery deck was a young newspaperman from Columbus, Ohio, William Dean Howells, then twenty-four years of age, who watched with misgivings as the water widened between ship and dock. He had seldom been away from home, but now he was sailing for Europe, as one of Lincoln's political appointees, to be American consul at Venice, four thousand miles from family and friends. It was, moreover, a dismal day in a dismal season of United States history. The early optimism of the North over the swift end of the Civil War already had been dashed by the rout at Bull Run and the unexpected military strength of the South. Another unhappy chapter was soon to unfold in the capture of Mason and Slidell from the British ship *Trent* on the day before Howells sailed.

The chance to go to Europe had come to Howells in return for writing a campaign biography of Lincoln the year before. He had obtained his elementary and secondary education at the compositor's desk of his father's newspapers and as a reporter for several Ohio papers, and his diplomatic appointment was his admission to postgraduate study abroad. Although many of his friends were in the army, he quieted his conscience by assuring himself that there was also a war to be waged on the diplomatic front. He hoped to combine education and government service and to be of more use to his country in the employ of the State Department than in the army. The opening sentence of *A Fearful Responsibility,* written in 1881, probably reflects Howells's attitude of twenty years before: "Every loyal American who went abroad during the first years of our great war felt bound to make himself some excuse for turning his back on his country in the hour of her trouble."[1] In the previous spring he had written Oliver Wendell Holmes, Jr., that he had been offered the rank of private in a company of his Columbus friends but did not know what he would do.[2] The tone of the letter indicates extreme reluctance to join the army, and even before writing it he had made application for a diplomatic appointment.[3] He does not seem to have considered enlisting again, and after reaching Venice he wrote to his sister Victoria that he hoped to stay in Italy his full four years.[4]

The voyage to Europe was uneventful though rough, and for three days Howells endured the agony of seasickness. He wrote to J. J. Piatt that "the ocean trip was not pleasant; it began with sea-sickness and ended in England. It was foggy, cold, and cheerless, and I did not feel that I had got my money back until I reached Germany. . . ."[5] Fourteen days out of New York, after touching Queenstown, Ireland, where Howells caught his first glimpse of Europe, the ship dropped anchor in the Mersey River at

[1] AFR, p. 3.

[2] Undated; MS at Harvard. This letter appears to be a fairly prompt answer to Holmes's announcement of his enlistment in April, 1861.

[3] He first applied in March, 1861, and when immediate action was not taken he renewed his application in June. See a group of seven letters recommending Howells for a diplomatic appointment to Munich among the appointment papers of the State Department in the National Archives, Washington, D. C.

[4] LinL, I, 47.

[5] "Awaiting His Exequatur . . . ," *The Hesperian Tree,* John J. Piatt (ed.), p. 427. This is a letter from Howells to Piatt dated Jan. 27, 1862.

Liverpool. Already he was homesick and silently agreed when a weather-beaten American sea captain, a fellow passenger on the *City of Glasgow,* observed: "Well, gentlemen . . . I'd rather be hung in America than die a natural death in this country."[6]

Taking a noon train for London, Howells passed quickly through Liverpool, and after he left the dirty, foggy port, the sun broke through the clouds. He was enchanted with his first sight of the trim, green English countryside, which seemed familiar from his reading of Tennyson and Dickens, but this pleasure was fleeting. In London he stayed at the Golden Cross Hotel near Trafalgar Square, because David Copperfield had stopped at that hostelry;[7] but he was considerably more enchanted by the inn's venerable appearance than Dickens, who had called it "a moldy sort of establishment in a close neighborhood." The British capital at first proved a fascinating place—from the parks which he visited the day after arriving to the rush-hour traffic jam which he viewed from the top of an omnibus in the Strand just before leaving. Nevertheless, as he rode outside the crowded bus, peering into the foggy evening, the nostalgic young American found himself telling the "conductor" of the wonders of High Street in Columbus.[8]

After the initial excitement of London wore off, pride in America and incipient Anglophobia dominated his emotions. He was annoyed at the lack of patriotism of an American he overheard telling of the corruption in American politics,[9] and he found English public opinion hostile to the United States. His anti-British attitude deepened

[6] "Letters from Europe," Ashtabula *Sentinel,* Jan. 22, 1862, p. 1. First printed in the *Ohio State Journal,* Jan. 9, 1862, p. 2.

[7] "Overland to Venice," *Harper's Monthly,* CXXXVII (Nov., 1918), 840.

[8] "Letters from Europe," Ashtabula *Sentinel,* Feb. 5, 1862, p. 1. First printed in the *Ohio State Journal,* Jan. 30, 1862, p. 1.

[9] "Overland to Venice," p. 840.

when he learned of the *Trent* affair, which exploded on the diplomatic horizon a few hours after he left England, and he wrote to the *Ohio State Journal* during the dark days of December, 1861, when war with England was a real possibility, that he had discovered in London that not only the press was in sympathy with the South but the public as well.[10] He told his sister in January: "I felt so bitter towards the English that I was glad to get out of England, where I was constantly insulted by the most brutal exultation of our national misfortunes."[11]

Leaving London on November 27 after a three-day stay in England, Howells took an evening train to Folkstone and the midnight channel packet for France. He landed before dawn at Boulogne and immediately continued on to the French capital. In Paris he rode about "deliciously lost and incapable of the slightest French"[12] during a day's experience which cost him only eleven francs. He left the city by a way different from that originally planned and traveled overland through Germany instead of via train to Marseilles and steamer to Genoa. The fear of seasickness and a fondness for the German language and literature apparently dictated the change,[13] and he entrained for Stuttgart on November 28, following the only all-rail route to Italy.

Howells had planned to push on from Stuttgart the next day, but the American consul, a former resident of Cincinnati, urged him to tarry. He remained three days in that little German capital—long enough to meet the old king

---

[10] "Letters from Europe," Ashtabula *Sentinel,* Feb. 12, 1862, p. 1. First printed in the *Ohio State Journal,* Jan. 31, 1862, p. 1.

[11] LinL, I, 47.

[12] "Awaiting His Exequatur . . . ," p. 427.

[13] Howells wrote his Columbus friend Dr. S. M. Smith on Oct. 3, 1861 (MS at Ohio Hist. Soc.), that he hoped to sail from New York to Bremen in order to see the German cities and travel through a country where he could speak the language.

of Württemberg on the street and to squeeze in a side trip to the village of Marbach, where Schiller was born. The stopover also provided an introductory lesson in his European education, for his aesthetic sense was lacerated by the "sensual" nudes in the Württemberg art galleries. When he wrote his impressions of Stuttgart a few months later,[14] he exposed his youthful Midwestern prejudices, owning that German art gave him a bad opinion of the sort of civilization which produced it. "For my own part," he brashly asserted, "I like not over-ripe sausages and far-smelling cheese, nor their principle as developed in morals and aesthetics."[15] Not only German art but also the class structure of German society repelled him, and the young republican was glad to continue his trip towards Italy.

Howells stopped only overnight in Munich, the city he had originally requested in his consular application, before going on to Vienna, where another congenial American consular representative, an Illinois German, went about the city with him.[16] During his two days there, he gave all his attention to seeing Vienna, a city which in 1861 was still capital of the Hapsburg Empire and home of Johann Strauss. Winter had set in, however, and Howells was glad

---

[14] "A Little German Capital," *Nation*, II (Jan. 4, 1866), 11-13. It is not clear just when this article was written, but it was rejected by the *Atlantic* in a letter from H. M. Ticknor to Howells dated Oct. 6, 1863 (MS at Harvard), apologizing for the delay in reporting on the contribution. It seems likely that this article is the one referred to in a letter from Howells to his father on Aug. 22, 1862 (LinL, I, 60).

[15] *Ibid.*, p. 13.

[16] In "Overland to Venice," p. 843, Howells declared that the incident which he used as the plot for his story "At the Sign of the Savage" (*Atlantic*, XL, July, 1877, 36-48) happened to him when he passed through Vienna in December, 1861. There is no reference to such an incident either in the letter to his family written just after arriving in Venice (LinL, I, 41-44) or the letter to Piatt ("Awaiting His Exequatur . . ."). This incident, as reported in 1918, sounds suspiciously like the short story, so that one might conclude after studying the two items that Howells refreshed his memory of his trip to Venice from the fiction which he had written in 1877.

to hurry on to Venice. When the train pulled out of the Vienna station, half an inch of frost coated the window-panes; then for twenty-four hours the cars toiled over the frigid mountains towards Italy. By Friday night Howells was traveling across the plains of Friuli, where mild Adriatic breezes dispelled the Austrian cold. Changing trains at Trieste, he continued on to Venice, arriving at five o'clock Saturday morning, December 7.

From the station to St. Mark's Square he glided by gondola "up the Grand Canal, with its sad old palaces on either side, and through an hundred secret, winding streets of water, to the door of the Hotel Danieli."[17] It was an eerie, silent city, and except for the rhythmic dipping of the gondolier's oar there were few sounds to break the early morning quiet. He was awed by the solitude of the spectacle and not a little apprehensive as his boatman turned into a small and dimly lighted canal leading to the water-door of the hotel.

Thus he began the experience that was to give him, in his own words, "four years of almost uninterrupted leisure for study and literary work" and "a wider outlook upon the world."[18] Five hours after registering at the hotel, he started exploring the city that was to be his home for four years, the scene of his early married life, and the birthplace of his first child.

EARLY MONTHS IN ITALY

When Howells reached Europe he discovered that his United States citizenship and diplomatic status were not the enviable distinctions he had imagined. Europeans too often regarded Americans as semibarbarians, and they generally held consular officials to be scoundrels. In the ab-

[17] LinL, I, 43.
[18] H. H. Boyesen, "Real Conversations—A Dialogue between William Dean Howells and Hjalmar Hjorth Boyesen," *McClure's*, I (June, 1893), 6.

sence, then, of already existing American prestige Howells had to draw on his own integrity and genius for making friends to create a reservoir of good will abroad. His success in overcoming the obstacles and his distinction in serving his country made his appointment one of the happy accidents of the spoils system.[1]

The reputation for social ineptitude which traveling Americans had acquired in Europe was hardly more than a minor annoyance, even though the wits among the privileged orders had seized on the uncouth American as a stock figure for jokes. Howells laughed away the unflattering attitude typified in a story he enjoyed telling of the American who was invited to a court ball in a little German capital. This homespun Yankee appeared at the function in the sartorial splendor of coat and dickey and during the fervor of the dance pulled off his coat—much to the consternation of German officialdom. Thereafter, reported Howells, it was stipulated on cards of invitation to visiting Americans that shirts were to be worn.[2]

Howells's greatest embarrassment in assuming his new duties stemmed from the political huckstering of public office which made incompetence, if not downright turpitude, seem a distinguishing characteristic of most American diplomats prior to 1861. "For the twenty years of my first knowledge of European matters our representation abroad was a disgrace to America," wrote William J. Stillman, painter and art critic who had been Howells's fellow-consul at Rome; and to document his censure he recalled a diplomat at Naples who had been notoriously dissipated even in

[1] T. S. Perry wrote (Century, XXIII, Mar., 1882, 680): "This appointment was one of the sort which, doubtless, the stern civil service reformer will have to condemn, in public, at least; but in private he will only congratulate himself upon it, as an Englishman might have done for the unsound system which found a place in Parliament for men like Pitt and Burke."

[2] See letter from Howells to Richard Hildreth dated Dec. 22, 1861; MS at Harvard.

that city of easy standards, a minister to Germany who had been found drunk in the streets, and a certain chargé d'affaires in Constantinople who had hoisted the American flag over his favorite brothel.[3] For his own part, Howells soon discovered that his credit in Venice had been destroyed by a rascally predecessor who had gone home leaving his bills unpaid.

The greatest obstacle blocking good consular representation before the Civil War was the uncertainty of remuneration, but in 1861 Congress appropriated funds to pay annual stipends of fifteen hundred dollars to consuls in specified cities, making it possible for men of Howells's caliber to go abroad. Previously the only profitable posts had been in busy ports where fees were plentiful from American shipping. After the war, however, the salary statute was allowed to lapse, and Howells wrote critically in 1865 that a consulship was neither "a career for any man ambitious of distinction and usefulness," nor "a support for those willing to go into exile for a livelihood."[4]

Despite Howells's later concern for the appointment of competent, full-time consular officials, his own duties during his years in Venice were slight. In his entire first year only four American ships called at Venice, and three left in ballast because of the fear of Confederate privateers.[5] As far as he could determine, there was not one dollar of American capital invested in Venice. The city, moreover, was languishing in the last years of the Austrian occupation, and in his first report to the State Department Howells wrote that this situation was slowly strangling trade.[6] The

[3] W. J. Stillman, *The Autobiography of a Journalist*, I, 370-371.

[4] "Our Consuls in China and Elsewhere," *Nation*, I (Nov. 2, 1865), 552.

[5] *Letter of the Secretary of State . . . for the Year Ended September 30, 1863*, pp. 360-362. Although dated Oct. 5, 1863, this report is for the calendar year 1862.

[6] *Letter of the Secretary of State . . . for the Year Ended September 30, 1862*, pp. 376-380. The data in the remainder of this paragraph are from this source.

commerce of the new Kingdom of Italy had been diverted
to Ancona and Ravenna because of Austrian duties, and
Venice was a port of little importance to Austria, whose
main outlet to the sea was through Trieste. The decline
of the city as a port, however, was only one of the troubles
besetting the unhappy community, for in addition the
grape and silkworm culture in the Province of Venetia had
suffered from a blight of the vines and mulberry trees for
several successive years. Of the 113,127 natives of Venice,
nearly one-third were classed as poor, and an even 10 per
cent were on relief.

As a result of the commercial decline of Venice and of
the Civil War Howells had ample time for study, writing,
traveling, and entertaining American visitors. Among his
light duties he later remembered dealings with Richard
Hildreth, the historian-consul at Trieste, over an an "American" sailor who had jumped ship but later confessed to
being British,[7] and he recalled that on another occasion he
had labored to free an American citizen's property from
the Venetian courts.[8] One of Howells's most frequent duties
was to say "no" to Continental soldiers who wished to offer
their services to the United States Government. The experiences of Ferris, the American consul in *A Foregone Conclusion,* must have been based on Howells's own dealings with
such volunteers:

Hardly a week passed but a saber came clanking up his dim
staircase with a Herr Graf or a Herr Baron attached, who ap-

[7] LF&A, pp. 98-99. The recollection is corroborated by a letter Howells
wrote to F. W. Seward, assistant secretary of state, on June 30, 1862 (MS in
National Archives) in which he reports receiving from the Venice police department a rebate of $1.37, this sum representing an overcharge for transporting
one John Dayly to Trieste. Note also the fictional treatment of this or a
similar incident in the story of the wanderings of Lemuel Barker's roommate,
recounted at a Boston lodging house for homeless men (*The Minister's Charge,*
p. 108).
[8] *Ibid.,* p. 95; *s. v.* De Bauernfeind.

peared in the spotless panoply of his Austrian captaincy or lieutenancy, to accept from the consul a brigadier-generalship in the Federal armies, on condition that the consul would pay his expenses to Washington, or at least assure him of an exalted post and reimbursement of all outlays from President Lincoln as soon as he arrived.[9]

When Howells was not refusing such soldiers of fortune, he was likely to be rejecting impossible schemes originating in America. Once he received a neatly lithographed circular, signed by a well-known promoter, asking him to cooperate in "the introduction of horse-railroads in Venice."[10] The idea was so absurd that he hardly thought it necessary to reply, but scarcely less fantastic was the proposal of his own father to export to Venice oars made in Jefferson, Ohio. In this case he took the trouble to explain that the cheapness of oars in Venice and their difference in construction from the Ohio product made the plan unfeasible.[11]

Howells spent nearly three months waiting for the Austrian Government to send his exequatur giving him authority to act as consul, and all the while his predecessor, J. J. Sprenger, held the job and drew the salary. The outgoing consul, however, was an obliging fellow, and Howells wrote his family that "this ex-consul has acted in the kindest manner. . . . But for his protection, I should already have been grievously cheated in one hundred ways."[12] While awaiting credentials, Howells lived in the same house with Sprenger in the street known as the Frezzeria behind St. Mark's Square. He remained there until a few

    [9] AFC, p. 7. J. L. Motley had the same experience in Vienna, and he wrote soon after taking up his duties as Minister to Austria that "I could have furnished half-a-dozen regiments since I have been here . . ." (George W. Curtis, ed., *Correspondence of John Lothrop Motley*, II, 56: letter to daughter Mary dated Jan. 27, 1862).
    [10] "By Horse-car to Boston," *Suburban Sketches*, p. 91.
    [11] LinL, I, 68.
    [12] *Ibid.*, p. 44.

days after taking official charge of the consulate on February 24.[13]

The first days in Venice were packed with excitement for the young man who still looked at life through the rose-tinted glasses of the romantic. The city was as beautiful as he had dreamed it would be, and he was glad to be there despite homesickness and loneliness. In sending photographs to his sister, he wrote that they were but "a faint illustration of the glorious things I see in Venice every day. As for describing the place . . . the task is simply hopeless; it's as much as anyone can do to enjoy them."[14] Even the swindles of the gondoliers, the extortions of his bootblack, and the incessant demands of the beggars for soldi failed to seem less than charming.

Meanwhile the study of Italian went ahead rapidly. On his arrival in Venice Howells wrote that he could not have mustered enough Italian to call for help if his gondolier had tried to dispose of him in a dark stretch of a lonely canal. By the middle of January, however, he had learned enough to talk to the gondoliers, and later in the same month he wrote to Piatt that while he was "incapable of expressing anything but the simplest sentiments of the phrase-books," he was improving fast. He added that "if I get through the first six months, I'll know enough Italian to begin to talk fluently, and then I shall do splendidly."[15] There is no doubt that Howells rapidly became fluent in Italian, for by the next year he was reporting meetings of the Venetian Institute of Sciences, Letters, and Arts,[16] and

[13] Howells's letter to F. W. Seward dated Feb. 24, 1862 (MS in National Archives), reports the arrival of his exequatur and incloses a receipt for the consular property.

[14] LinL, I, 46-47.

[15] "Awaiting His Exequatur . . . ," p. 428. When he had been in Venice nearly eleven months, Howells wrote S. P. Chase: "Of myself I have little to tell you. I've learned Italian, and I've written some things" (Nov. 1, 1862; MS at Penn. Hist. Soc.).

[16] "Letters from Venice," Boston *Advertiser*, Mar. 27, 1863, p. 2.

before leaving Italy he was mistaken for an Italian by reason of his exceptional linguistic proficiency.[17]

Early in his Italian sojourn he made the acquaintance of G. Antonio Tortorini, the Italian friend "Pastorelli" in the sketch called "An Old Venetian Friend."[18] Tortorini had studied English with the outgoing consul, and he soon became Howells's inseparable companion. The ruddy-faced Italian was, at the age of fifty-six, a retired apothecary and mayor of a little town near Padua named Monselice, where he had a country estate and lived in the summer. He and Howells tramped about the city together during the spring of 1862, the Italian practicing his English and the young American, not yet proficient in Italian, glad of the company on his rambles.

By late February the friendship had progressed so far that Tortorini assumed the dual role of doctor and nurse when the consul contracted a serious illness after an all-day tramp around the city one damp Saturday.[19] The retired pharmacist found him in bed with a fever and on no account would permit him to call an Italian doctor. As a skilled apothecary, he prescribed remedies and went to a near-by shop himself for the medicine. Howells wrote to his mother, when he was convalescing, that one morning, after giving him his medicine, "the dear old fellow stooped down and kissed me. . . ."[20]

During his ten-day illness Howells's spirits drooped under the depressive influence of homesickness and financial difficulties. After he had waited almost three months for his exequatur, the authority to act finally came from Vienna, but when he counted his money there was not enough to

[17] IJs, p. 163.

[18] *Harper's Monthly*, CXXXVIII (Apr., 1919), 634-640. Unless otherwise indicated, the material pertaining to Tortorini in this and following paragraphs is from this article.

[19] See LinL, I, 52-53.   [20] *Ibid.*

last until he drew his first quarter's salary. At this point Tortorini came to his assistance. As Howells remembered the transaction fifty-seven years afterwards, the Italian went to his strong box, which he kept at the home of a countess friend, and extracted twelve gold sovereigns, a coin which had been obsolete for many years. The only condition he attached to the loan was that Howells should repay the debt in gold sovereigns.

Early in March, after Tortorini had gone house-hunting with him, Howells moved to quarters more in keeping with the dignity of the United States Consulate than those occupied by his predecessor. He found suitable rooms on the Campo San Bartolomeo near the east end of the Rialto Bridge, through which passed the Merceria, the main thoroughfare between the bridge and St. Mark's Square. The Italian then invited his young friend to visit him in the country in June, and Howells wrote his family that he intended to go, promising to write about the experience for his father's newspaper;[21] but the visit was postponed until 1865, when he and his wife visited Monselice together.

Now, in full possession of the consular office and equipped with more pretentious living quarters, Howells was ready to begin his Italian journeying. In December he had invited Richard Hildreth to come to Venice and in return had been asked to visit Trieste. He knew his fellow consul as the author of the antislavery novel *Archy Moore,* which he had seen in French and Italian translations on the bookstalls in Venice and remembered as a "powerful piece of realism."[22] No doubt he was as eager to talk to an author again as he was to see more of Italy. In mid-March he left for Trieste on the dingy night steamer which smelled of fish and was so small that he worried over being seasick again. But the Adriatic was like glass, and

[21] *Ibid.,* p. 54.   [22] LF&A, p. 97.

he stood on deck watching the skyline of Venice recede
until the last landmark, the slender campanile in St. Mark's
Square, sank below the horizon.

"The city looks more like an American town than any I
have yet seen in Europe," he wrote of his first sight of
Trieste.[23] He had found himself, upon debarking, in a
bustle of activity which contrasted sharply with the quietness
of Venice. Eagerly he looked about at the broad streets,
new houses, and busy, polyglot population as he rode in a
hack from the dock to Hildreth's villa on the outskirts of the
city. Howells remembered the historian as a "tall thin man,
absent, silent: already a phantom of himself, but with a
scholarly serenity and dignity."[24] On the same occasion he
recalled that Hildreth, who was always reading, could be
aroused only with difficulty from his books. On the last
night of Howells's brief visit Hildreth was so engrossed in
Paradise Lost that nothing could keep him from finishing
it, not even his guest's nervous fear of missing the midnight
boat.

Howells followed the usual sight-seeing routine in
Trieste, visiting the ruins of the Temple of Jupiter, the Cathedral, and Archduke Maximilian's castle at near-by Miramare. One morning he climbed the hills behind Trieste
where he could see the city and harbor spread out below
him. He watched peasants trudging to market beside their
produce carts and women bent over their washing by a
hillside brook. Spring was in the air, the peach and almond
trees were in bloom, and violets and cowslips lined the foot-
paths and dotted the slopes of the barren, treeless hills. All
these sights and smells he drew in with the avidity of youth
and saved for subsequent literary capital.

[23] "Letter from Europe," Ashtabula *Sentinel*, May 14, 1862, p. 1. This letter
is dated Apr. 13, 1862.
[24] LF&A, p. 98.

FRIENDSHIPS, VISITORS, AND MARRIAGE

After four months in Venice Howells found that the novelty of foreign residence palled in the face of financial embarrassment and unfamiliar Italian social mores. In March he complained that his expenses amounted to two florins (one dollar) a day despite the utmost economy, and he recalled nostalgically how well he had eaten for three dollars and a half a week in Columbus, Ohio.[1] By April, however, when he began drawing his consular salary, his criticism of Italy shifted from the high cost of living to the paucity of social life. He hungered now for the society and the gay round of parties which had made the winter of 1860-1861 in Columbus the happiest of his life. He wrote his sister late in the month:

> I presume I shall be quite as much alone throughout my whole stay in Venice, as I am now. . . . What with their political discontents, and the natural effect of their mode of education, the Venetians are eminently unsocial. There are no parties, nor anything of that kind. . . . As for seeking women's society for intellectual pleasure, as I used in Columbus, it is a thing so far from their knowledge, that they could not understand it. Young ladies *never* receive calls, and a young lady cannot go upon the street unless accompanied by her mother or brother. If she went alone she would lose her character.[2]

In spite of his loneliness he denied that he was homesick and insisted that nothing was further from his mind than leaving Italy. He detailed plans for continuing his Italian studies, taking up French, and reading the Latin and Greek classics. He planned to save enough money to start life afresh when he returned, and he had begun keeping a journal from which he hoped to make a book about Venice.

At the time he needed it most, Howells made the

[1] See LinL, I, 53-54.
[2] *Ibid.*, p. 58.

acquaintance of Eugenio Brunetta,[3] a young Italian whose
friendship helped mitigate the Consul's indictment of Venetian society. He was a tall, swarthy youth of nineteen or
twenty years, the son of a lumber merchant, and in the
spring of 1862 he was preparing for the University of Padua.
Evening after evening the two young men walked together,
discussing literature, from the Campo di Marte at one end
of the city to the Public Gardens at the other. Often they
attended the Malibran Theater, where they saw the comedies
of Goldoni performed. Brunetta was learning English and
Howells was rapidly acquiring proficiency in Italian.
Brunetta lent Howells his favorite Italian novels, and the
consul tried to interest the Italian in the latest works of
Dickens. After Howells was married, Brunetta became a
frequent visitor at the Consul's apartment on the Grand
Canal, and when Howells and his wife made a two-months'
tour of Italy in 1864, they left baby Winifred and the consular office in joint custody of Mrs. Howells's brother Larkin Mead, Jr., and Brunetta.[4] This friendship lasted a lifetime, kept alive by correspondence after 1865 and renewed
in the winter of 1882-1883 when Howells revisited Italy.

[3] This is the "Biondini" of whom Howells wrote in his sketch "A Young
Venetian Friend," *Harper's Monthly*, CXXXVIII (May, 1919), 827-833. Despite
the late date of this sketch, the facts check with those of Howells's published
and unpublished letters. There are, in addition, five letters from Brunetta to
Howells in the Howells Collection at Harvard. The material in this paragraph
and the next is based on this article.

[4] Perhaps it was then that Mead conducted his courtship of Marietta da
Benvenuti, who had lived above the Howells family in Casa Falier, with
Brunetta acting as interpreter. They were married Feb. 26, 1866, and lived
happily together in Florence until Mead's death in 1909. Neither could speak
the other's language when the courtship began, but it flourished nonetheless,
with Brunetta as interpreter. Howells describes this romance amusingly in
"A Young Venetian Friend." Despite the statement (VL, I, 130) that "we
never knew their names," the Venetians from Zara, who lived over the Howells
apartment in Casa Falier, were the Benvenutis. Positive identification of this
family may be made from the inscription under a photograph of Marietta da
Benvenuti in a family album in the Howells Collection at Harvard and from
Mildred Howells's annotations in LinL, I, 131.

In his later years Brunetta lived in Verona, where he held a professorship in a technical school, and few of Howells's friends went to Italy without a letter of introduction to this old comrade.

Through his friendship with Brunetta, Howells met Signorina Perissenotti, a brilliant young Venetian girl, whose acquaintance he cultivated in spite of the taboos of local society.[5] The relationship grew out of Brunetta's knowing an elderly law clerk, the same individual who later became the title character in Howells's short story "Tonelli's Marriage." This friend worked for an old Venetian lawyer who had been compromised in one of the demonstrations against the Austrians some years before and lived in complete retirement with his niece and her mother. The niece, however, under the chaperonage of "Tonelli," had managed to obtain a measure of freedom. Howells admitted that the affair must have seemed very irregular when he and Brunetta joined the girl and her chaperon in St. Mark's Square; "but nothing could have been more decorous, and evening after evening we walked together, she talking Italian poetry and Venetian patriotism, and the secretary keeping her literary and revolutionary vivacity in bounds."[6] Howells continued his friendship with these people after he brought his bride to Venice, and on one occasion the girl and her mother allowed the consul and his wife to take them to the opera. The current *dimostrazione* against the Austrian occupation, by precluding Italian attendance at the opera, kept the bulk of the native population away from the theater; but occasionally the love of music overcame patriotic scruples. At this particular performance the girl and her mother sat well back in the box where they could not

[5] The identification of this girl may also be made from the photograph album cited above. When Howells wrote "Tonelli's Marriage," she provided a prototype for the heroine of that story.
[6] "A Young Venetian Friend," p. 827.

be seen.[7] After the unification of Venice with the Kingdom
of Italy Signorina Perissenotti married a member of the
Italian Senate but continued to live in Venice. In 1883 when
the Howells family revisited Italy, they called on their old
friend but found her absent from the city.

Despite the dislocations caused by the Civil War, there
were American travelers in Venice during most of the
forty-three months that Howells lived there. One of the
earliest and most important was Charles Hale, younger
brother of Edward Everett Hale and editor of the Boston
Advertiser, who paused in Venice in the spring en route to
Egypt. He took an immediate liking to Howells, a feeling
which was reciprocated, with the result that the two men
were together constantly during the visit.[8] Hale knew
Longfellow, Lowell, and Holmes and indulgently let the
consul talk about his literary idols; but Hale was more than
a link with the literary Boston of which Howells aspired
to become a part. He subsequently played a prominent role
in the consul's literary career by opening the columns of
the *Advertiser* to the letters which ultimately became *Venetian Life.*

The most distinguished person to visit Venice that spring
was J. L. Motley, the American minister to Austria, who
traveled as far as Venice to meet his youngest daughter returning from a winter spent with family friends in Rome.[9]
He was an impressive individual with a thick mane of hair,
piercing, deep-set eyes, and a well-groomed blond beard, and
Howells remembered him as "one of the handsomest men

[7] Cf. VL, I, 91: "Last winter being the fourth season [1863-1864] the
Italians had defied the temptation of the opera, some of the Venetian ladies
yielded to it, but went plainly dressed, and sat far back in boxes of the third
tier, and when they issued forth after the opera were veiled beyond recognition."
[8] See LF&A, p. 91.
[9] Herbert and Susan [Motley] St. John Mildmay (eds.), *John Lothrop
Motley and His Family,* p. 118.

I ever saw . . . altogether a figure of worldly splendor."[10] While he was in Venice, Motley put on his court clothes and called on the Austrian lieutenant-governor, protesting successfully, as Howells recalled, censorship of the Consul's mail. During the stay the Minister and his subordinate held long talks about literature as they explored the city by gondola, and Howells later helped his chief in his historical research by arranging for a scholar-friend named Barozzi to copy documents from the Venetian archives.[11]

Later the same year Howells dealt with Motley on a very different sort of business—the affairs of a naturalized American whose inheritance was tied up by litigation in the Venetian courts. He solicited Motley's help in the matter, but the Minister declined to act, explaining patiently that the case was a legal problem and beyond the province of the State Department.[12] Howells was not satisfied, however, and annoyed his superior by pressing the issue. In his second letter Motley answered testily that "it is taking considerable responsibility to give advice in regard to matters subject to the decision of high legal tribunals, in your private capacity," and he went on to lecture the Consul on his duties, declaring that "it is the very essence of a diplomatic agent's duty not to act except on instructions . . . from his government."[13] But the sequel to the story was a victory for Howells's persistence, for Motley finally exerted himself in the case, and the naturalized American received his property.[14]

[10] LF&A, p. 94.

[11] There are seven letters pertaining to this research written from Motley to Howells in 1862-1863 in the Howells Collection at Harvard.

[12] Aug. 7, 1862; MS at Harvard. This letter, pertaining to the litigation involving Vincenzo de Bauernfeind, is marked "private" and is one of two written on the same date.

[13] Aug. 11, 1862; MS at Harvard.

[14] See letters from Motley to Howells dated Feb. 20, 1863, and from Vicenzo de Bauernfeind to Howells dated Sept. 26, 1864; MSS at Harvard.

The spring and summer months brought discouraging war news from home. The indecisive but costly Battle of Shiloh had been fought in April, and McClellan's retreat before Lee in the Seven Days' Battles at the end of June gave new life to Southern hopes. Motley's abiding faith in the Union's ultimate victory failed to reassure Howells, whose "whispered misgivings of the end" brought an instant rebuke from the historian during his visit.[15] To make the situation doubly hard to bear, Southerners then in Europe flaunted their defiance and made no secret of their optimism. In July Howells visited Milan and Lake Como, and from the deck of a lake steamer saw a Confederate flag waving boldly over a shallop before the landing of a stately villa. The Italians on the steamer did not recognize the banner, the Germans debated its nationality, and the Englishmen grinned knowingly. Howells blushed in silence and later wrote: "Of all my memories of that hot day on Lake Como, this is burnt in deepest; for the flag was that insolent banner which in 1862 proclaimed us a broken people. . . ."[16] By the end of the summer he apparently thought the Confederacy could not be destroyed and was willing to have the North accept a negotiated peace. Perhaps he was nursing a guilty conscience when he wrote his father in August:

I've been dreadfully discouraged about the war. . . . We

[15] LF&A, p. 93.

[16] IJs, p. 292. When the account of this visit to Como was first published as "Minor Italian Travels," *Atlantic*, XX (Sept., 1867), 337-348, Howells added to the above passage: "It has gone down long ago from ship and fort and regiment, and they who used to flaunt it so gaily in Europe probably pawned it later in the cheap towns of South France, whither so much chivalry retired when wealth was to be wrung from slaves no more forever" (p. 342). M. M. Hurd objected to this passage (see LinL, I, 121), so Howells deleted the reference to the private misfortunes of the Southerners and made the passage read: "It has gone down long ago from ship and fort and regiment, as well as from the shallop on the fair Italian lake" (IJs, p. 292). In the 1901 edition of IJs the entire passage was deleted.

can't treat with the South on the basis of our defeats, unless we mean to yield everything. We must conquer before we can think of peace. When we have gained two or three battles, I suppose we'd better stop and let the South go. . . . If we only had met secession with entire leave to secede when this first began, we should to-day have been a stronger and freer and better people than ever we were before.[17]

In the summer of 1862, while Howells was growing increasingly aware of his loneliness, he became engaged to be married. He must have proposed to Elinor Mead of Brattleboro, Vermont, shortly before August, for on the twenty-second of the month he was anxiously awaiting a letter from home "on a subject very interesting to me"[18] —a subject which Mildred Howells in editing her father's letters identified as his engagement. Howells seems not to have been engaged when he went abroad, because he had written Hildreth soon after arriving in Europe that there was neither a Mrs. Howells nor any prospect of one.[19] His family wanted him to come home to be married, but he could not leave his consular post for more than ten days at a time; hence it was arranged for Larkin Mead, Jr., to accompany his sister to Europe. In October, before final arrangements were made, however, Howells had misgivings and in a dark mood of homesickness seriously considered writing his fiancée not to come. Nevertheless, plans were completed and the marriage was set for late December.

Elinor Mead was the oldest daughter and the fourth of nine children of Larkin G. Mead, a lawyer of Brattleboro, Vermont. She was two months younger than Howells, slight, fair, quick, intelligent, and artistic. Howells met her during his Ohio days, having wooed her in the winter of 1860-1861 when she was visiting her cousin Laura Platt in

[17] LinL, I, 60-61.   [18] *Ibid.*, p. 61.
[19] Dec. 22, 1861; MS at Harvard.

Columbus, but published records of this courtship are extremely meager. Howells himself, writing when the memory of his wife's death was still vivid, passed over this phase of his life in two sentences.[20]

The arrangements called for marriage in England as soon as Larkin and Elinor Mead reached Europe; the wedding trip was to be the journey back to Venice. Howells reckoned without taking into account British marriage laws, and he discovered that he could not be married in England without a seven days' residence. The young couple first tried to get married in Liverpool, then London, and finally in desperation pushed on to Paris. Four or five discouraging days elapsed between the ship's arrival and the marriage. Mrs. Howells later told Mrs. T. B. Aldrich: "The new gloves I had so proudly put on as we left the ship were all out at the fingers, and my spirit was like my gloves, torn and frayed at the edges."[21] The ceremony was ultimately conducted quietly on December 24 at the American Legation in Paris by a Methodist minister reading an Episcopal service. The bride wore a combined wedding and going-away costume, a simple brown dress and coat with a close-

[20] It is impossible to say with any assurance where Howells met Elinor Mead. The letters which passed between them before their marriage, if extant, are not yet available. The "two sentences" in which Howells discussed the gay social life in Columbus in the winter of 1860-1861, stated briefly that he met her and "we were married the next year . . ." (Years of My Youth, p. 225). This would place the meeting perhaps in January or February, 1861. The source of the statement that Miss Mead visited her cousin in Columbus that winter is Mildred Howells (LinL, I, 12), and it is partly corroborated by the reference to "a visiting young lady from New England" (LF&A, p. 3). Against this evidence is the memory of M. D. Conway, who wrote in his memoirs that Howells visited him in Cincinnati at the time he was writing his biography of Lincoln (June, 1860) and there met his future wife at the home of a Miss Nourse, a teacher (Autobiography, Memories and Experiences, I, 309). Conway's memory is supported by a letter Howells wrote him Mar. 24, 1863: "Though I've never heard directly from you, I used to hear a great deal about you in letters from Cincinnati. You have an additional merit in my eyes because you met Elinor there" (Autobiography, I, 427).

[21] Mrs. T. B. [Lilian Woodman] Aldrich, Crowding Memories, p. 90.

fitting little bonnet trimmed with a single bridal rose.[22] The bride and groom and Larkin Mead spent Christmas visiting the Louvre while they waited for the evening train to take them to Italy.

Little is needed to complete the record of Howells's first year in Venice. There were additional visitors from America during the late months of 1862, the most prominent being Samuel Bowles, editor of the Springfield (Mass.) *Republican,* who spent the summer in Baden-Baden and Switzerland in an effort to regain his health and, with his brother Benjamin, made a short trip to Venice, probably in September.[23] Another guest, one whose friendship lasted beyond Howells's Italian years, was James Lorrimer Graham, a charming young dilettante who visited the city with his wife in December. When the Consul left for England to meet his fiancée, Graham gave him a letter of introduction to Trübner and Company,[24] later the London publishers of the first edition of *Venetian Life.*

Another important and lifelong friendship which Howells made during his first year in Venice was that of Padre Giacomo Issaverdenz, with whom he corresponded for thirty-five years. This priest was a brother in the Armenian monastery at San Lazzaro on an island in the Venetian lagoon which "every tourist who spends a week in Venice goes to see" and "is charmed with."[25] Padre Giacomo, though born in Smyrna, had lived with an English family in his youth, and one of his regular assignments at the

[22] This detail is from *ibid.,* p. 89; other wedding data are from LinL, I, 61-63.

[23] When Howells later recalled Bowles's visit to Venice (LF&A, p. 113), he did not state when it took place. Bowles's presence in Switzerland at this time may be verified in G. S. Merriam, *The Life and Times of Samuel Bowles,* I, 364-385.

[24] This letter, dated Dec. 10, 1862, is preserved in the Howells Collection at Harvard.

[25] VL, I, 248. This is the same monastery where Byron studied Armenian.

monastery was to conduct English-speaking visitors through the buildings and grounds. It was undoubtedly in the course of his duty that the Consul met him, and after Howells brought his wife to Venice, their clerical friend sometimes took breakfast with them in their apartment on the Grand Canal, occasionally bringing with him another member of the Armenian community.

1863

There were few more enchanting places to spend a honeymoon than Venice, even the decadent, shabby Venice of 1863. It was true that the gondoliers no longer sang as they rowed, but few cities in the world had so nearly retained the physical appearance of their great days. Howells took his bride to an apartment he had rented in Casa Falier on the Grand Canal.[1] and there they spent the first sixteen months of a long and happy life together. As long as they remained, the charm of the venerable mansion held —especially of their balcony overlooking the canal. Above them was the family of Mrs. Howells's future sister-in-law, and on the same floor lived their landlord, Edward Valentine, who also was British consul, a staunch friend, and later Winifred Howells's godfather.

The year 1863 was a happy one, for the loneliness of the first year vanished, and Howells set to work on the projects he had planned for his residence abroad. He wrote his mother contentedly in April that his life was uneventful but happy,[2] and under the influence of Elinor, whose sketchbook was soon filled with scenes from Venetian life, he began to study art and re-examine the paintings of the Venetian masters. In March he was dickering with a bookseller, apparently unsuccessfully, for a commission to write some

[1] They paid two florins (one dollar) per day both at Casa Falier and later at Palazzo Giustiniani, to which they moved in 1864. See VL, II, 250.
[2] LinL, I, 68-69.

biographical sketches of the Venetian painters,[3] and it may
have been at this time that he translated a German guidebook to Venice.[4] He also was reading one of the most
fascinating autobiographies he had ever read, the memoirs
of the eighteenth-century Venetian dramatist Carlo Goldoni. Still another project he kept tentatively in mind was
the preparation for teaching modern languages, "in case I
should find on my return to America the intellectual life
of the country yearning more decidedly for professors of
modern languages than for journalists or even poets."[5]

During his second spring in Italy Howells was still
aspiring and perspiring to become a poet, but he dropped
a prose anchor to windward early in the year when he submitted to the *Atlantic* the first of the sketches which ultimately became *Venetian Life*. He had sold a long narrative poem to the magazine in November, "Louis Lebeau's
Conversion," and this acceptance was enough recognition
to keep alive the poetic urge, even though rejected manuscripts began to accumulate. But in March he resumed in
the Boston *Advertiser* the interrupted newspaper correspondence begun fifteen months earlier in the *Ohio State
Journal*. His intention was to write a monthly newsletter
for Charles Hale's paper, but before the end of the year his
sketches written for the *Atlantic* were returned, and he
offered them to Hale, who accepted eagerly. The *Advertiser* then published these literary pieces, in which Howells
incorporated the meager budget of news from Venice.

In the first of the newsletters Howells reported a meeting of the Venetian Institute of Sciences, Letters, and Arts,[6]
where he heard a paper by Professor Angelo Messadaglia
of the University of Padua, whom he knew as a translator

[3] *Ibid.*, p. 65.
[4] *Ibid.*, II, 136, and VL (1907 ed.), p. 419.
[5] LinL, I, 65-66.
[6] "Letters from Venice," Boston *Advertiser*, Mar. 27, 1863, p. 2.

of Longfellow. In his next letter he discovered a bright
spot in the general gloom of Venetian commerce, the revival of mosaic painting, and he described a visit to Antonio
Salviati's factory in a palace on the Grand Canal, where he
had seen two hundred artisans engaged in making mosaics
that rivaled the Byzantine originals in St. Mark's Cathedral.[7] This craft fascinated Howells so much that he wrote
about it in his consular reports for the next two years and
gave it several pages in *Venetian Life*. Salviati was properly
grateful for the publicity and invited Howells to his glass
works when he returned to Venice in 1882.[8]

By the end of March the waters of the Adriatic were
warming up, flowers were blooming in profusion on the
islands of the lagoon, and on the mainland spring had
arrived.[9] The Howells family was ready for a day's excursion into the country, and in mid-April they made a
visit to Torcello, an island in the lagoon five miles away.
Howells wrote his mother:

We went partly to see the old Cathedral (built A.D. 600), but
principally to do our good old Giovanna a pleasure. She is fifty
years old, and has never been out of Venice—never "out of these
stones," as she says. We took her and her two children, Beppi
and Nina, who fairly went wild to see grass and flowers
growing.[10]

That was the expedition amusingly described later in *Venetian Life,* and Giovanna, of course, was the fabulous domestic who practiced nepotism in the grand manner and
came with the apartment in Casa Falier. She has been im-
mortalized in *Venetian Life* as the flower of serving-women

[7] "The Revival of Mosaic Painting in Venice," Boston *Advertiser,* May 2,
1863, p. 2.
[8] See VL (1907 ed.), p. 422.
[9] See letter from Howells to Conway dated Mar. 24, 1863, contained in
Autobiography, I, 426.
[10] LinL, I, 69.

who exerted such tyranny over the newly married couple
that they had to move across the Grand Canal to get away
from her. What happened to her after the Consul left
Venice, the record does not say. When Howells revisited
the city in 1883, he looked for Giovanna but found no trace
of her among the inscrutable stones and dark canals.[11]

Late in April Howells and his wife made their first trip
away from the environs of Venice, visiting Larkin Mead,
who was studying art in Florence.[12] In 1863 Venice and
Florence had not yet been linked by railroad; hence the
travelers had to go by carriage from Padua to Ferrara and
from Bologna to their destination. The last lap they accomplished by diligence in an all-night ride over the Apennines. Their brief visit to the Tuscan city was spent in the
usual routine of sight-seeing, looking up places associated
with Dante, visiting the Uffizi and Pitti galleries, and trying
unsuccessfully to get into Casa Guidi, where the Brownings
had lived. They saw the house which Hawthorne had occupied during his stay in Florence, called at the studios of
various American sculptors, and watched Italy's new King
Victor Emmanuel review his troops.

The journey to Florence was the only important traveling which they undertook in 1863. There were two short
trips to the home of Petrarch at Arquà, less than three
hours away, in the late summer and autumn, but by the
time they returned to Venice at the beginning of May, they
knew that Elinor was expecting a baby in December.
Among the plans they made for this event was the arrange-
ment that Mary Mead, Mrs. Howells's youngest sister,
should come to Venice before the infant was born.[13]

[11] See VL (1907 ed.), p. 417.

[12] Although Howells wrote to his mother on April 18 (LinL, I, 69) that the
trip was planned for May, the journey actually was completed in time to be
described in a newspaper letter dated May 3 ("From Venice to Florence and
Back Again," Boston *Advertiser*, May 25, 1863, p. 2).

[13] Tentative plans also were made for Howells's sister Aurelia to come with
Mary Mead, but her visit never took place. See LinL, I, 76.

While making preparations for the baby, Howells laid
plans to entertain his old Ohio friend, Moncure Daniel Conway, whom he had known earlier as editor of the Cincinnati *Dial*. In April, 1863, Conway had gone to England to
represent the Boston Abolitionists in a series of talks on
slavery and secession, but before his departure Howells had
invited him to Casa Falier, where "we have a piano and a
balcony on the Grand Canal, and the most delightful little
breakfasts in Venice."[14] Renewing the invitation in his
next letter, the Consul rhapsodized: "Come at once . . .
for now the bathing begins. . . . A beach like velvet under
your feet—waves of amethyst, and purple, purple heavens
full of mellow light. *That's* bathing on the Lido. . . . You
shall live upon green peas, young beets, strawberries and ice
cream as we do now."[15] Such importuning was irresistible,
and by the time Conway visited Venice he was badly in
need of the sympathy of old friends and the sanative powers
of a Venetian summer. In June he indiscreetly and without authorization wrote the Confederate agent J. M. Mason
pledging the efforts of the Abolitionists to end the war if
the South would agree to emancipate the slaves. Mason
published the letter, and the deafening repercussions from
America were still ringing in Conway's ears when he
reached Italy in July. Howells comforted his guest in that
dark moment and suffered with him, but the error turned
out to be trivial. The Consul wrote Edmund C. Stedman
the next month that Conway was "a sadder and wiser man
for his essay in diplomacy."[16]

In return for sympathy Howells exacted news of home
from his guest and a large quantity of good literary talk.
During the visit the two men discussed books long and

[14] *Autobiography*, I, 426.
[15] May 12, 1863; MS at Columbia Univ. This letter exists only in a copy
in Conway's handwriting.
[16] LinL, I, 72.

earnestly as they sat on the balcony overlooking the Grand Canal or took their coffee in the Square prior to an early morning ramble through the byways of the city. While Howells transacted occasional consular business, Mrs. Howells escorted Conway through the galleries and churches, and in the evenings the three dropped into a café where they watched the promenaders and listened to Howells read parts of a "novelette in poetic form" which he then was writing.[17] Conway also arrived in Venice in time to help the Consul and other compatriots celebrate the Fourth of July. All the visiting Americans gathered in a flag-draped parlor at Casa Falier and under a portrait of George Washington drank toasts to the United States. An additional guest was a "fair Venetian" who played the piano accompaniment for patriotic songs.[18]

As the summer of 1863 drew to a close, Howells was probably happier than he had been at any previous time in his life. The fog of uncertainty over the outcome of the Civil War began to lift, and when the news of the Battle of Gettysburg and the capture of Vicksburg reached Europe late in July, the North's victory finally must have seemed inevitable. At the same time, Howell's marriage and approaching parenthood had brought contentment which he had never known. The hard, grinding toil of his youth seemed far behind him, and life in Venice was a perpetual round of reading, writing, and studying in a tranquil atmosphere of domestic felicity.

When Howells wrote Stedman in August, he reported enthusiastically on his literary prospects.[19] Frank Foster, one of his publishers in Columbus, had set up a firm in New

[17] *Autobiography*, I, 429. The "novelette in poetic form" was *No Love Lost*, which at that time was still called "Disillusion." See also letter from Howells to Conway, May 23, 1863; MS at Columbia Univ.
[18] "Letters from Venice," Boston *Advertiser*, July 28, 1863, p. 2.
[19] LinL, I, 70-72.

York and accepted his long narrative poem for publication. Mrs. Howells was busily engaged in making sketches to illustrate the volume. The Consul also had a portfolio of prose sketches of life in Venice, to which he kept adding while awaiting disposition of other sketches then in the office of the *Atlantic*. To make his happiness complete, he had sold his first poem to *Harper's Monthly*, "St. Christopher," for publication in the December issue.

During this period of exhilaration Howells entertained another distinguished visitor from the United States, Henry Ward Beecher, who was ending a European speaking tour on behalf of the North. He bounced into Venice for a few days accompanied by Dr. John Raymond, president of Vassar College. After escorting his guests around the city on a hot day, Howells wrote that he had just left Beecher in the Academy of Fine Arts, "one limp and helpless mass of enthusiasm and perspiration."[20] These visitors were present for the Emperor's birthday, celebrated by an annual procession of lantern-lighted gondolas on the Grand Canal,[21] and three days later on August 19 they left for Germany and home.[22]

The day after Beecher left Venice, Howells and his wife set out for Arquà in the Euganean Hills near by to visit the home of Petrarch. They made the short railroad trip to Padua, and when it began to rain they stopped over to look at churches for the rest of the day. Spending the evening at Pedrocchi's Café with Professors Frattini and Messadaglia of the University, they had a full evening of literary talk, discussing the "distinguished American writers, of whom intelligent Italians always know at least four . . . Cooper, Mrs. Stowe [everyone had read *La Capanna di Zio Tom*], Longfellow, and Irving."[23] The next morning

[20] *Ibid.*, p. 72.
[21] See LinL, I, 61, for description of this celebration in 1862.
[22] "Letters from Venice," Boston *Advertiser*, Sept. 11, 1863, p. 2.
[23] IJs, p. 212.

they went on by carriage to Arquà. At the little stone cottage where Petrarch once had lived the pilgrims plucked ivy and fig leaves for mementoes and wrote their names on the much-inscribed walls. Howells added his name to the others, reflecting gaily that "this passion for allying one's self to the great, by inscribing one's name on places hallowed by them, is . . . without doubt, the most impertinent and idiotic custom in the world."[24] The visit to Arquà was more than a literary pilgrimage, for Howells wrote home the following month that in all this voyaging "we shall have another purpose besides that of entertaining ourselves, which will appear later or not, according as success attends it."[25] Apparently he planned to make a magazine article out of the excursion, and late in September he went back to Arquà to gather more material.[26]

Howells passed an important milestone in his literary career in the last quarter of 1863 when he abandoned efforts to place his Venetian sketches with the *Atlantic* and offered his work to the Boston *Advertiser*. The magazine had kept his contributions an unconscionable length of time, and in October H. M. Ticknor advised him, somewhat apologetically, that "not one of the MSS you have sent us swims our sea. . . . I don't believe that you are more disappointed at this than I am."[27] But Howells already had anticipated this final rejection by asking Charles Hale to get his manuscripts for him, and at the end of the month he gave the *Advertiser* a chance to buy the articles at five dollars a column.[28] Hale

[24] *Ibid.*, p. 225. First printed as "A Pilgrimage to Petrarch's House at Arquà," *Nation*, I (Nov. 30, 1865), 685-688.

[25] LinL, I, 75.

[26] The first of these visits to Arquà may be dated from Howells's letter to Conway of Aug. 22, 1863 (MS at Columbia Univ.), written after returning to Venice; the second is conjecturally placed in late September. In Howells's letter of Sept. 17, he speaks of planning to revisit Arquà in a few days (LinL, I, 75), and in IJs, pp. 231-232, he describes but does not date the second visit.

[27] Oct. 6, 1863; MS at Harvard.

[28] LinL, I, 77. Curiously enough, he also had offered the sketches to John

accepted readily, but even before receiving this proposal, he had written: ". . . you must by no means discontinue your letters. . . . They are very much liked. . . ."[29]

After Howells had arranged for publication of the sketches, the household at Casa Falier settled down quietly to wait for the baby. The monotony was broken at the end of October by the arrival of a New York newspaperman and his wife. These Americans commandeered their consular representative's services as cicerone, then went on to Egypt.[30] Their place was taken by an English artist who came for his annual visit to paint sunsets.[31] November slipped away uneventfully, although late that month Elizabetta Scarbro, the "Bettina" of *Venetian Life,* was hired as a nurse for the baby; early in December Mary Mead arrived to begin a visit which lasted as long as the Howells family remained in Italy. Finally, on December 17, the baby was born, and the father announced in a letter to his wife's cousin:

We have,—unless I dreamed all last night—a little daughter, whom we call Winifred. I write at 10 A.M., and I compute her age at exactly nine hours. As yet, her features have that somewhat blurred effect visible in young ladies of her age; but she is understood to be the image of her father. . . .[32]

1864: "THE TURNING POINT OF MY LIFE"

The year 1864 brought the pleasures and increased responsibilities of parenthood and the most memorable

Swinton of the New York *Times* three days before he wrote Hale. See letter dated Oct. 22, 1863; MS at Boston Pub. Lib. Swinton, of course, was not editor of the paper, which was still under Henry J. Raymond.

[29] Oct. 13, 1863; MS at Harvard. Beginning Apr. 1, 1864, Hale raised Howells's space rate to one pound sterling per column, an effective increase of four dollars, since a pound cost nine dollars in New York or Boston during the Civil War. See Hale's letter to Howells dated May 9, 1864 (MS at Harvard), announcing the new rate.

[30] LinL, I, 78.

[31] "Letters from Venice," Boston *Advertiser,* Nov. 21, 1863, p. 2.

[32] LinL, I, 80.

winter in a century and a half.[1] Snow fell repeatedly and lay unmelted for weeks, while the lagoon was frozen for miles around. Under the windows of Casa Falier great sheets of ice rose and fell with the tide for a month, and the visible misery throughout the unprepared city was great. Howells wrote cheerfully, however, at the end of January that the members of his household were enjoying Venice very much that winter. They were going frequently to the theater and opera and even taking walks on the Molo when the weather relented. The consular establishment, already doubled by the addition of Mary Mead and the baby, was further augmented by an American artist, Miner Kellog of Cincinnati, and his wife. Mrs. Howells, moreover, after recovering from her confinement, began entertaining both Italian acquaintances and whatever Americans chance brought to Venice. "Elinor has a little coffee and cake and cards Saturday evening," wrote Howells, "and we see friends that night—principally the Przemysl who grows more delightful and brilliant the better she is known to us."[2]

While Howells was enjoying great domestic happiness in Venice, the reception which his poetry was meeting in England and America was as cold as the unusual Italian winter. Frank Foster had procrastinated so long in bringing out "Disillusion" that it became apparent he was reluctant to go through with his agreement. He wrote in January that costs were up 50 per cent over the preceding year,[3] and in March that poetry in his opinion was unsalable.[4] In London, meanwhile, Conway was having no luck in finding a publisher for a volume of Howells's poetry and

[1] See "The Winter in Venice," VL, I, 49-67.
[2] Howells to M. D. Conway, Jan. 26, 1864; MS in the Berg Collection, New York Pub. Lib. The "Przemysl" probably was the Polish-born Countess Capograssi, whose photograph may be found in the previously mentioned family album.
[3] Jan. 21, 1864; MS at Harvard.
[4] Mar. 8, 1864; MS at Harvard.

wrote gloomily: "I have consulted and worked for your
poems. I have waited and waited on publishers, hoping to
get some good tidings to send you."[5] Finally in May he
sent the manuscript back, saying that everyone praised the
poems but would not risk a penny "except on a man so
famous here that their returns are sure."[6]

After a winter of being cooped up in a damp palace on
the Grand Canal, Howells was eager to get away from
Venice, and when the first warm spring days arrived he
took his wife and sister-in-law on a ten-day tour of Lom-
bardy.[7] The first stop was in the old signorial city of
Vicenza, where they inspected the ancient basilica restored
by Andrea Palladio and walked down an avenue of Venetian
Gothic palaces which made them feel "as if the Grand
Canal had but just shrunk away from their bases."[8] At the
opera they were delighted with the tacit defiance of Austria
by a beautiful young woman, whose red and green fan
made a bold display of the forbidden Italian colors against
the white background of her dress. In Verona they were
awed by the massive amphitheater which completely dwarfed
a modern circus performing where once had been played
the sterner sports of the Romans.[9] Other tourist attractions
in Verona kept them busy during the remainder of their
stay: the home of the Capulet family, Juliet's tomb, the
tombs of the Scaligeri, and the ruins of the Roman theater.

[5] Jan. 10, 1864; MS at Harvard.   [6] May 11, 1864; MS at Harvard.

[7] This trip is described in "Stopping at Vicenza, Verona, and Parma," IJs,
pp. 293-320. The visit to Mantua resulted in the article "Ducal Mantua," first
printed in the North American Review, CII (Jan., 1866), 48-100, and later
included in the 1872 edition of IJs. The dates of this trip have been obtained
from the diary which Howells kept of his travels in 1864. The diary is in the
Howells Collection at Harvard. They were in Verona Mar. 12; Mantua, Mar.
15; and Modena, Mar. 18.

[8] IJs, p. 294.

[9] This circus, barely mentioned in IJs, p. 302, inspired the article "Sawdust
in the Arena," first printed in "Life and Letters," Harper's Weekly, XL (Oct.
3, 1896), 966, and later in Literature and Life, pp. 187-192.

After visiting Mantua, where the Consul's wife created a stir of local interest by sketching a group of peasant women washing clothes on the banks of a millrace, the travelers pushed on through Modena, a city in which "the badness of our hotel enveloped the city in an atmosphere of profound melancholy."[10] The last stop on the trip was Parma, which they found as full of paintings by Correggio as Venice was of Titians and Tintorettos. Howells, the linguist of the party, was fascinated by the Parmesan dialect, which suppressed the last syllable of every word "as if language were not worth the effort of enunciation."[11]

Returning to Venice about March 20, Howells threw all his energies into the writing of his first important piece of criticism, an article on "Recent Italian Comedy," which he labored over until mid-May, and then submitted to the *North American Review*. In April he began to think of returning home, although he was not to leave Venice for another fifteen months. His plans for the future, however, were beginning to take shape, and he decided not to apply for reappointment to his consular post if Lincoln were re-elected. He felt that he had derived nearly all the benefit he could from his stay in Europe and his mind was full of busy schemes to justify a return home. The next month he wrote home that he was planning an autumn trip to Rome, after which he wanted to leave Italy.[12]

In the midst of these plans came the staggering news of the sudden death of his younger brother John on April 27. It was a crushing blow, for Howells had been particularly close to his brother and had hoped great things for him. He

[10] IJs, p. 313.   [11] *Ibid.*, p. 317.

[12] LinL, I, 82-83. This letter, which is merely dated "Venice, 1864," was written, Howells says, the day before news was received of the death of his brother John. The news came either on May 16 or shortly thereafter, because Howells began a letter to Conway on May 16 (MS at Columbia Univ.) but was interrupted, presumably by the announcement of John's death, and did not finish it until May 22, when he added a postscript relaying the sad news.

had written from Venice to his brother Joe when John was
seventeen: "Why not send Johnny to College, and let one
Howells have the stamp of the schools?"[13] After the boy
had been sent to a military school in Cleveland, Howells
had written him an affectionate letter of fraternal advice
and nostalgic reminiscence. "Do you remember," he had
asked Johnny, "what a good cry we had together that night
I left home, when I came upstairs and kissed you, in
bed?"[14] The death of his brother evoked one of the tender-
est and most poignant poems which Howells ever wrote,
penned as he sat sleepless at daybreak in his palace on the
Grand Canal:

> Distance wider than thine, O Sea,
> Darkens between my brother and me![15]

The loss was doubly hard to bear, coming as it did immediately after an illness which left Howells so nervous
that it was a torture to write. He thought that the sickness
had been brought on by overworking himself in the preparation of his paper on Italian comedy, but the subsequent
acceptance of the article was more than adequate compen-
sation for his illness. The heartache caused by his brother's
death, however, was not to be assuaged so easily.

Although the month of May ended on a note of sadness,
it had begun with nothing more disheartening than a shift
to new quarters. On May 1 Howells had moved his family
from Casa Falier to Palazzo Giustiniani on the west side
of the Grand Canal where the waterway doubles back on
itself and leads to the Rialto Bridge. This magnificent but
drafty old Gothic palace commanded a sweeping view of

[13] *Ibid.*, p. 73.

[14] *Ibid.*, p. 74.

[15] "Elegy on John Butler Howells," *Poems*, p. 100. The elegy is incorrectly
dated "Venice, Wednesday Morning, at Dawn, May 16, 1864" *(Poems,* p. 104),
but the correct date, Wednesday, May 25, may be obtained from the Ashtabula
Sentinel, June 29, 1864, p. 1, where the poem was first printed.

the Grand Canal, and the Howells apartment, while scantily furnished, contained a bedroom with a ceiling of carved and gilded wood panels fifteen feet high. The parlor was built on the same generous proportions and was adorned with two great Venetian mirrors and a good painting of a miracle of St. Anthony.[16]

As he began his third summer in Italy, Howells planned the literary exploitation of the March tour of the Lombard cities. He originally projected a series of lectures which he intended to work up along with his book on Venice. His notion was to get ready several talks on such cities as Padua, Verona, Mantua, Modena, and Parma. In June he was busy compiling notes on Mantua and working every day in St. Mark's Library; but instead of becoming a lecture this research went into the historical essay "Ducal Mantua." He had recovered fully from his illness in May, and though he was working hard, he delighted in the task and felt no ill effects.

The hot, sultry weeks of summer passed in a steady round of labor punctuated by occasional holidays at the beach, but the uncertainty of the future cast its shadow. During July Howells looked forward to the second visit of Charles Hale and planned to talk over with him the postwar outlook for newspaper work. The Boston journalist had been appointed Consul-General at Cairo and was then on his way to Egypt via Trieste, having purposely routed his itinerary so that he could visit the *Advertiser's* Venice correspondent.[17] Howells had already asked his advice about an editorship in the eastern United States, and Hale had replied before sailing: "I have no doubt that you will be able to . . . obtain a position either in Boston or in New York that will be comfort-

[16] VL, II, 249.
[17] Hale wrote from Vienna on Aug. 3, 1864 (MS at Harvard), that he expected to be in Venice on the seventh and was to sail from Trieste on the twelfth.

able, honorable and promising."[18] In early August editor
and contributor spent several pleasant days together, talking literature, revisiting historical places, and discussing the
Consul's prospects.[19] Hale's great faith in his friend at that
time must have been deeply appreciated, for Howells knew
that he soon ought to give up his sinecure and return
to America, even though the future was uncharted and
insecure.

Against a drab background of literary toil and gnawing
anxiety flashed the electrifying news that the *North American Review* had accepted his article. Howells had sent off
the essay prayerfully in May, hoping that the new editors of
the journal, Lowell and Charles Eliot Norton, would see
merit in it. Much labor had gone into the composition of
the paper, and he knew it was good; but his wildest dreams
could not have encompassed the literary opportunities which
the article opened for him. Consider the effect of the following letter on an earnest young man of twenty-seven as
he breathlessly rips it open and reads:

MY DEAR SIR,—Your article is in print, and I was very glad to
get it. . . . Write us another on "Modern Italian Literature,"
or anything you like. I don't forget my good opinion of you
and my interest in your genius. . . . I have been charmed with
your Venetian letters in the *Advertiser*. They are admirable,
and fill a gap. They make the most careful and picturesque
study I have ever seen on any part of Italy. They are the thing
itself.

                              Your friend,
                              J. R. LOWELL[20]

Lowell occupied one of the brightest places in Howells's
literary firmament, and during the Consul's two visits to

[18] May 17, 1864; MS at Harvard. Only Hale's reply is extant.
[19] See letter from Hale dated Alexandria, Egypt, Sept. 6, 1864 (MS at Harvard), thanking Howells for a pleasant visit.
[20] Charles Eliot Norton (ed.), *Letters of James Russell Lowell*, I, 338.

Cambridge in 1860 and 1861 the poet-editor had been more than cordial, but their correspondence had lapsed during the Italian sojourn. The effect of the above letter was an immediate upward surge in the young man's morale, and he promptly sat down and wrote an answer which is almost pathetically grateful in tone.[21] The letter ran to more than one thousand words, recalling the circumstances of Howells's meeting with Lowell in 1860 ("I thought that . . . you might have forgotten") and recounting his labors and disappointments of the past three years. It went on to outline his plans for returning home, bringing out the Venetian letters in book form, and writing additional articles on Italian subjects. Four days later Howells wrote to his father, quoting Lowell's note in full, in a letter that painted an optimistic picture of his literary prospects. In referring to Lowell's compliments, he wrote: ". . . this certainly opens up a prospect for me and gives me standing. If I had only got the letter a year ago! How I could have worked! But that is spilt milk."[22]

This letter made an indelible impression on Howells. A note from Lowell ten years later evoked the reply that "this letter looked exactly like that letter you wrote me at Venice accepting my 'Recent Italian Comedy': I got it from the *postiere* . . . and . . . went up to heaven at once."[23]

Again in 1895 Howells spoke of this letter:

Before I left Venice, however, there came a turn in my literary luck, and from the hand I could most have wished to reverse the adverse wheel of fortune. I had labored out with great pains a paper on recent Italian comedy, which I sent to Lowell . . . and he took it and wrote me one of his loveliest letters about it, consoling me in an instant for all the defeat I had undergone.[24]

[21] LinL, I, 84-87.   [22] *Ibid.*, p. 88.   [23] *Ibid.*, p. 188.
[24] LF&A, p. 100. First printed as "Roundabout to Boston," *Harper's Monthly*, XCI (Aug., 1895), 427-438.

Fifteen years later at the age of seventy-three he returned to
the same topic when *Harper's Bazar* began a series of articles
by eminent men on "The Turning Point of My Life." He
then believed that Lowell's letter had been the decisive
factor in turning him away from poetry towards prose.
Actually, his youthful poetic aspirations had slipped away
gradually during his three years abroad, and Lowell's letter
was more a much-needed accolade than an instrument of
decision. Nevertheless, he still remembered "the thrill of
joy and hope and pride which that note gave me, a trumpet
call to battle, which echoed and reechoed in my soul and
seemed to fill the universe with its reverberation."[25]

Howells scarcely had time to reply to Lowell's encouraging note before further family troubles in Ohio threatened
the bright future. His father wrote on July 31 that brother
Sam, who had enlisted the previous year, was sick and that
brother Joe might be drafted for military service.[26] Joseph
A. Howells, who was four years older than William, by
1864 had taken over a large measure of the responsibility
of running the family newspaper, the Ashtabula *Sentinel*.
Apparently the father asked the son to be prepared to return
home from Venice to take his brother's place if the threatened draft came about. Howells was dismayed at the possibility, although he promised to fill his brother's position
if need be. He wrote his father that he doubted his ability
to conduct a publishing business but added: "Your wish
must be law with me . . . and I cannot think of anything
more unworthy than my shrinking from a duty of the
kind."[27]

While he waited for developments in the situation at
home, the Consul interrupted his writing and study in Sep-

[25] "The Turning Point of My Life," *Harper's Bazar*, XLIV (Mar., 1910),
165.
[26] Only Howells's reply (LinL, I, 87-91) is extant.
[27] LinL, I, 87-88.

tember for a five-day trip to Bassano and its environs,[28] his purpose being to make literary capital of the Cimbrian mountaineers who inhabited the near-by mountain tops. Although Bassano was little more than thirty miles away, the trip took two hours by train and a half-day by carriage. Making Bassano their base, the Howells household traveled by mule up the steep mountain slopes to the Cimbrian settlements, where they found a quaint Germanic people who had lived unassimilated in Italy since the second century. On their way back to Venice the travelers stopped at Possagno, the birthplace of the sculptor Canova.[29]

Before and after this junket to Bassano Howells entertained American visitors: Cousin Edward Howells and his niece, the first of kith and kin whom he had seen for three years, and Motley for the second time. The Minister to Austria had come down with his family from Vienna and once more was interested in arranging for research in the Venetian archives.[30] Several weeks after Motley left, Howells received news from home that the draft crisis had passed, ending the possibility that he might be needed at home. The suggestion that he seek another consular term, however, elicited a flat rejection when he wrote his mother at the end of the month:

Father speaks of my taking office for four years more. I doubt if I could manage it, and if I could, I wouldn't. . . . I want to go home to live, "be it ever so humbly." I am sure it will be better than the proudest life here. I only consent to remain here till spring because I think I see very great advantage in doing so; and as soon as I have notes for half a dozen papers on Italian cities I shall be off for home.[31]

[28] This trip, which took place from Sept. 14-18, is dated from the diary previously cited. For Howells's account of it see IJs, pp. 235-250, 274-284.

[29] I have found no evidence that Howells visited Possagno before this occasion, Sept. 18, 1864, despite the reference to a planned visit in his letter of Sept. 17, 1863 (LinL, I, 75).

[30] Motley's Correspondence, II, 186.   [31] LinL, I, 91.

Howells added that his book of Venetian sketches was nearly ready for publication—"but three chapters more to copy"; simultaneously he was negotiating with Trübner in London in an effort to place the book.

On the eighth of November[32] he began a two months' leave of absence, and after installing Larkin Mead as vice-consul, he set out for Rome with his wife and Mary Mead.[33] Following the road to Florence, which they had taken eighteen months before, the travelers paused for two days of sight-seeing in Ferrara before continuing to Bologna, where they stayed overnight, November 11. The weather was bad and the autumnal rains had made the roads over the Apennines impassable; hence the shorter route to Rome by way of Florence was out of the question, and they detoured through Genoa. Leaving Bologna on a noon train, November 12, they reached Genoa at midnight and embarked the following night on a ship for Naples. Storms buffeted the little coastal steamer, and a day was added to the normal passage when the ship was forced into port the second night at the Island of Elba. Howells was seasick once more and thankful to debark at Naples on the evening of November 16. The travelers made their headquarters in that city for the next eleven days, taking a two-day side trip to Capri and a day's excursion to Pompeii. On November 27 the entourage moved northward, and the next three and one-half weeks were given over to exploring Rome.

When the tourists left the Italian metropolis on Decem-

[32] This date is given in IJs, p. 9, while the rest, except for the date of return, may be reconstructed from the narrative and checked from Howells's diary in the Harvard Library. The arrival back in Venice on Dec. 24 was reported in a letter from Howells to F. W. Seward dated Dec. 31, 1864 (MS in the National Archives).

[33] The record of this trip is too well preserved in IJs, pp. 9-195, 251-258, to need more than the clarification of a few dates here. Howells covers the journey in ample detail and in chronological order.

ber 21, they debated all the way to Città Vecchia whether or not to take the steamer to Leghorn. A glimpse of the rough sea and sodden sky convinced them that an overland trip would be pleasanter; so they mounted the diligence and reached Grossetto without undue incident. On the far side of the city, however, the swollen waters of the Ombrone River provided the most exciting adventure of the journey. The diligence drove to the river bridge along an inundated highway, but when it approached the span, it could go no farther. In trying to turn back, the driver ran off the highway, upsetting the carriage in three feet of the muddy flood waters. Clothes, luggage, and passengers were thoroughly soaked, and the travelers were forced to wade ashore and retrace their steps to Grossetto, where they waited for the river to subside. The record of the journey ends at Leghorn, except for a brief description of near-by Pisa; but the Apennines no doubt were still impassable, and it is likely that they returned through Genoa, arriving in Venice on Christmas Eve.

RETURN TO AMERICA

Howells began the year 1865 with enough travel experiences stored in his journal and memory to fill the second book which he planned to write. He also had come back from Rome with an idea for another *North American Review* article.[1] These projects, together with the uncompleted essay on "Ducal Mantua," kept him busy during the remainder of the winter. By the end of January he had nearly finished the article on "Italian Brigandage," and he must have sent it off to Lowell promptly, for it was accepted and published in July. At the same time, he was working on the first of his travel sketches based on the recent journey to Rome. He sent a series of articles to the Boston *Ad-*

[1] "Italian Brigandage," *North American Review*, CI (July, 1865), 162-189.

vertiser, his first contribution to that paper in six months,
and three were published at one-month intervals beginning
in March. As the winter ended, Howells wrote to the artist
David D. Neal in Munich: "We get on in the old, dull way
here: my wife paints, and I scribble, and so we contrive to
pass the time."[2]

By spring Howells was eager to go home, and he applied
for another extended leave of absence. He had told Lowell
the preceding August that he intended to resign either at
Christmas or in March, but when the time came to make the
break, he decided to hold his consular job open in case
prospects for literary work in the United States proved un-
favorable. Although he kept himself hard at his writing in
the winter of 1864-1865, he was restless and knew the return
must come soon. "I find myself almost expatriated," he had
told Lowell, "and I have seen enough of uncountryed
Americans in Europe to disgust me with voluntary exile . . .
but with what unspeakable regret I shall leave Italy! . . .
in a year or two more of lotus-eating, I shouldn't want to
go home at all."[3]

In the middle of March Howells wrote that the government had half promised him—"or has not wholly refused"[4]—a leave of absence, and when the leave came he
intended to be off for home. More than three and one-half
months were to elapse, however, before he finally received
authorization to quit his post. By June his impatience at
the delay prompted him to write to Motley in Vienna,

[2] Mar. 15, 1865; MS at Harvard.
[3] LinL, I, 85-86.
[4] Howells to David D. Neal, Mar. 15, 1865; MS at Harvard. Howells
applied for leave in a letter to F. W. Seward on Jan. 9, 1865 (MS in National
Archives) and was informed that the request would not be granted at that time
though kept on file. He made his request on grounds that if the State Department planned to renew his appointment during Lincoln's second term, he should
be allowed a visit home before starting another four years in office. He repeated his request for a leave again on April 12 and May 15 in successive
letters becoming more urgent in tone.

apparently suggesting that he might leave without official sanction. Motley replied stiffly: "I should think that your going home from Venice to *America* without permission would be deemed grave dereliction of duty."[5]

Spring passed slowly and uncertainly in the anxious and fretful household of the American consul. In April came word that Trübner would not publish *Venetian Life* unless Howells agreed to find an American publisher who would take half of the edition. The London firm wrote that they had just published two books on Italy and both were failures.[6] News of Lee's surrender at Appomattox came at the end of April to cheer the expatriates, but a few days later the report of Lincoln's assassination cast its shadow over the North's victory.[7]

In late May or early June, while waiting for permission to leave, the Consul and his wife slipped out of Venice to the country near Padua to see their old friend Tortorini.[8] For three years he had urged them to visit him at his home in Monselice, and at last they went. Perhaps they expected the stay to be trying, as it turned out to be, but in the state of mind they had reached by the end of May, it is doubtful if any visit could have been successful. They were sick of their residence abroad and longed for America. Mrs. Howells, moreover, seemed to have grown delicate in the Venetian climate. Hence an experience they undoubtedly would have found picturesque two years before was intolerable in in 1865. Howells wrote later that Tortorini's dinners were so bad that they cut short their visit. Such dishes as rice

---

[5] June 10, 1865; MS at Harvard.   [6] Mar. 30, 1865; MS at Harvard.

[7] Howells wrote to W. H. Seward, May 1, 1865 (MS in National Archives): "Sir—I cannot refrain from uttering my share of the national sorrow which every American citizen feels with the poignancy of a personal grief, in view of the untimely loss of the great and good man whom the people had called, after a term of most ardent, devoted, and triumphant service, to continue at the head of their affairs, and whom a horrible crime has removed. . . ."

[8] See "An Old Venetian Friend," pp. 634-640.

soup, boiled beef, fried brains, and strawberries in wine were completely unpalatable, and they heaved a great sigh of relief when they finally left Tortorini's villa and feasted at Pedrocchi's in Padua.

During this period of anxious waiting Howells's spirits drooped and the future looked increasingly gloomy. The chance of a newspaper editorship in Cleveland had presented itself only to elude his grasp. He despaired of finding any editorial position, particularly in New York, where he had been assured by a recent journalist-visitor to Venice that newspaper editorships were almost impossible to obtain. He was so homesick and tired of Europe that he could stay hardly a day longer; yet it seemed utter rashness to return in the face of such uncertainties. Added to these problems were his brother's shortcomings as a literary agent. Joseph Howells had failed both to get back from Foster the long poem which had been scheduled for publication nearly eighteen months before and to inquire about articles which Howells had submitted to *Harper's Monthly* but not heard from. Nevertheless, the Consul kept his pen going from morning to night, writing more travel sketches and making translations from the Italian poets to go with his articles on modern Italian literature.

Finally on June 21 Howells received notice that he had been granted a four months' leave of absence. Writing his father on the same day, he outlined plans for leaving Venice on the first of July and spending ten days in London before sailing for home.[9] An unidentified literary lady had given him a letter of introduction to Anthony Trollope, and with that novelist's help (which was not offered) he hoped to place *Venetian Life* with a more intrepid publisher than Trübner. Just how he traveled across Europe to England does not appear in the surviving records, but he had writ-

[9] LinL, I, 94.

ten David Neal in March that he intended to visit him in Munich on the way home. At all events, Howells left Venice for London on the third of July.[10] About the twentieth of the month he sailed from England with his wife, daughter, and Mary Mead on the steamship *Asia,* and landed in Boston on August 3, 1865. He had returned to the United States with a wife, a child, and a rich store of impressions and experiences. In four years abroad he had progressed from a callow writer of newspaper paragraphs and imitative verse to a competent literary craftsman on the threshold of a long and fruitful career.

[10] See letter from Howells to F. W. Seward dated June 28, 1865 (MS in National Archives), announcing that he would leave Venice on July 3 after turning his office over to Larkin Mead as vice-consul.

II. Literary Apprentice

VENETIAN LIFE

THE MOST important product of Howells's Italian sojourn was *Venetian Life,* his first book after returning from Europe and his first outstanding literary success. Lowell had no hesitation in saying flatly that it was "the best book ever written about Italy,"[1] and his opinion was attested by the prompt acclaim of the critics and the rapid exhaustion of the first edition. The book maintained its popularity for half a century, passing through numerous editions and reprintings, and in 1893 when Howells estimated that there were forty thousand copies in print,[2] it was still selling briskly. As late as 1907-1908 three editions were brought out in less than a year to supply the demand of the American tourists and the author's wide following.

Venetian Life was the climactic accomplishment of Howells's long newspaper apprenticeship, the result of an ample experimentation and practical experience in writing about travel. He had first turned his hand to this literary genre as early as 1860, when he contributed travel letters to the *Ohio State Journal* and the Cincinnati *Gazette* on the occasion of his literary pilgrimage to Boston. Between engagements on the *Journal,* while he was a reader for the publishers Follett and Foster, he broadened his experience with this type of literature by editing and rewriting a book on Chile.[3] When he went abroad he planned to send back

---

[1] LinL, I, 112. As reported by Howells in a letter to his sister Victoria dated June 17, 1866.

[2] Boyesen, *op. cit.,* p. 8.

[3] [C. B. Merwin], *Three Years in Chili* (Columbus, 1861). See William M. Gibson and George Arms, *A Bibliography of William Dean Howells,* pp. 17-18.

travel letters, and he made arrangements before leaving to write for the *Journal;* but he contributed only three letters, all written in December, 1861, none of which bears any resemblance qualitatively to the polished and mature sketches of *Venetian Life.* He quit writing for the Columbus paper when he found that "I couldn't avoid politics, and them I'm forbidden to touch."[4] During the two years of uninterrupted leisure which followed his arrival in Venice he achieved a certain maturity of style and viewpoint. When the bulk of the *Venetian Life* sketches appeared in 1864, the youth of promise in 1860-1861 had already become an artist of considerable competence.

Howells first mentioned plans for the book in April, 1862, when he wrote his sister that he was keeping a journal "from which I hope to make a book about Venice."[5] He later recalled that he had gone about the island city noting impressions and registering sensations in this diary and had borrowed whole pages from it when he was composing the sketches.[6] The earliest published part of the book was the description of a day's ramble along the Lido, which appeared in the Ashtabula *Sentinel* on July 30, 1862 (p. 1), carrying a June 29 dateline. This article, which had been extracted from a private letter, later turned up in *Venetian Life* in the chapter "Some Islands of the Lagoons." It seems likely that both accounts of the day's outing were compiled from the journal. The final version, as it appears in the book, varies only slightly from the letter in the *Sentinel,* but the later account affords a typical example of the way Howells worked over his material. Between the first version and the last he looked up the history of the little town of Malmocco at the southern end of the Lido, and his final report on the day's experience contains an historical

[4] LinL, I, 54.   [5] *Ibid.,* p. 57.
[6] "Author to the Reader," VL (1907 ed.), pp. xiv-xv.

embellishment in addition to observations along the way.

Serious work on the sketches began in 1862, and by the following January the first group of them had been submitted to the *Atlantic*.[7] The work continued throughout 1863 after Howells took his bride to Venice. To supplement his observations, he read voluminously in the library of St. Mark's, while his wife transcribed sheaves of notes, and after the *Atlantic* had kept his contributions nine months, he then offered the articles to the Boston *Advertiser*.[8] Even before the magazine had finally rejected the sketches, he had outlined plans for his book to Salmon P. Chase, secretary of the Treasury, whom he had known as governor of Ohio. He told Chase that he was writing "in the desultory fashion proper to such work" some sketches of Venetian life in which he hoped to give an accurate idea of how the people lived. "Literary travel," he continued, "seldom consents to treat of such small interests as go to form a knowledge of countries, being too generally devoted to experiences of bed bugs, tables d'hote, galleries, and so forth. . . ."[9] Howells concluded that such a book as he proposed would have the merit of novelty. Previously Chase had challenged: "If you do not give us a very charming book, we shall all be greatly disappointed. You must beat Ruskin."[10] By the end of October Howells had completed approximately fifteen of the articles which ultimately

[7] Howells wrote Conway on Aug. 22, 1863 (MS at Columbia Univ.), that "I have had some Venetian Sketches . . . in that purgatory [the *Atlantic* office] for seven months."

[8] I suspect that Howells revised these sketches after getting them back from the *Atlantic* before sending them to the *Advertiser*. At least he must have recopied them, because he was worried about their legibility. See LinL, I, 78.

[9] Oct. 3, 1863; MS at Penn. Hist. Soc. Howells also wrote Swinton on Oct. 22 (MS at Boston Pub. Lib.) that his sketches would be "views of life among all classes of this interesting people—the living human interest predominating over the sentimental and historical relish, which I could not help also imparting." A similar statement of purpose may be found in VL, I, 119.

[10] Aug. 25, 1863; MS at Harvard.

found their way into the book.[11] After he sold his work to the *Advertiser,* the articles began appearing at frequent intervals, and between January 18 and July 23, 1864, seventeen letters, the bulk of *Venetian Life,* were printed.[12]

The month after the series of letters had ended in the *Advertiser* Howells began putting them into shape for book publication. There was little rewriting to do except for a transitional paragraph here and there or an occasional page of added material. He told Lowell in August:

I wrote the Venetian studies laboriously enough, adding and altering, re-writing and throwing away as my wont is, and now when I come to put them together for a book, I find my account in all that work, for I shall have to change the printed matter very little.[13]

Howells added, however, that he had plans for several new chapters, one on Venetian painting and others on the Venetian national character. He carried out this project, incorporating the material on painting into the chapter "Churches

[11] See LinL, I, 77-78. Howells wrote Hale on Oct. 25, 1863, that he on hand three times as much material as the *Atlantic* had just refused. Since he listed eleven sketches, I estimate the number completed to be fifteen. Even before the *Atlantic* had turned down his contributions, fragments of what later became *Venetian Life* had appeared in Howells's *Advertiser* newsletters: June 29, material on Venetian holidays; Sept. 11, information on the churches and pictures of the city; Sept 29, a report on the commencement exercises at the Armenian college in Venice.

[12] The last of the nonliterary newsletters (though parts of these also went into the book) appeared in the *Advertiser* on Nov. 21, 1863 (p. 2), and the first of the literary series began Nov. 26 (p. 2), a piece on the sentimental errors about Venice, which became part of VL, chap. i. The Nov. 26 article could have been one of those rejected by the *Atlantic,* because Hale had sent them to Howells when he wrote Oct. 13, and there was just time for Howells to have returned one. He obviously kept the bulk of the sketches on hand until he received an answer to his letter to Hale of Oct. 25 (probably early in December) before sending the whole series which began running in January. One other *Advertiser* letter belonging to the literary series, however, was published before the end of the year—Dec. 8 (p. 2)—the essay on the Venetian winter; and it may also have been a rejected *Atlantic* sketch.

[13] LinL, I, 84.

and Pictures" and using the studies of Italian character in the last three chapters of the book. Even though these chapters were substantially new, fragments of all four had been published in the newspaper letters. The only entirely new chapter was a short one which Howells had not planned when he wrote Lowell, the chapter called "A Daybreak Ramble." Soon after writing Lowell, he told his father that he expected to have the book done by November,[14] and in late October, as we have noted, there were only three more chapters to copy.[15] By the time he left for Rome in November the manuscript was ready, but finding a publisher willing to gamble on an unknown author was an obstacle yet to be overcome.

The negotiations for book publication of *Venetian Life* dragged on for a full year before the final arrangements were completed. In late August or early September Howells submitted part of his book to Trübner.[16] A month later, after Howells sent him a copy of Lowell's note praising the sketches, the publisher asked to see the entire manuscript;[17] but the London firm was unwilling to take the risk, and Howells was forced to wait until he could find an American house to underwrite half the edition.[18] When he visited London on his way home in July, 1865, he carried the manuscript from one publisher to another, hunting without success for a firm which would give him better terms than Trübner,[19] but fortunately for Howells, one of

[14] *Ibid.*, p. 89.   [15] *Ibid.*, p. 92.
[16] See letter from Trübner & Co. to Howells dated Sept. 8, 1864; MS at Harvard.
[17] See letter from Trübner & Co. to Howells dated Oct. 8, 1864; MS at Harvard. Lowell's note is reproduced in "1864: 'The Turning Point of My Life,' " chap. i.
[18] As I have noted earlier, Trübner offered in March, 1865, to publish the book if Howells could get an American publisher to take half of the edition. The arrangements called for printing 1,000 copies, and Trübner offered half profits on the 500 which were to be marketed in England.
[19] LF&A, pp. 101-102.

the passengers on the steamship *Asia* was Melancthon M. Hurd of the New York publishing house of Hurd and Houghton. The two men struck up a lasting friendship, playing ringtoss and shuffleboard together on deck during the day and euchre at night in the saloon, and the result was Hurd's acceptance of the American edition of Howells's book.

The arrangements for Hurd's undertaking the venture, however, were not made during the voyage; the following month, while Howells was free-lancing in New York, he met Hurd on the street and over a restaurant table proposed the book. Writing his wife a few hours later, Howells reported breathlessly that Hurd had "figured the matter over, and accepted: didn't want to see the manuscript: knew it was good."[20] When Hurd read the book later, he was delighted with it and wrote from Lancaster, New Hampshire:

> I took a copy of your *Venetian Life* with me, which I had had bound for the occasion and am now reading it. I cannot refrain from expressing my delight at its freshness, originality and humor. . . . I believe you have the materials (in portfolio and brain) for a first class novel or poem.[21]

Hurd's acceptance released Howells's father and brother from a tentative agreement to take the American edition if no one else would, and the author then sent his manuscript off to London. But six more months were to elapse before the first English edition reached the public on June 2, 1866, nineteen months after the manuscript had been completed.

The first edition of *Venetian Life* was a financial failure even though a literary success. The English edition came out with three pages of errata tipped in, and when the London publishers sent a balance sheet a year later, How-

[20] LinL, I, 98.
[21] July 5, 1866; MS at Harvard.

ells found himself almost owing Trübner money. After charging for corrections and a commission on sales, the company had authorized Ticknor and Fields, as their agents, to pay him ten shillings. He wrote Hurd in September: "I propose to give the sum to Mr. Trübner for the benefit of South American and Oriental literary men, and to take my pay in glory, so far as England is concerned."[22] The American edition did not appear until August 25 and was made up of imported sheets, but because of the great number of errors Howells cancelled thirty-three sheets and replaced them with corrected leaves printed in the United States.[23] In 1907 he remembered:

As for the American edition, I spent my whole percentage from it in replacing certain portions of the London sheets with corrected pages, where the errors seemed too gross. I had then gone to live in Cambridge, where errors, especially in foreign languages, were not tolerated; these were in Italian, and worse yet, they were my own blunders.[24]

Beginning with the second edition, *Venetian Life* began to show a profit, and early in 1869 Howells wrote Hurd that he was "most agreeably surprised at the amount of your very welcome cheque: my most soaring expectation did not fly higher than half of it."[25] The check included royalties on both *Venetian Life* and *Italian Journeys* (published a year later), but the former was the better seller.

The careful, painstaking labor which went into *Venetian Life* paid a handsome dividend when the book reached the reviewers. For a young, unknown writer Howells fared

---

[22] LinL, I, 120-121.

[23] Gibson and Arms, *op. cit.*, p. 20.

[24] VL (1907 ed.), pp. xx-xxi. Actually Howells made a little money from the first American edition of VL. Hurd sent him a statement dated April 6, 1867 (MS at Harvard), showing half profits to be $97.49, but after charges for corrections had been deducted, the balance was $29.95.

[25] LinL, I, 153. Hurd and Houghton issued at least five reprintings of the book by the end of 1868.

well among the critics, and even though Trübner had done a poor job of printing, the reviewers were charmed and expressed unanimous surprise at finding among the flood of travel books something different and eminently readable. The London *Athenaeum,* the first journal to review the book, recognized in the sketches "certainty of hand and brightness of colour,"[26] and subsequent reviewers found that the absence of conventional guidebook materials—the descriptions of churches and palaces, statues and paintings —gave the work charm and originality. The *Westminster Review* rejoiced that the "book does not revel in new descriptions of thrice-described Palaces, and is not inordinately stuffed out with scraps of half-digested Venetian history."[27] This review correctly attributed its appeal to the vignettes of everyday life in Venice and realistic treatment of Italian character. The most enthusiastic notice, in the *Contemporary Review,* praised it as lavishly as the publisher himself might have:

It is the very model of what a light book of travels ought to be. The author can instruct without prosing, and describe without boring. But moreover he is a genuine poet, with a loving eye for the beautiful, and the keenest sense of humor. The writing is positively creative. Every object is seized from the point of view of a gifted painter.[28]

Despite its intrinsic merits *Venetian Life* owed some of its immediate success to the fortuitous timing of its publication. The Seven Weeks' War between Prussia and Austria, which resulted in the cession of the Province of Venetia to the new Kingdom of Italy, brought Venice into

[26] No. 2014 (June 2, 1866), p. 734.
[27] XXX (July, 1866), 236. This journal, it might be noted, was published by Trübner & Co.
[28] *Contemporary Review,* II (Aug., 1866), 594-595. The book also was noticed by Conway in the *Fortnightly Review,* and by the *Pall Mall Gazette.* See Howells's letter to Conway dated Mar. 10, 1867 (MS at Columbia Univ.).

the news. The reviewer for the London *Spectator* used the
book as an excuse for discussing the important events taking place in Continental politics, and the relationship between the Venetians and Austrians during the years of
occupation, as observed by Howells, occupied the most
prominent position in this notice.[29] American reviewers,
writing after the New York publication of the book on August 25, also noted an historical value in the work, and both
Charles Eliot Norton in the *Nation*[30] and George William
Curtis in *Harper's Monthly*[31] recognized that it described a
period in the life of Venice which already had come to an
end. Norton, for example, compared *Venetian Life* with the
account of the city written by William Beckford in the
period immediately preceding the fall of the Venetian
Republic.

None of the reviewers of *Venetian Life* applauded with
more enthusiasm than Lowell,[32] who heaped lavish praise
on his young friend's first serious bid for literary recog-

[29] "Reprinted from the *Spectator*," *Littell's Living Age*, 4th Ser., II (Sept. 8, 1866), 758-761.

[30] III (Sept. 6, 1866), 189.

[31] "Editor's Easy Chair," XXXIII (Oct., 1866), 668.

[32] *North American Review*, CIII (Oct., 1866), 610-613. The Gibson-Arms bibliography notes that the *North American Review* index ascribes this review to Norton, but it almost certainly was written by Lowell. Not only is it listed in G. W. Cooke's *A Bibliography of James Russell Lowell* (Boston, 1906), p. 27, but also there is the letter to Hurd (LinL, I, 114) in which Howells thanks his publisher for advance copies of the book, adding: "I shall send it to Mr. Lowell, who says he will notice it in the next *N. American Review*, and to Mr. Norton, who, I think, will review it in the *Nation*, though of course I can-not state my expectation to him." Lowell had previously written Howells (Oct. 17, 1865; MS at Harvard): ". . . see if I don't say a good word for it when it is published." The marked file in the *Nation* office attributes the notice in that journal to Norton, and it seems unlikely that he would have reviewed the book twice. Moreover, between the two reviews there is a notable factual discrepancy in the matter of citing Howells's length of residence in Italy, a situation which makes it even more unlikely that the same person wrote both notices. On the basis of careful examination of both external and internal evidence I have no hesitation in pronouncing the *North American Review* notice to be Lowell's.

nition. "We know of no single word," declared the editor-poet, "which will so fitly characterize Mr. Howells's new volume . . . as 'delightful,' "[33] and he went on to strew his pages with such flattering terms as "charm of tone," "minute fidelity to nature," "refined humor," and "airy elegance," showing a lack of restraint which might have turned the head of a less steady neophyte. But Lowell was on safe ground in bestowing his highest praise on Howells, and his crystal ball was unclouded when he predicted that a great deal would be expected from one "who at his years has already shown himself capable of so much."[34]

Lowell, of course, felt a warm personal regard for Howells, having printed his first *Atlantic* poem and his first article in the *North American Review*, and he actually was more interested in the author than the book. The idea of the young self-taught Westerner storming the citadel of Eastern culture fascinated Lowell, who for six years had watched Howells's progress towards intellectual and artistic maturity. With a sense of proprietorship and discovery he recalled the circumstances of Howells's first offerings to the *Atlantic* and how he had discovered that his contributor was a product of the "rough-and-ready West," who had passed from the compositor's desk to a newspaper editorship without advantage of college training. "But there are some men born cultivated," concluded Lowell.[35]

The educational value of Howells's four years in Europe was a further matter on which Lowell speculated at considerable length. Having known the young man before and after his consular years, he was better qualified than any other critic to evaluate the broadening process which had taken place between 1861 and 1865. The sudden transplantation from Ohio, "where the log-hut was but yesterday turned to . . . brick and mortar," to Italy with its "imme-

[33] *Ibid.*, p. 612.   [34] *Ibid.*, p. 613.   [35] *Ibid.*, p. 611.

morial permanence of grandeur" presented a spectacle
which captured Lowell's imagination.[36] He could think
of no experience which would more effectively quicken
the perceptions of a sensitive individual than "the constantly recurring shock of unfamiliar objects."[37] One can
expect, he observed, "something like seeing from fresh
eyes," especially those that open on marvels "so utterly
alien to their daily vision and so perdurably novel as
Venice."[38] Lowell recognized that Howells had cultivated
his mind and expanded his horizons during his foreign residence, and with shrewd insight he wrote: "Venice has been
the university in which he has fairly earned the degree of
Master."[39]

Lowell's publicly expressed opinion of *Venetian Life*
was hardly more flattering than the private letters which
Howells received from his literary friends. The young author had astutely arranged for complimentary copies of the
book to be widely distributed,[40] and his foresight was rewarded by an enthusiastic response. Longfellow read it
with much pleasure and regretted that he had missed so
many things in Venice during his youthful travels. "Your
book," wrote Longfellow, "is full of light and color, and
that insight into life, without which a book is not a book,
but a volume only. I heartily congratulate you on your
success."[41] The next day Bayard Taylor recorded his impressions, writing that he read the volume at a single sitting
and venturing the opinion that it would be a "permanent
contribution to our literature." He was the most articulate

[36] *Ibid.*, p. 612.   [37] *Ibid.*   [38] *Ibid.*, p. 613.

[39] *Ibid.*, p. 612. The reviewer for the *Round Table* (IV, Sept. 8, 1866, 90)
closed the book with a similar feeling, describing it as a genuine work and
not a compilation, "something that grew out of the author's mind and with
it—the fructification of his experience. . . ." This notice probably was written
by the librarian Justin Winsor. See LinL, I, 114.

[40] See letter to Hurd, LinL, I, 114.

[41] Aug. 25, 1866; MS at Harvard.

commentator on Howells's prose style and recognized the artistic workmanship when he wrote:

The style is exquisite, and I don't know any young writer in the country who has selected a better basis upon which to build. It is remarkably *plastic:* the refining processes are never seen: it becomes grave without the slightest heaviness or dullness, and runs, as if spontaneously, into light and sparkle. A prose style without humor is like unleavened bread, but your loaf is aerated through and through. You interfuse the element of humor with faultless tact—or, I should say, *instinct.* Then, over the whole book there is the bloom, the subtle *something* (always suggesting perfume to my mind), which the poetic faculty gives to the prose of a poet. It is altogether a delightful book, and you may be well satisfied to have written it.[42]

Such praise from Longfellow and Taylor, two older and well-established writers whom Howells admired greatly, must have been heady wine for the ex-Consul, but the sincere words of Francis Child, written before Howells had become his Cambridge neighbor and while the book was still in press, probably were equally satisfying. Professor Child expressed pleasure that the Venetian letters were going to be available in book form so that he could reread them, and added: "During the war I cared *nothing* for literature. Thoughts not bloody were nothing worth to me. And yet, I read those [Venetian letters] with great zest.... Before your letters the Venetians were as unreal to me as Shakespeare's Bohemians."[43]

After eighty-six years *Venetian Life* is still a readable book, comparing favorably with the best of Howells's multitude of works. The style is sure, the detail well chosen and deftly handled. There are humor and pathos, color and

[42] MS at Harvard.
[43] Dec. 18, 1865; MS at Harvard.

movement, and the reader gains an over-all impression of meticulous workmanship. Howells begins with a chapter on the sentimental errors about Venice, correcting historical inaccuracies and exposing anachronisms perpetuated by such Romanticists as Byron, and goes on to sketch realistically the relationship between the Italians and their Austrian masters. Although his official consular position prevented his criticizing the foreign rule, it is clear from the start that he is not writing a conventional travelogue, and as one reads, this opinion is strengthened. He does not hesitate to attack corruption in the Church, and he is frequently critical of Old World social mores. Always interested in people—gondoliers, domestic servants, tradesmen, aristocrats—he shows a genuine affection for the Italians, but at the same time he recognizes and catalogues their faults.[44]

The book is essentially a socioeconomic study of Venice with a prominent thread of autobiography running through it. Unobtrusively added are engaging bits of history, lively anecdotes, amusing incidents, and characterizations which foreshadow the novelist to come. The book follows a chronological pattern, although the chronology is distorted on occasion for artistic purposes. Some of the chapters are predominantly biographical, some mainly descriptive. The de-

[44] It would be instructive to know more of the book's reputation in Venice. Howells himself was anxious to learn how the book was received in Italy and wrote Taylor, who had just returned from Europe (Sept. 18, 1868; MS at Cornell): "Sometime I hope you'll let me know what people you met in Venice, and just what they said of *Venetian Life*. Larkin Mead had [*sic*] already given me hints that the book was not wholly acceptable to them. 'Ben scritto si; ma troppo severo,' said one friend. I should be very sorry to have done them injustice. They had a great deal to bear." When Howells returned to Venice in 1883 the Crown Princess of Germany was there and asked to meet the author of VL (see VL, 1907 ed., pp. 412-413), and on another occasion Howells was entertained on board an English steamer where there were a Montenegrin princess and half a dozen other thrones, principalities, and powers who had read VL (see Howells's letter to William Cooper Howells dated May 20, 1883; MS at Harvard). During the same visit to Venice Howells reported finding VL on sale in the foreign bookstore (see VL, 1907 ed., p. 419).

scriptive chapters run the gamut of Venetian life, depicting the national character, native holidays, the opera and theaters, the islands of the lagoons, the churches and pictures, and various other aspects of the city and its inhabitants. In all these chapters the autobiographical element is present, giving life and movement to the exposition. At the same time, in the predominantly biographical chapters there is ample description to lend color and background to the narrative. The different types of matter are distributed throughout, giving the work the general effect of variety.

"The book is distinctly a youthful book,"[45] asserted Howells in 1891 when he wrote a new preface for it, and the excitement of being young amid fabulous surroundings is ably communicated. Not only is the book full of accurately observed detail reported in a pleasing manner, but it is also on firm footing when it delves into political, social, or economic history. Howells read widely in preparing his manuscript, and he cites or quotes at least a dozen writers on Venice, chiefly Italian, the most frequently used authority being the Venetian historian Mutinelli. He leans on Ruskin for his art criticism, quotes the travel letters of Thomas Gray, and supports, in addition, his observations on Venetian life by extensive reading from the works of Venetian literary men. Chief among these is Goldoni, whose plays were repeatedly performed while Howells was in Venice.

The study of Howells as an essayist and novelist properly begins with an analysis of *Venetian Life,* for his later writings derive from the travel-book genre. *Suburban Sketches* (1871) follows directly from this book of Venetian sketches and in a sense does for Cambridge what its predecessor had done for Venice. The incidents of everyday life and descriptions of his friends and acquaintances in Venice give way

[45] VL, I, vi.

to observations on his activities and neighbors in Cambridge. His early novels also derive, though less directly, from *Venetian Life,* for this first book is in many respects an auto-biographical romance with the author as the leading character. There is only a quantitative difference between Consul Howells, who plays the hero of *Venetian Life,* and Consul Ferris, who takes a subordinate role in *A Foregone Conclusion* (1875). In his subsequent career as a novelist Howells treated with minute fidelity the lives and surroundings of his characters, employing the same type of accurate observation and vivid detail. He was to grow as a psychologist and as a contriver of plots, but he set the pattern for his particular brand of realism during the years in Venice.

No other book which Howells wrote was so much added to, edited, reprinted, and revised as *Venetian Life,* and it occupied a place in his affections never attained by later successes. The first American edition had scarcely gone on sale before a new edition was called for,[46] and Howells spent the month of September, 1866, preparing the second edition, which appeared in January of the following year.[47] It was subsequently kept in print between 1867 and 1907 by three different publishers who in turn held the rights to the book, Hurd and Houghton, James R. Osgood, and Houghton Mifflin. In the second edition Howells revised and expanded his consular report for 1864 to make a chap-

[46] Hurd and Houghton advertised the book in the *Round Table* on Aug. 18, Sept. 1, and Sept 15, but on Sept. 22 VL was dropped from the advertisement containing the rest of the company's trade list.

[47] On Sept. 13 Hurd wrote Howells (MS at Harvard) about arrangements for the new edition and offered a 10 per cent royalty. Howells wrote E. P. Whipple on Sept. 15, 1866 (MS at Yale), that he was then preparing the book for a second edition. Howells also wrote his father in September postponing a visit to Ohio until the revision of the new edition was finished. The date of this letter (LinL, I, 115), which is given as "Cambridge, Sunday, Sept. 20/66" is incorrect, inasmuch as Sept. 20 was not a Sunday. Sept 2 seems a more likely date, especially since Hurd had mentioned a second edition (LinL, I, 114) even before the publication date of the first edition.

ter on Venetian commerce.[48] In 1872 when Osgood became the publisher, a new and enlarged edition was brought out, and again the author added a new chapter, one which had previously been printed in the *Atlantic* as "A Year in a Venetian Palace."[49] This increment rounded out the record of the Consul's years in Venice and appeared in the 1872 edition as "Our Last Year in Venice," an account of the final fourteen months of Howells's Italian sojourn.

The next edition of *Venetian Life* (1885) was published by Houghton Mifflin, the firm which brought out all subsequent American issues of the book, but no new material was included. In 1891, however, Howells wrote a new preface and the book was published again,[50] this time handsomely in two volumes with illustrations in aquatint. This edition supplied the trade for the next sixteen years. Then in 1907-1908 the publishing record of *Venetian Life* ended with issuance of three new editions just before the original copyright expired. In order to make these editions really new, Howells wrote a ten-page introduction, "Author to the Reader," and a seventeen-page concluding chapter, "Venice Revisited," drawing upon his return trip to Venice in 1883.[51] One of these editions was a two-volume, limited, autographed issue selling for fifteen dollars, and the others were one-volume trade editions. After the second of the two trade editions was issued in 1908, the book was not reprinted, but of all Howells's many works *Venetian Life* to-

[48] *Letter of the Secretary of State . . . for the Year Ended September 30, 1864*, pp. 462-467.

[49] XXVII (Jan., 1871), 1-14.

[50] The title page carries the date 1892, although the book was published Oct. 7, 1891. See Gibson and Arms, *op. cit.*, p. 40.

[51] In the preface to the 1891 edition Howells wrote that he preferred not to emend the book despite the faults he knew it contained, but in 1907 he made minor changes (see "Author to the reader," p. xi), pruning some of the youthful exuberance, altering some of the bolder conclusions about Venetian social customs, and toning down some of the more critical passages on the Catholic Church.

day turns up most frequently on the shelves of the secondhand dealers.[52]

ITALIAN JOURNEYS

Soon after Howells laid plans for the literary exploitation of his Italian residence, it became obvious that he
would have material for at least two books. The first was
to contain sketches of life in Venice, and the second was to
record his travels in other parts of Italy. By November,
1864, he had finished preparing *Venetian Life* for the press,
and for the remaining eight months of his stay in Italy
he was busily engaged in gathering material and making
drafts of articles on Italian subjects. When a two months'
leave of absence came his way in November, he leaped at
the opportunity to make an extensive tour of Italy. He carried along his notebook in customary fashion and recorded
his impressions of the sights and sounds in Naples, Rome,
and other cities visited along the way. When he returned
to his consulate at the end of 1864, he set about writing the
sketches which became the major part of *Italian Journeys*.

At the time Howells departed for Naples and Rome he
had already made a half-dozen short trips to cities in northern Italy. All of these minor travels were to find a place
in the book, and all but one were to be serialized in newspaper or magazine before book publication, following the
pattern set by *Venetian Life* and further establishing the

[52] This observation is based on my own experience in hunting for Howells
titles. This chapter has described only the editions of VL which contained
new material or were actually new editions printed from new plates. The
book was reprinted many times, and by 1895 nineteen editions or issues had
been brought out. I have not traced the reprintings beyond that date. It
was reprinted in Great Britain by Howells's publisher David Douglas of
Edinburgh and by Longmans, Green in 1891. Trübner also brought out a
second edition in 1867, and the book appeared in the 1880's in a Tauchnitz
edition for continental Europe. See the appropriate volumes of *The British
Museum Catalogue of Printed Books*, *The English Catalogue of Books*, and
Kayser's Bücher Lexicon.

procedure Howells was to use throughout his career. The initial excursion which he made outside Venice, his trip to Trieste in 1862, was described in the Ashtabula *Sentinel* on May 14 of that year, but his report was completely rewritten before it appeared in *Italian Journeys*. The journey to Florence thirteen months later, however, provided three-fourths of the section called "The Ferrara Road," and the account of this trip in the Boston *Advertiser,* "From Venice to Florence and Back Again," represents the earliest published portion of the book. The two visits to Petrarch's house at Arquà, the trip to Lake Como, and the excursion to Bassano and Possagno were first described in the *Nation* and the *Atlantic* after Howells returned home. Only the visit to Vicenza, Verona, and Parma did not appear in print before book publication.

Howells began the year 1865 with a notebook full of material gathered during his tour of southern Italy in the preceding November and December. In January, as we have seen, he put these travels into letters, three of which appeared in the Boston *Advertiser* in March, April, and May as "The Road to Rome and Home Again." This trio of sketches, however, covered only the visit to Ferrara and the voyage from Genoa to Naples. Additional articles which were submitted to the paper at the same time were not used, and after returning from Italy six months later Howells went to the *Advertiser* office to learn what had become of them. The managing editor returned "half a dozen unprinted letters," and Howells then published them in the *Nation.*[1]

The first of these articles to appear in the *Nation,* "A Day in Pompeii," came out the month before E. L. Godkin, the editor, hired Howells as a staff writer. It brought a welcome gale of praise from Lowell, who wrote with

[1] LF&A, p. 103.

characteristic enthusiasm: "I read the article about Pompeii without the least suspicion whose it was, and found it charming. Why, here is somebody, I said to myself, who writes about Italy just as I would like to have written if I could."[2] This auspicious beginning was followed by other travel sketches in subsequent issues of the *Nation* between October, 1865, and December, 1866, and the "half a dozen" letters which Howells remembered getting back from the *Advertiser* grew to eight before the series was finally completed.[3] Long before all the articles had been printed, he had moved to Cambridge to assist Fields in editing the *Atlantic*.

Howells finally managed to place the last four installments of *Italian Journeys* with the *Atlantic* in February, March, July, and September, 1867, five years after he first had submitted a travel sketch to the magazine and nearly a year after becoming assistant editor. These four articles scraped the bottom of his Italian barrel and rounded out the collection of papers he was getting together for the new book. "Forza Maggiore" took the Howells family to Leghorn from Rome; "A Glimpse of Genoa" closed a gap in the previous journey southward. The article "At Padua" was based on a visit to that city in 1863, and "Minor Italian Travels" disposed of the miscellaneous peregrinations of the entire Venetian sojourn.

Before the second edition of *Venetian Life* was off the press, Howells was negotiating for publication of his next book, planning to call it "The Road to Rome." Hurd ob-

---

[2] *Letters of James Russell Lowell*, I, 350.

[3] It seems likely that the last two letters, "Capri and Capriotes" and "Roman Pearls," were written after Howells went to the *Atlantic*. The sketches had been appearing in the *Nation* at almost one-month intervals, but between the first six articles and the last two, three months passed. Since the last two sketches began appearing in July, more than four months after Howells went to Cambridge, it is my guess that he was unable to work these sketches into the *Atlantic* and as second choice passed them along to the *Nation*.

jected to the Catholic connotation of the title and suggested instead "Memorable Places in Italy,"[4] but in the end they compromised on *Italian Journeys.* Late in December, 1866, Hurd wrote that he had discussed the publication of the book with his partner Houghton and the firm probably would want to bring it out. The decision, he added, was to be deferred until after the company's February inventory.[5] Eight months later, when the September, 1867, issue of the *Atlantic* appeared,[6] serialization of the travel articles was completed, and the book could then go to press.[7] On November 25 Howells wrote his mother that "my new book is now ready, and I'll send you a copy early in the week."[8] Soon after the publication date he informed his sister: "My new book's out, and I've seen some half dozen notices, all very favorable."[9]

The subsequent publishing history of *Italian Journeys* was less spectacular than that of *Venetian Life,* but the book was reprinted many times and sold briskly during most of Howells's lifetime.[10] In 1872, the same year that *Venetian Life* was expanded, Osgood also brought out a new and enlarged edition of *Italian Journeys,* adding the seventy-eight page essay "Ducal Mantua," which previously had been printed in the *North American Review;* but after this supplement was incorporated there were no further additions. The book received its last important reprinting when simultaneous English and American editions were brought

[4] Hurd to Howells dated Dec. 19, 1866; MS at Harvard.

[5] Dec. 29, 1866; MS at Harvard.

[6] The magazine customarily came out about the tenth of the month before the date of issue. See LinL, I, 117-118.

[7] See Howells's letter to Hurd of Sept. 8, 1867 (LinL, I, 121), reporting that Houghton had just written the book was ready to go to press.

[8] LinL, I, 122.

[9] *Ibid.,* p. 124. Letter dated Dec. 8, 1867. On Dec. 7, 1867, Hurd and Houghton advertised the book in the *Round Table* (VI, 382) as "lately published."

[10] For example, up to 1888 I have traced twelve editions and reprintings.

out in 1901, the former under the imprint of William
Heinemann and the latter by Houghton Mifflin. A limited,
de luxe issue appeared in time for the Christmas trade and
was followed by a less pretentious printing for "The Park
Street Library" series. In 1907 Houghton Mifflin used the
plates again to issue *Italian Journeys* as volume five of
"The Atlantic Library of Travel."[11]

Although Howells seldom revised the text of his books,
he was unable to let some of his youthful observations stand
in the new 1901 edition of *Italian Journeys*. Rereading the
book in his old age, he found himself doubting his earlier
taste, judgment, and veracity. "From time to time it seemed
to me," he wrote, "that I was aware of posing, of straining
. . . and I had a sense of having put on more airs than I
could handsomely carry."[12] In the light of his attitudes at
the age of sixty-four he pruned with a free hand, cutting
away twenty-three pages and three entire subchapters. His
deletions included both autobiographical detail and personal judgments on places and people. His account of
breakfasting in Bologna with a "purse-proud English Jew,"
for example, is excised along with animadversions on
Frenchmen met aboard the steamer he took from Genoa to
Naples. Two of the entire sections omitted, the account of
a visit to some Protestant schools in Naples and a report
on colored statuary seen in Rome, are among the duller
parts of the book and were well taken out; and the essay
"Ducal Mantua," which is trimmed of ten pages, is tight-
ened up and improved. On the other hand, the deletion of
the section called "The Ferrara Road" removed a good
character sketch and a poetic description of the road between Padua and the Po River. All changes considered,

[11] See Gibson and Arms, *op. cit.*, p. 53.
[12] IJs (1901 ed.), p. v. Howells also wrote a new, two-page introduction
to this edition.

the book is improved artistically but at the expense of making the volume less of a personal document.

After the book made its first appearance in December, 1867, Howells again was applauded by the reviewers for a performance of undeniable excellence. One of the most cordial of the critics was Henry James, who found the author a charming writer and the most satisfactory of American travelers. Howells had, moreover, an eye for the small things of nature, art, and human life, which enabled him "to extract sweetness and profit from adventures the most prosaic."[13] But James went beyond the superficial praise of the reviewer and recognized the solid literary character of the book when he wrote:

This charm of style Mr. Howells's two books on Italy possess in perfection; they belong to literature and to the center and core of it,—the region where men think and feel, and one may almost say breathe, in good prose, and where the classics stand on guard.

. . . .

Mr. Howells is, in short, a descriptive writer in a sense and with a perfection that, in our view, can be claimed for no American writer except Hawthorne. . . . Mr. Howells is the master of certain refinements of style, of certain exquisite intentions (intentions in which humor generally plays a large part), such as are but little practised in these days of crude and precipitate writing.[14]

The reviewer for the *Nation,* noticing the book about the same time as James, believed that its realistic appraisal of Italy might disappoint some readers, but for his own part he was thankful for anything Howells had chosen to give the public. This critic went on to say: ". . . though

[13] *North American Review,* CVI (Jan., 1868), 336.
[14] *Ibid.,* pp. 337-339.

Mr. Howells's books are pervaded by sentiment, it is sentiment satirized—satirized not with the least bitterness; on the contrary, with unfailing good nature and cheerfulness. . . ."[15] He concluded that the author was a traveler who treated the places he visited with "loving disparagement," and went on to exclaim: ". . . we should say that as a humorist he is the superior of all other American writers."[16] If there was doubt in anyone's mind that Howells by 1868 had "arrived," in the literary sense, the reviewers of *Italian Journeys* dispelled it. The appearance of a new star in the literary firmament was typically observed by *Harper's Monthly,* which saw Howells as "a new author whose name must grow to honor in our literature" and a writer from whose work gleams "the soft auroral light of something more than talent."[17]

The critical approval which *Italian Journeys* received was once more matched by the warm approval of Howells's friends. Less than a week after the book appeared a former Italian traveler, George Stillman Hillard, expressed his delight: "About a thousand years ago I was in Italy, and wrote a book about it,[18] which may be found now and then in the garrets of old houses. . . . How exactly you paint what I felt and feel!"[19] Howells enclosed this letter when he wrote to Hurd three days later, saying that he was "particularly proud of it because it was not provoked by a presentation copy. . . ."[20] When Howells and Bret Harte began corresponding in 1869, the California writer praised all of Howells's books, writing specifically of *Italian Journeys* that he liked it so much that as a "lazy man and a fastidious one, I should have been willing to have seen Italy by proxy.

[15] VI (Jan. 2, 1868), 11.   [16] *Ibid.*, p. 12.
[17] "Literary Notices," XXXVI (May, 1868), 815.
[18] *Six Months in Italy* (Boston, 1853).
[19] Dec. 12, 1867; MS at Harvard.
[20] LinL, I, 125.

I think you have such a rare faculty of not liking things in a likeable manner."[21]

Despite its literary merits, *Italian Journeys* performed a utilitarian service as a guidebook for countless English-speaking tourists who traveled from Naples to Trieste with the volume in hand. The most sensitive and articulate of the travelers compared the portrait and the subject and were delighted with the likeness. Such a tourist was Howells's friend John Fiske, the historian, who wrote his wife enviously from Naples after visiting Pompeii: "And now what's the use of saying anything about it except to tell you to read what Howells says. . . ."[22] The following year when Charles Dudley Warner toured Italy, he sent Howells a volume of Carducci's poems and at the same time reported finding and rereading with "intense enjoyment" a chance copy of the book. "Your handling of the English language," added Warner, "charms me to the core."[23]

Howells considered *Italian Journeys* a better book than *Venetian Life,* but the public thought otherwise,[24] and the critic viewing the two works with the perspective of eighty years is obliged to agree with the public. *Italian Journeys* has the light touch and the charm of style which the reviewers found, but it lacks the unity of the earlier work, and the greater diversity of the subject matter weakens the total impression. The book is much like *Venetian Life,* however, in its exploitation of the strangeness and charm of distant places and in its incisive delineation of Italian character. The industry which made the earlier volume a finished piece of prose is evident also in the stylistic polish of *Italian Journeys.* Hence in the matter of subject and

[21] Bradford A. Booth, "Bret Harte Goes East: Some Unpublished Letters," *American Literature,* XIX (Jan., 1948), 320.

[22] Ethel F. Fiske (ed.), *The Letters of John Fiske,* p. 317. Letter dated Apr. 2, 1874.

[23] Aug. 1, 1875; MS at Harvard.   [24] See LinL, I, 153.

style the latter book is in reality a continuation of the former.

But there is one aspect of the second book which shows the author's further literary development—the handling of dramatic incident. There are numerous episodes which read like chapters from Howells's later novels, and the execution of this travel narrative prepares the way for his subsequent travel fiction. The account of the voyage from Genoa to Naples on a stormy sea aboard a tiny coasting steamer, for example, is written in the manner of fiction with a gallery of interesting passengers who speak their parts like characters in a novel. The chapter "Forza Maggiore," which James called "a real masterpiece of light writing,"[25] describes the near disaster which Howells experienced in the flood waters of the Ombrone River near Grossetto. It would be instructive to have a contemporary letter recounting this experience in order to determine exactly how the author managed the events to achieve a dramatic effect.

Fortunately enough, it is possible to make such a study of a lesser episode, the author's visit to Trieste, which originally was described in the Ashtabula *Sentinel* on May 14, 1862, and later incorporated into the chapter called "Minor Travels." Howells customarily prepared his travels for book publication by reading through his newspaper letters and notebooks, accepting, revising, or rejecting the material he had written previously, as the occasion warranted. In the case of the *Sentinel* letter, he found the early account totally unusable and rewrote it from start to finish. An examination of the revised version gives an insight into Howells's creative process. The two articles—the section in *Italian Journeys* and the newspaper letter—are of almost exactly the same length, but in revising the early account, Howells

[25] "Review of *Italian Journeys*," p. 339.

telescoped the first five hundred words into one sentence and eliminated a rather tedious account of the overnight trip by steamship from Venice to Trieste. Then he brought up to the first page from the second half of the *Sentinel* letter a report on one of the more interesting features of Trieste, the bora. A comparison of passages describing this fierce wind gives some indication of his stylistic development between 1862 and about 1867. The Ashtabula *Sentinel* version follows:

It was pleasant enough in Trieste, then, but there are times when the weather is not so good humored. In the winter, a terrible wind which they call Borea, (after the classical north wind of nearly the same name,) sweeps down from these hills, and freezes everything as it goes. The streets of Trieste are then almost impassable, such is the force of the wind, and any lady venturing out is instantly converted into a parachute. This wind comes periodically, and its approaches are always felt before its full fury bursts upon the people. There is a story— I do not say it is true—that the peasants on the adjacent mountains have one of their number appointed to announce the coming of the Borea. The sentinel takes his place in a certain current of air. As soon as he feels the freezing breath of the Borea, he sounds upon a horn, and all the peasants below, immediately hang on to something.

The parallel description from *Italian Journeys* has acquired a polish not present in the former passage. For this account of the wind Howells switched from the formal *borea* to the dialectal *bora,* and he no longer cared to doubt the authenticity of the warning system. Other refinements over the earlier version also are apparent:

. . . looking at those rugged acclivities [the mountains behind Trieste], with their aspect of continual bleakness, you readily believe all the stories you have heard of that fierce wind called the Bora which sweeps from them through Trieste at certain

seasons. While it blows, ladies walking near the quays are sometimes caught up and set afloat, involuntary Galateas, in the bay,
and people keep in-doors as much as possible. But the Bora,
though so sudden and so savage, does give warning of its rise,
and the peasants avail themselves of the characteristic. They
station a man on one of the mountain tops, and when he feels
the first breath of the Bora, he sounds a horn, which is the signal
for all within hearing to lay hold of something that cannot be
blown away, and cling to it till the wind falls. This may happen in three days or in nine, according to the popular proverbs.[26]

He then concludes this passage with an embellishment
gathered from his extensive reading, a description, taken
from a note to one of Dall'Ongaro's ballads, of the sea and
hills before and after the wind.

In addition to his stylistic progress, Howells's treatment
in *Italian Journeys* of his return trip from Trieste shows the
apprentice novelist and dramatist at work. In the newspaper letter the voyage home is told in about three hundred
and fifty words, ignoring the dramatic possibilities of the
scene. Briefly the situation is this: Howells climbs into a
hack and orders himself taken to the wharf despite the
driver's protest that the steamer does not leave for Venice
that night. He insists and the driver takes him from one
dock to another until finally they find a vessel getting up
steam. It appears larger than the ship on which he had
come; so he questions the steward before embarking to
make certain that Venice is the destination. Once aboard,
he finds that he is the only passenger, and the situation
gives him a queer feeling which recalls the Flying Dutchman and Poe's "MS Found in a Bottle." He again queries
the steward and discovers that he is not on the regular
packet but a vessel which has been diverted from the
Trieste-to-Alexandria service to take on an extraordinary

[26] Pp. 264-265.

cargo at Venice. Howells finds that he was allowed passage because he happened along when the ship was ready to sail and seemed determined to come aboard. After learning the true situation, the Consul goes to bed and awakes the next morning within sight of Venice.

When Howells rewrote the incident for *Italian Journeys,* he recognized the dramatic possibilities of this material and expanded it to one thousand words. The details are now somewhat different: as the hack driver clatters from one pier to another, the Consul grows increasingly alarmed and wonders what the papers will have to say when his body is found floating in the bay the next morning. Finally they drive up to a steamer puffing at its dock, and Howells climbs aboard just in time for the departure. After reaching the deck he realizes that this is not the ship on which he came, and the only person in sight is the mute steward who guides him below to an elegant saloon and leaves him alone. The terrified Consul sits alone in the saloon thinking of the Flying Dutchman and Poe's story. He summons the steward:

> *Was* this the steamer for Venice?
> *Sicuro!*
> All that I could do in comment was to sit down; and in the mean time the steamer trembled, groaned, choked, cleared its throat, and we were under way.
> "The other passengers have all gone to bed, I suppose," I argued acutely, seeing none of them. Nevertheless, I thought it odd, and it seemed a shrewd means of relief to ring the bell, and pretending drowsiness, to ask the steward which was my state-room.
> He replied with a curious smile that I could have any of them. Amazed, I yet selected a state-room, and while the steward was gone for the sheets and pillow-cases, I occupied my time by opening the doors of all the other state-rooms. They were empty.

"Am I the only passenger?" I asked, when he returned, with some anxiety.

"Precisely," he answered.

I could not proceed and ask if he composed the entire crew —it seemed too fearfully probable that he did.[27]

At the conclusion of this effective scene the Consul goes fearfully to bed and awakens in broad daylight when the steward, now a cheerful-faced fellow, brings in breakfast. It is only at this point that the author discovers the facts of the strange situation and why he is the only passenger. The whole scene is handled skilfully, and one concludes from reading this exhibit that Howells's literary apprenticeship in Venice was profitably spent.

POETRY

The young man who sailed for Europe on board the *City of Glasgow* in November, 1861, was a poet whose idols were Longfellow and Heine, but his literary productions in Venice during the Civil War years followed a gradual transition from poetry to prose, from Romanticism to Realism. This evolutionary process was accompanied by frustration and disappointment over rejected manuscripts, and it did not take place without an emotional readjustment. Howells discovered before returning home that he had reached his poetic peak in 1860, the year in which he sold his antislavery poem, "The Pilot's Story," to the *Atlantic,* but during 1862 and 1863 he kept trying to restrike the same popular note of that melodramatic narrative. The weakness of his poetry, as Howells himself later recognized, lay in its derivative character, and his initial poetic success had been achieved in spite of this serious defect. His first contribution to the *Atlantic,* for example, had sounded so much like Heine that Lowell had withheld publication for sev-

[27] IJs, p. 271.

eral months in order to make sure that it was not a translation from the German poet.[1] In 1861, just before sailing
for Italy, Howells had asked Lowell to criticize some imitative verses that Fields had rejected for the *Atlantic*,[2] but
Lowell seems not to have answered his letter, apparently
thinking it a kindness to ignore poems so undistinguished.
When the correspondence between the two men reopened
in 1864, Lowell promptly warned: "You must sweat the
Heine out of you as men do mercury."[3]

The strenuous effort which Howells made in 1862 to
continue his career as a poet was moderately successful, but
the year beginning in mid-1863 was a period of multiple
discouragements. As we have seen, Conway was unable to
find a London publisher for a volume of verse; the *Atlantic*
rejected several poems; and Foster went back on his agreement to publish the long narrative "Disillusion." At the
same time, Howells was publishing his Venetian letters in
the Boston *Advertiser,* and their success, plus Lowell's acceptance of the essay on "Recent Italian Comedy," turned
him irrevocably to prose. Recalling his disappointments
during his consulship, he remembered:

During the four years of my life in Venice the literary intention was present with me at all times and in all places. I wrote
many things in verse, which I sent to the magazines in every
part of the English-speaking world, but they came unerringly
back to me, except in three instances only, when they were
kept by the editors who finally printed them.[4]

Actually, the three instances were four, but Howells's mem-

[1] LF&A, p. 26.
[2] Howells to Lowell dated Sept. 29, 1861; MS at Harvard. This letter inclosed copies of verses, still unpublished, entitled "Drowsihed" and "Coming."
[3] *Letters of James Russell Lowell,* I, 338. This warning was given in the
same letter praising the Venetian sketches and accepting "Recent Italian
Comedy."
[4] LF&A, p. 91.

ory of his poetic frustration was based on a persistent editorial indisposition to accept his poems between 1862 and 1865. At least eleven of his poetical efforts, however, owe all or part to his residence in Venice. One of these was never published; another was printed privately in Venice; a third appeared in the Ashtabula *Sentinel;* and the remaining four came out in the years after his return from Italy.

"Did you get the poem I sent you for the *Atlantic?*"[5] Howells wrote his father early in March, 1862, referring to "Louis Lebeau's Conversion," a narrative like "The Pilot's Story" in the hexameters of Longfellow. This poem was the first literary product of his foreign residence, although the subject matter properly belongs to his Ohio years. The author began working the material into poetic form soon after reaching Venice, and when he wrote his sister in January he reported: "I have already sketched a poem—a lovestory, which I call 'Louis Lebeau's Conversion.' The scene is a camp-meeting one, and I think the poem will be successful."[6] He added that the idea had come to him the preceding September when he had listened one evening to his mother and father tell of old-time revival meetings.

The charm and novelty of Venice furnished an effective setting for the poem, affording Howells a chance to use a flashback narrative technique. Beginning

Yesterday, while I moved with the languid crowd on the Riva, Musing with idle eyes on the wide lagoons and the islands,[7]

he goes on to sketch the Venetian scene on a bland December day, then switches to the contrasting locale of the poem, the frontier country of Ohio in the early days of the nineteenth century. At the end of the narrative, after telling the story of the old sinner Lebeau's conversion, he re-

[5] LinL, I, 55.
[6] *Ibid.,* p. 49.
[7] *Poems,* p. 32. All references to poems are to the 1886 edition.

turns to the exotic setting of Venice for his concluding
lines.

The poem was good enough to be accepted by the *Atlantic,* although publication was delayed by the well-in-
tentioned corrections of William Cooper Howells, who
acted as agent in submitting it to the magazine. The Consul wrote his sister in late April:

I hope, dear Vic, that if father was hurt by anything I said to
him of the correction of my poem . . . that you excused me all
you could. Father knows nothing of the principles of the verse
in which the poem is written, and I'm afraid his correction has
been the death of it.[8]

Apparently Howells already had asked the *Atlantic* to return the piece, for on May 7 H. M. Ticknor wrote: "I send
you back your 'Louis Lebeau.' I hope you will not keep
him forever. . . ."[9] By the end of the summer the manuscript had been resubmitted to the magazine, and it was
scheduled for publication in November.

Another poem which Howells wrote during his residence in Venice, perhaps even before he composed the
much longer "Louis Lebeau's Conversion," was "Sweet
Clover," published by *Harper's Monthly* in 1866 after he
returned home. Although the verses are merely dated
"Italy, 1861," they speak of

> . . . these December skies,
> As bland as May's in other climes,[10]

a climatic comparison which recalls the opening lines of
the other poem. In addition, "Sweet Clover" is such a
poem as Howells must have had in mind when he wrote
Stedman in August, 1863: "Some happy day, I hope our

[8] LinL, I, 57.
[9] MS at Harvard.
[10] *Poems,* p. 51

wives may meet, in America, when we will read them all
the forlorn and desperate verses of our bachelorhood."[11]
This poem consists of forty-four lines written in the octo-
syllabic, four-stress "In Memoriam" *(abba)* stanza and de-
picts a rejected lover in Venice who suffers the cruel pangs
of unrequited love after he receives from America a packet
of returned love letters scented with sweet clover.

After writing and marketing "Louis Lebeau's Conversion," Howells "idled away" the last months of his first
year in Venice in a sort of homesick despair,[12] but after his
marriage in December, 1862, the poetic muse returned.
Three months after bringing his bride to Venice, he composed "By the Sea," a lyric which he contributed to the
Commonwealth.[13] This is an undistinguished poem which
he forgot when he later recalled that his verses during his
Italian years had found magazine publication only in three
instances, but it seems to celebrate a rekindling of the creative spark:

> I walked with her I love by the sea,
> The deep came up with its chanting waves,
> Making a music so great and free
> That the will and the faith, which were dead in me,
> Awoke and rose from their graves.[14]

During the following happy summer of his first year of
married life Howells produced a fair quantity of verse, including the most curious of all his poetic flights—an epi-
thalamium. Written in honor of the Zeni-Foratti nuptials,
this poem was privately printed at the University of Padua
after Professor Frattini had translated it into Italian, and

---

[11] LinL, I, 72.

[12] See Howells's letter to Lowell dated Aug. 21, 1864 (LinL, I, 85).

[13] Dated "Venice, March 24th," these verses no doubt were the lines inclosed in Howells's letter to Conway of Mar. 24, 1863. See *Autobiography*, I,
426.

[14] *Poems*, p. 97.

when Howells sent his father a copy, he wrote that the original English had never been published.[15] Who Zeni and Foratti were does not appear in the record of Howells's years in Venice, but it was the custom in Italy when people married for a friend to write congratulatory verses for private circulation among the happy couple's well-wishers, a tradition which is duly recorded in *Venetian Life* and again in the story "Tonelli's Marriage." Adding piquancy to the meager information available on this unique composition is the fact that no copy of it is known to have survived.[16]

All through the autumn of 1863 Howells thought that his poetic star was in the ascendancy, and with good reason. As we have noted, he already had found a publisher for the ill-fated "Disillusion," the chief literary product of the summer, and in mid-September he received word of his first sale to *Harper's Monthly*. This good news, surprisingly enough, came from his publisher Foster, who had encountered the editor of the magazine just before writing Howells a business letter about the long verse-narrative.[17] Howells promptly relayed the information to his sister Annie:

The editor of *Harper's Magazine* has accepted a poem of mine, with an illustration by Elinor, both of which will appear as the opening paper of *Harper's* for December. The poem is called "Saint Christopher," and the illustration represents an old gateway and statue in Venice, not far from where we live.[18]

The composition itself is a good descriptive piece, creating in nine subdued quatrains a brief mood of repose, and when it was published with Mrs. Howells's sketch of the venerable ivy-covered figure of the saint, the two items together made

[15] LinL, I, 76.
[16] This is one of the few items which Gibson and Arms in their extensive bibliographical research were not able to find.
[17] Aug. 21, 1863; MS at Harvard.
[18] LinL, I, 76.

an effective layout for the opening pages of the magazine. The verses probably were written in July during the visit of Conway, who recalled in 1904 that he and Howells had repeatedly visited and admired the old statue.[19]

Soon after Foster agreed to publish "Disillusion," Howells overflowed with plans for pyramiding his expected triumphs into a great poetic reputation. He wrote Stedman exuberantly of the poem in press and went on to say: "There is another poem 'nearly ready,' and if the public were half so eager as I am, how much would I not give them."[20] Unfortunately, the editors and publishers, if not the public, lacked Howells's enthusiasm, and this poem was stillborn. It was to have been named "Ordeals," and the plan of the work called for four parts, each dealing with one aspect of the Civil War: the mourners, the comforters, the comrades, and the victors. No copy of this unpublished poem is extant, but it seems likely that this was the work which Howells remembered many years later as "a long poem in the *terza rima* of the *Divina Commedia*," dealing with the war in "a fashion so remote that no editor would print it."[21] By the end of the year his high hopes had given way to despair. He felt he had been chasing celebrity all his life to find only a glimpse of it now and then. Since he commenced writing, many others had outrun him in popularity, and sometimes he felt bitter and despondent at what he considered their unmerited good fortune. What he thought his best and greatest efforts never saw the light of publication, but gradually he learned patience if not wisdom.

[19] *Autobiography*, I, 431. The poem is dated "Venice, August, 1863," but it must have been sent to the magazine from Italy at least by Aug. 1, since Foster's letter announcing acceptance is dated Aug. 21.

[20] LinL, I, 71. Letter dated Aug. 16, 1863.

[21] MLP, pp. 204-205. Howells wrote Conway on May 16, 1864 (MS at Columbia Univ.): "The poem (Copperhead) which I read to you in Venice, I continued more patriotically and more or less mystically, and sent it to the *Atlantic*." It seems impossible to say whether this was a later version of the same poem or still another poem on a Civil War (?) theme.

Another shattering blow to Howells's poetical fortunes occurred the following spring when Conway returned the manuscript volume of poems from London after failing to find a publisher. He wrote regretfully that his friend would have to finance publication himself if he wanted a London imprint, and the only encouraging result of Conway's efforts was a note of faint praise from Robert Browning.[22] Howells was still interested enough to write Trübner for an estimate on bringing out a duodecimo volume of one hundred and fifty pages,[23] but when the publisher replied that such a book would cost about forty pounds in a boarded edition of five hundred copies,[24] Howells dropped the project. Perhaps he could have afforded the expense, but by the middle of 1864 he knew that his poetic star had set.

If one discounts some trivial newspaper verse, the only important poem which Howells published in 1864 was the elegy on the death of his brother, which appeared in the Ashtabula *Sentinel* in June, but he was persistent even though discouraged. In analyzing his meager success, he must have realized that "The Pilot's Story," which had been well received, and the poem which the *Atlantic* had last accepted from him, "Louis Lebeau's Conversion," were well-contrived narratives in which the story perhaps overshadowed the versification. Consequently, when he found in Volta's *Storia di Mantova* the romantic tale of Federico, the third Marquis of Mantua, he used the material to write another narrative poem, this time a ballad which he called "The Faithful of the Gonzaga."[25]

[22] Conway left the poems for Browning to read, and the English poet acknowledged them in a note which Conway sent Howells (undated but inclosed in a letter from Conway to Howells dated Aug. 5, 1863; MS at Harvard): "I have read the 'Pilot's Story' and liked it much: the other verses show similar power and beauty. I wish the author well with all my heart. . . ."

[23] May 16, 1864; MS at Harvard.

[24] June 4, 1864; MS at Harvard.

[25] Howells quotes this episode from Volta in his essay "Ducal Mantua." See IJs, pp. 365-367.

The faithful of the House of Gonzaga, according to
Volta, were six young men who followed young Federico
into exile when he refused to marry the Duke of Bavaria's
daughter. Following a period of banishment, during which
the followers and Federico suffered great privations, the
Duke of Mantua relented and allowed his son to return.
After his homecoming the young man thought better of his
intractability and married the beautiful Margherita. Howells embroiders this story by supplying his ballad with an
extra thread of romance. The young duke of the poem
leaves home because he is in love with a girl other than his
father's choice. This girl follows Federico, disguised as a
minstrel, and in the end sacrifices herself to bring about the
reconciliation of the young duke and his father.

Despite previous rebuffs Howells sent the ballad to the
Atlantic, and while it was under consideration he wrote
resignedly to Lowell: "I wish you could see a longish ballad of mine now awaiting refusal at the *Atlantic* office,
called 'The Faithful of the Gonzaga.' "[26] His pessimism
was well founded, but the ballad had an interesting subsequent history.[27] Even before Howells wrote Lowell,
Charles Hale had made his second visit to Venice on his
way to Egypt, and liking the ballad, he made a copy which
he sent to his brother Edward Everett Hale. The older
Hale interested himself in the composition and placed it
with Robert Bonner's New York *Ledger,* from which Howells received fifty dollars, twice as much as the *Atlantic* had
paid for "The Pilot's Story."[28]

[26] LinL, I, 86.

[27] Described in LF&A, p. 91.

[28] See letter dated Feb. 23, 1865 (MS at Harvard), from Charles Hale & Co.,
Boston, transmitting four pounds for travel-letters and fifty dollars for the
poem sold to Bonner by E. E. Hale. Gibson and Arms were not able to find
a copy of the *Ledger* which carried the poem, but the ballad must have been
published in the late winter or early spring of 1865.

One of Howells's first acts upon returning from Europe was to hunt a new publisher for "Disillusion." He finally had obtained the poem from Foster, who had kept it nearly two years, and he lost no time submitting it to Fields, but the Editor of the *Atlantic* found the composition too long and unpalatable. He wrote quite bluntly: "I regret extremely that it does not seem to me up to your mark."[29] He would have taken the passages descriptive of Venice, however, if the author had been willing to prune away the story. In September Howells went to New York to seek his literary fortune, taking the manuscript with him; and when he persuaded Hurd to bring out *Venetian Life,* he also put in a word for the poem. Howells wrote his wife after meeting the publisher: "He made very cordial inquiries about you and wants to look at 'Disillusion,' with your illustrations."[30]

Hurd must have liked the poem at that reading, and perhaps he agreed to bring it out if *Venetian Life* found public favor. Such a situation is suggested by the publisher's response that "you have two books already in the press"[31] when Howells first broached the idea of *Italian Journeys.* The first book, of course, was the second edition of *Venetian Life,* published in January, 1867, and the second must have been "Disillusion," for Howells wrote his Ohio friend J. M. Comly in December that "I shall publish a longish poem either in the coming spring or fall—probably spring."[32] A year later when *Venetian Life* was in its fourth reprinting the poem had not yet made its appearance, although Hurd still reluctantly planned to issue it. Nevertheless, the publisher began looking for a graceful way out and wrote Howells that G. P. Putnam might be interested

[29] Aug. 18, 1865; MS at Harvard.
[30] LinL, I, 98.
[31] Dec. 19, 1866; MS at Harvard.
[32] Dec. 23, 1866; MS at Ohio Hist. Soc.

in printing the poem in his magazine. To this the author promptly replied: "I'm very much obliged for the hint about Putnam. Should you have any objection to his publishing my Venetian poem before you book it?"[33] Hurd then made one more effort to discourage Howells: "Have you asked your wife's advice on this matter? . . . every author has a peculiar fondness for his first production, as a mother has for her first baby."[34] Ultimately the publisher found a chance to withdraw entirely, for Putnam was interested not only in printing the poem in his magazine but also in issuing it as a book. Finally in November, 1868, five and a half years after it had been written, it appeared in print as *No Love Lost: a Romance of Travel*.[35] The misgivings of Foster and Hurd proved valid: the book was a financial failure. When Howells recalled this episode in his old age, he remembered sending back the royalty check after the publisher complained of losing money on the venture.[36]

This romance in verse was scarcely worth the trouble it cost Howells to get it published. The poem was written in 426 lines of unrhymed hexameters, the meter which he thought "one of the measures best adapted to the English speech."[37] Told in the form of letters, the plot concerns a pair of American lovers who plight troth before the young man goes off to war and live to regret their vows. The action takes place in Venice, where the ex-lovers meet after the Civil War. The girl, thinking her former lover dead, is suffering from a guilty conscience, because she has not remained true to the memory of the dead hero. But the

[33] LinL, I, 125.
[34] Dec. 30, 1867; MS at Harvard.
[35] Although the poem carried the date 1869 when published as a book, it was issued on or before Nov. 12, 1868. See Gibson and Arms, *op. cit.*, p. 21. It appeared about the same time in *Putnam's Magazine*, N. S., II (Dec., 1868), 641-651.
[36] "The Turning Point of My Life," p. 165.
[37] LF&A, p. 203.

young veteran is equally happy to find his fiancée in love with another, for he too has placed his affections elsewhere during their separation. All ends happily when the lovers cancel the outworn vows and flee to the charms of their second choices.

The passages descriptive of Venice, which Fields liked, contain the most effective lines of the poem and are handled perhaps as skilfully as anyone had managed this subject since Byron wrote Canto iv of *Childe Harold* (1818). Howells wrote of the sights and sounds of the old city with sensitivity and affection, and the result is often genuinely poetic. At the same time, the entire work is leavened by a mild satire on American tourists, anticipating somewhat the disparaging attitude of Mark Twain's travelers in *The Innocents Abroad* (1869). For example, the character Fanny, the hero's new love, looks at Venice with a jaundiced eye, finding it a city where

Palaces and mosquitoes rise from the water together,[38]

while the other members of this girl's family are no doubt drawn from traveling Americans such as Howells met while consul, typical of whom are Fanny's brother and aunt. The former talks of nothing but

Passports, policemen, porters, and how he got through his
    tobacco,—[39]

while the latter goes about chattering a kind of pidgin Italian:

"Quanto per these ones here?" and "What did you say
    was the prezzo?"[40]

A very different sort of poem from *No Love Lost*, though also inspired by the exotic background of Venice, was "The

[38] *Poems*, p. 183.   [39] *Ibid.*, p. 182.   [40] *Ibid.*, p. 184.

Mulberries," written during Howells's Italian sojourn but not published for half a dozen years after his return. One of his more pleasant Italian diversions on warm spring days was to purchase mulberries from street vendors, and when he ate this fruit he recalled the boyhood pleasure of climbing a tree in Morgan's pasture to pick berries. In 1900 he recalled nostalgically:

They used to sell the mulberries from their baskets in front of St. Mark's Church in Venice, as well as on the Rialto Bridge; but I put the transaction on the bridge in the poem, probably for some convenience of the rhythm. The Venetian mulberries were always luscious and of twice or thrice the bigness of the small wild fruit I had known. They were grown on the Lido, or on the mainland somewhere; possibly at Mestre or Fusina, or in the gardens of the Giudecca; pleasant names all to my eye and ear.[41]

Howells used this pleasant experience in Venice as a point of departure for calling up the childhood memory, composing in relaxed four-stress quatrains verses which re-emphasize in their mood the *Weltschmerz* of the author's youthful Romanticism.

The last published verse which he wrote from the hoard of his Italian experiences was "Pordenone," an excellent poem of slightly more than two-thirds the length of *No Love Lost*. Although it is composed in rather monotonous hexameters, the poem creates a good picture of life in Venice in the sixteenth century when Pordenone and Titian were rivals. The author invented a love-jealousy and peopled his poem with the caustic Pietro Aretino, the architect Jacopo Sansovino, and Tintoretto. The lines show a familiarity with the history of Venetian art, and the dra-

---

[41] "The Mulberries in Pay's Garden," *The Hesperian Tree*, J. J. Piatt (ed.), p. 433. This essay was also published in book form under the same title with the poem as an appendix.

matic elements of the story are manipulated successfully. Using the flashback, Howells once again began with a contemporary description. His Renaissance setting is evoked by the crumbling remnant of Pordenone's frescoes on a wall of the Augustinian convent adjoining the church of San Stefano.

The date of composition of "Pordenone" is not yet known, but the chapter in *Venetian Life* on "Churches and Pictures," written in 1864, contains a commentary on the fresco which inspired the poem. The author added to this passage the information that he had made up the story of the love-jealousy in his own use of the material. The poem languished in manuscript at least eighteen years before H. M. Alden accepted it for *Harper's Monthly,* and Howells, recalling this tardy appearance, wrote in 1912: "I still do not think it was very bad, though the reader who turns to it in my 'Poems,' so called, may not agree with me."[42] When these hexameters finally came out in November, 1882, the author was in Europe for his first return trip since his consular days.

ESSAYS AND CRITICAL BEGINNINGS

Not only did Howells return from Italy an articulate and discerning traveler, but he also came back a critic and essayist of unusual promise. The pleasure and stimulation which he received from Lowell's acceptance of his article "Recent Italian Comedy" encouraged him greatly at the outset of his long and distinguished career as a critic. His initial contribution to the *North American Review* began an association with that journal which did not end until four years before his death. When Lowell opened the pages of the review to him in 1864, he provided the chance the

[42] J. Henry Harper, *The House of Harper,* p. 319. Howells contributed an eight-page paper on his relationship with Harpers to this history of the firm.

young author needed to get his writings into a journal of recognized importance. By the time Howells went to Cambridge to be assistant editor of the *Atlantic* in February, 1866, he already had published articles in three of the most recent issues of this magazine.

Howells chose wisely both the subject for "Recent Italian Comedy" and the editors to whom he submitted the essay. It is hard to see how he could have failed to place it. Not only were Lowell and his coeditor Norton intensely interested in Italian literature, but the article in itself was a competent enough performance to command editorial respect. Howells had worked on the essay for several months, and the result was a meticulous and well-documented study. Soon after the article was set in type, Norton wrote Lowell that he liked it, adding that the piece was pleasantly written and full of agreeable information. He hoped that his coeditor had asked the author to write again.[1] After the autumn number of the magazine appeared, another competent student of Italian literature—Longfellow—noted in his journal that one of the good articles was "Modern Italian Comedy."[2]

The article does more than review a handful of plays which Howells had seen during his residence in Venice; it is a compendious survey of nineteenth-century Italian comedy. Beginning with an analysis of contemporary Italian prose, in which he finds that only in the theater is the representation of modern Italian life to be found, he goes on to consider political and economic conditions in nineteenth-century Italy and to relate to them the sterility of Italian

[1] Sara Norton and M. A. DeW. Howe (eds.), *Letters of Charles Eliot Norton*, I, 275-276. Letter dated Aug. 10, 1864.

[2] Samuel Longfellow, *Life of Henry Wadsworth Longfellow*, III, 47. Entry for Oct. 1, 1864. This entry is interesting in that Longfellow recorded Howells's name as author of the article, information which he could not have obtained from the review, since contributions were unsigned. Hence he must have known of the article before he read it.

fiction. In the drama he discovers a richness of contemporary, everyday incident which is represented by an abundance of creative effort quite unknown in English literature. Linking Italian comedy of his century to the tradition deriving from the popular *commedia dell'arte* of the late Renaissance and its successor, the Goldonian theater, he argues that the essentially dramatic character of the Italian people provides a logical basis for a viable dramatic literature in Italy. He speaks from careful, firsthand observation, and his exposition is cogent and ably argued.

After thirteen pages of social, economic, political, and literary background he takes up the contemporary drama in a discussion that is solidly informed and based on wide reading in the dramatic literature. Although two of the writers included are transitional figures between the time of Goldoni and the mid-nineteenth century, the article treats of ten modern playwrights and covers with more or less thoroughness twenty-two plays. Most of the dramatists in the article are no longer remembered even by the Italians,[3] although two of the four who receive the most attention, Francesco Dall'Ongaro and Paolo Ferrari, are perhaps still considered among the minor writers of the century. He particularly liked the biographical dramas of Ferrari and thought *Goldoni e le sue sedici commedie nuove* a superb play. He also gives several pages to the forgotten Luigi Gualtieri, whose farce *Lo Spiantato* and seriocomic *L'Abnegazione* he admired greatly, and he enjoyed with reservations *La Statua di carne* of another playwright no longer remembered, Teobaldo Ciconi.

Not only does Howells treat the plays which he thought worth while, but this article is enlivened with exhibits from

[3] Only three out of the ten are even mentioned in A. Momigliano's *Storia della letteratura italiana*, a literary history used in recent years as a textbook in the Italian schools.

the absurdities he had read or seen enacted. One of these is a biographical drama by Paolo Giacometti, of whom he wrote: "No career which offers any salient point on which to hang a play seems to be safe from this voluminous and unscrupulous writer."[4] The play which Howells picked to illustrate his point is one based on the life of the precocious American child poet Lucretia Maria Davidson.[5] The plot is laid in Pennsylvania and the characters move about with a singular ignorance of Anglo-Saxon society. The play ends, reports Howells, when the poetess dies for love as the result of an unhappy attachment for a titled Englishman, one Sir Georgio Dorsey, "traveling in America for the purpose of kissing the tomb of Washington."[6]

Howells ends his article in agreement with Dall'Ongaro, who had written that the Italian drama was then at a great moment in its history, a moment when the shackles were falling away from art with the restoration of political liberty. Howells himself found in the plays of the mid-century a reflection of a society in transition and entertained high hopes for Italian literature following the unification of Italy. His article surveys adequately that portion of contemporary Italian literature which he found most interesting. It is ably and pleasantly written and compares favorably with his later critical writings. The article brought his work to the attention of American literary circles and even

[4] "Recent Italian Comedy," p. 395. On the other hand, Howells wrote of a tragedy by this author: "I should be puzzled to name the modern drama that surpasses La Morte Civile of Paolo Giacometti" (MLP, p. 207).

[5] Born in Plattsburg, N. Y., in 1808, daughter of a poor doctor, she began scribbling verses before fully learning to write. After a poverty-stricken childhood she was sent to school by friends and died in Albany of consumption before her seventeenth birthday. Her poetry, which is merely precocious juvenile verse, and her pathetic life caused her to be taken to the hearts of the Romantic poets. Southey, for instance, in the *Quarterly Review* (XLI, Nov., 1829, 289-301) reviewed her literary remains enthusiastically, comparing her to Chatterton.

[6] "Recent Italian Comedy," p. 396.

gained him a measure of recognition in Italy. Dall'Ongaro in Florence was much pleased and through an American living there sent Howells a note of appreciation, the first communication in a literary correspondence between the two men.[7] Shortly before returning home, Howells wrote his father: "My article on *Comedy* has made me quite a reputation in Italy, amongst the Italian literati, and the English living in Italy. Curious, isn't it?"[8]

Following the acceptance of "Recent Italian Comedy," Howells redoubled his literary efforts. He already had begun work on "Ducal Mantua" when Lowell invited him to write something else for the *North American Review;* hence he replied: "I have notes enough on Mantua . . . to make you an article . . . if only I could find the title of some recent book to hang the review on."[9] Such a book was unavailable, however, and refusing to be daunted by this obstacle, he boldly selected a work which was neither recent nor likely to be seen by any of his readers.[10] He described it himself as a work with "little . . . to leaven statistical heaviness,"[11] adding that he had been forced to go back to the historians whose substance his author had desiccated in order to rehabilitate the ducal state of Mantua. Perhaps he held off submitting the article to the review until his return from Italy, in hopes of finding a better excuse for publishing the piece, because "Ducal Mantua" did not appear until January, 1866.[12] In the meantime he had published his second review article, "Italian Brigandage."

[7] See letter from Mrs. Jennie Jackson to Howells dated Florence, Mar. 27, 1865; MS at Harvard. Two letters from Dall'Ongaro (Aug. 8, 1869, and Dec. 1, 1870) to Howells survive in the Howells Collection at Harvard.

[8] LinL, I, 94.

[9] *Ibid.,* p. 86.

[10] Bartolomeo Arrighi, *Mantova e sua provincia* (Milan, 1859).

[11] IJs, p. 327.

[12] Apparently the essay had been recently submitted when Lowell wrote Oct. 17, 1865 (MS at Harvard): "I cannot answer clearly about the *time* of using the article till Mr. Norton comes home which will be within the week. But you may reckon on seeing it soon. . . ."

The essay on Mantua was based on a careful reading of material available in St. Mark's Library in Venice. It was his first attempt at historical writing and one which he did not repeat for many years until he wrote *Tuscan Cities* (1886) after a return visit to Europe. The article combines the travel sketch with history in a fashion that perhaps made it dull for the admirer of *Venetian Life* and at the same time too popular for the professional historian. Nevertheless, the essay was a significant early attempt to unite the two types of writing which he was able to combine more successfully later.

The essay, which is packed with solid and well-ordered information, treats the story of Mantua chronologically and weaves into the texture of the narrative an autobiographical thread. Beginning with the account of the founding of the city from the *Divina Commedia,* he next reports on its appearance in 1864, then goes on to sketch a full panorama of Mantuan history. Such figures as Sordello, whom he had already encountered in his reading, particularly interested him, but most of all he was fascinated by the saga of the Gonzaga family, which ruled the city for nearly four hundred years.

Howells's visit to Naples in November, 1864, and three recent books on brigandage gave him the idea for his second published contribution to the *North American Review*. This essay, "Italian Brigandage," is more nearly a conventional review article than "Ducal Mantua," but it also contains a large measure of historical exposition and works in another autobiographical note. A discussion of brigandage which takes place between the author and his guide on a mountain top in Capri supplies a point of departure for a colorful account of the guerrilla warfare between the brigands and the various governments which ruled the southern provinces. He delights in giving a sketch of the Calabrian bandit Fra Diavolo and is particularly vivid in describing the ruthless extermination of the brigands during the regime in Naples of Napoleon's subordinate Murat.

When Howells returned to the United States, he was regarded as an authority on Italy, and during his period as a free-lance writer in New York he exploited his interest and competence in Italian matters. Besides a review of a book on Dante, which will be considered later, in the months of September and October, 1865, he wrote three editorials on Italian topics for the New York *Times*. In "Spanish-Italian Amity" he commented on the significance of the reported betrothal of Victor Emmanuel's son to the daughter of the Queen of Spain and declared that the news showed the strength of the liberals in Spain rather than the strength of the Church in Italy. In the second editorial, "The Proposed Purchase of Venetia," discussing a news report that Italy had offered to buy Venetia from Austria, he concluded that the proposal no doubt aimed principally at keeping the Venetian question before the world. In the third of these editorials, "Marriage among the Italian Priesthood," Howells wrote on a subject which was to interest him later in his novel *A Foregone Conclusion*. Here he pegged his essay to a resolution adopted by an Episcopal church convention in support of Italian efforts to reform the clergy. Before he left New York for Cambridge, he again made use of his interest in Italian literature to write an obituary in the *Nation* for the Piedmontese statesman and novelist Massimo D'Azeglio.

III. Italian Literature

DANTE AND LONGFELLOW

"I RAN through an Italian grammar on my way across the Atlantic," wrote Howells in 1894, "and from my knowledge of Latin, Spanish and French, I soon had a reading acquaintance with the language."[1] After he took up his duties as consul, he plunged into the study of Italian literature with the enthusiasm of youth and an insatiable desire to know. He had limitless time for reading, and one by one Italian authors from Dante to the contemporary writers of the nineteenth century passed through his hands. Although he had not asked to go to Italy, the dividend which he received from the intelligent use of his fortuitous assignment to Venice was inestimable. It gained him admission to the intellectual society he thought most worth while when he went to live in Cambridge, and it furnished usable capital in his subsequent career as editor and writer.

Howells's acquaintance with Italian literature when he went to Italy was considerably less than his knowledge of the literatures of Spain, Germany, and France. He had cast a net into Italian waters a year before his departure, but he was fishing in the tame preserves of secondhand sources. Concluding an account of his work on the *Ohio State Journal* in November, 1860, he announced that he had been doing "a little French Revolution, Milton, Leigh Hunt's Autobiography, Italian Poets, and Faust."[2] Just what he was reading of the Italian poets he does not say, but he remem-

[1] MLP, p. 198. Howells's reminiscences of his Dante studies are covered in pp. 198-205.
[2] Howells to O. W. Holmes, Jr., Nov. 14, 1860; MS at Harvard.

bered in 1894 that he had gone to Italy with "a fairish general notion of Italian letters from Leigh Hunt, and from
other agreeable English Italianates."[3] Perhaps on the occasion mentioned he was reading Hunt's *Stories from the
Italian Poets*. He recalled that he had arrived in Italy with
the desire to read not only Dante, Petrarch, Ariosto, and
Tasso but also the burlesque poets such as Pulci and Berni,
a list including four of the five poets treated in Hunt's
book.[4]

He read the older writers in desultory fashion but made
little literary use of them in his subsequent writings. It is
therefore difficult to tell just how well acquainted he was
with Petrarch, Tasso, and others, and in contrast with the
evidence of his interest in the modern poets, novelists, and
playwrights the data are meager. A certain amount of reading in Petrarch must have preceded or followed his visits
to Arquà, and he returned to America with two copies of
a rare edition of Pulci's *Il Morgante,* one of which he gave
John Fiske.[5] When he visited Ferrara in November, 1864,
and was conducted through the prison where Tasso had
been confined for seven years, he confessed that he had not
read the poet's works, but in his literary reminiscences he
lists among books which once gave him pleasure two pastoral dramas, Guarini's *Il Pastor Fido* and Tasso's *Aminta.*
On the same visit to Ferrara he was much more interested in
Ariosto, whom he seems to have read, and he was thrilled
by a glimpse of the manuscript of *Orlando Furioso,* which
he described as the "noblest thing and best worthy to be
remembered."[6]

While the other older Italian poets did not succeed in

[3] MLP, p. 199.

[4] Dante, Ariosto, Tasso, Boiardo, and Pulci. In *Imaginary Interviews*, p. 221,
one of the imaginary members of a colloquy on the art of quoting well recalls
that he read this book as a boy.

[5] *Letters of John Fiske,* p. 165.   [6] IJs, p. 29.

capturing his interest, Dante became a literary passion. During his first year in Venice Howells began reading the *Divina Commedia* with an Italian priest who became the prototype of Don Ippolito in *A Foregone Conclusion.* Month after month this teacher guided his pupil's faltering steps through the successive depths of the *Inferno:*

My good priest sat beside me in these rich moments, knotting in his lap the calico handkerchief of the snuff-taker, and entering with tremulous eagerness into my joy in things that he had often before enjoyed. No doubt he had an inexhaustible pleasure in them apart from mine, for I have found my pleasure in them perennial. . . .[7]

As the study continued, sometimes the priest lost himself in the beatific vision and left Howells stumbling along in the philological wilderness. The Consul, however, persevered and eventually reached with the poet and his teacher the ineffable radiance of the *Paradiso.* The memory of the magnificent rhythm and sonorous voice of the teacher remained as a rich experience, and long after he had left Italy he could recall how the obscure meaning had shown out of the mere music of the poem when the priest read, "like the color the blind feel in sound."[8] These Dante studies must have continued well beyond his first year in Venice, for in August, 1863, he wrote Stedman of his "halting progress" through the *Divina Commedia,*[9] and the following year he added in a postscript to Lowell, as though the course had been completed: "I know *now* why you told me to study Dante."[10]

As a result of these studies Dante became a living personality and the poem a vital part of his literary background. When he visited Florence for the first time in 1863, he piously hunted up the landmarks associated with

[7] MLP, p. 203.   [8] *Ibid.,* p. 204.
[9] LinL, I, 70.   [10] *Ibid.,* p. 86.

the poet, although after sitting on the stone where Dante
was supposed to have watched the construction of Giotto's
Tower, he declared: ". . . I really cared very little about
it."[11] His first literary use of the *Divina Commedia* was in
his newspaper letter to the Boston *Advertiser* describing his
visit to Florence when he quoted the words of the unfor-
tunate Pia de'Tolomei *(Purg.* v. 133) in describing a statue
seen in a sculptor's studio. Later he used the same quota-
tion in *Italian Journeys* (p. 195) when his travels were interrupted by flood in the marshy maremma of West Tuscany where Pia was supposed to have died of a fever; and
about nine months before, he had visited Mantua with
Dante's description of that city's founding fresh in his
mind.[12] Nineteen years later in 1886, his historical re-
searches in *Tuscan Cities* were filled with allusions to events
and people described by Dante. Although Howells adorned
his writings with gems from the *Divina Commedia* and
learned long passages for his own amusement and to aston-
ish his friends,[13] he never regarded himself as a Dante expert. He left the writing of purely literary essays on the

[11] ."From Venice to Florence and Back Again." No doubt he later learned
that Dante died before the cornerstone of the campanile was laid.

[12] He quotes in his essay "Ducal Mantua" thirty-two lines translated into
English *terza rima* from *Inf.* XX, 55-93, the account of Mantua's founding by
Manto, the damned daughter of a Theban king. Although he does not spe-
cifically state that this translation is his, these lines do not agree with any of
the English translations made before 1864. I am indebted to Miss Frances
Lauman, assistant reference librarian of the Cornell University Library, for
checking Howells's version with these translations in the Cornell Dante
Collection.

[13] Howells reported (LF&A, p. 222) that when he called on Lowell he often
found him reading the *Divina Commedia,* "which he magnanimously supposed
me much better acquainted with than I was because I knew some passages of
it by heart. One day I came in quoting—

　　　　Io son cantava, io son dolce Sirena,
　　　　Che i marinai in mezzo al mar dismago.
　　　　　　　[*Purg.* XIX, 19-20]

"He stared at me in a rapture with the matchless music, and then uttered
all his adoration and despair in one word. 'Damn!' he said, and no more."

poet to his more scholarly friends such as Lowell and Norton.

The fortune of public office which sent Howells to Italy instead of Germany was one of the luckiest accidents of his career; and at the same time no study he could have undertaken while abroad would have been more fruitful in terms of personal satisfaction than the reading of Dante. He could not consciously have planned a better campaign to storm the literary citadel at Cambridge. His knowledge of Italian literature when he went to live in Cambridge in early 1866 cemented the bonds of friendship with Lowell and brought him a lifelong friendship with Norton; but most rewarding of all was the entry his Italian studies gave him to the Wednesday evening meetings of the Dante Club when Longfellow was revising his translation of the *Divina Commedia*.[14]

Longfellow was one of the Cambridge literary idols whom Howells had not met when he first visited Boston in the summer of 1860. The poet had then been at his summer home at Nahant, and the young visitor had returned to Ohio without seeing him. The two men met for the first time on a street in Cambridge on February 20, 1866, introduced by Norton, who had taken the new assistant editor of the *Atlantic* house-hunting. Longfellow was, Howells wrote Stedman, "such a looking poet as I should like to be . . . white locks, white beard, and autumnal bloom."[15] It was soon after this meeting that the poet invited his new acquaintance to attend the Dante Club.

The Dante Club met between 1865 and 1867, and despite the fact that Howells was late in starting, he was the fourth

---

[14] The best account of the Dante Club is contained in the chapter entitled "The White Mr. Longfellow," LF&A, pp. 178-211.

[15] LinL, I, 107.

most regular member of the group,[16] next to the translator himself, Lowell, and Norton. Longfellow wrote in his journal for Wednesday, March 28, 1866: "Dante Club; *Paradiso* XXII. Norton, Lowell, Fields, Akers, and Mr. Howells—formerly consul at Venice, poet and prose-writer; a very clever and cultivated young man."[17] This entry marks Howells's initial appearance at the weekly sessions, but in succeeding weeks his name, written in the poet's neat, round hand, appears frequently in the journal. He was present for most of the readings of the last twelve cantos of the *Paradiso* during the spring of 1866, and at the conclusion of the meetings for that year on June 13 he wrote his sister: ". . . we honored the close by sitting at supper till two o'clock in the morning."[18] At the May 30 meeting, when all but two cantos had been completed and the pleasant suppers which followed the readings were about to end, Lowell asked Longfellow if there was not "an Indian epic in an hundred thousand lines which he was going to translate next."[19] The club did not break up with the completion of the *Paradiso*, however, and the meetings were resumed during the winter and spring of 1866-1867.

The Wednesday night sessions of the Dante Club were a memorable part of Howells's first two years in Cambridge. The most select of the Italianate Cantabrigians gathered in Longfellow's study to appraise the translation as they listened to the poet read it in his deep, resonant voice. Lowell and Norton offered suggestions frankly and often during the readings, and frequently the translator accepted their criticisms, noting, as he went along, changes

[16] For this information I am indebted to the late H. W. L. Dana, who compiled it from the manuscript journals in the Craigie House in Cambridge.

[17] Samuel Longfellow, *op. cit.*, III, 71. The date of the entry in this source is incorrectly given as January 28. The March 28 date may be found in the manuscript.

[18] LinL, I, 112-113.

[19] *Ibid.*, p. 110.

in the margin of the proof sheet before him.[20] Howells remembered with admiration "the subtle and sympathetic scholarship of his critics, who scrutinized every shade of meaning in a word or phrase that gave them pause, and did not let it pass till all the reasons and facts had been considered."[21] The junior member of the group, just turned twenty-nine, had little to say during the textual criticism of the poem. He followed faithfully in his Italian Dante, content to enjoy silently one of the great intellectual experiences of his life. During the entire winter, he remembered, he ventured only one suggestion, which was "kindly, even seriously, considered by the poet, and gently rejected."[22] Other less scholarly members, such as Holmes and Fields, followed along tacitly with Howells, while one of the frequent visitors, Longfellow's old friend from Rhode Island, G. W. Greene, usually went to sleep. He dozed off by the fire with "the old terrier under his deep armchair, breathing in a soft diapason with him, till the hour of supper came. . . ."[23]

At the conclusion of the week's canto, the scholars adjourned to the dining room, where they were joined by the poet's less Italianate friends. Although six or eight was the usual number attending the literary part of the meetings, there seldom were less than ten or twelve at the supper table. It was during this part of the evening that "Holmes sparkled, and Lowell glowed, and Agassiz beamed,"[24] and

[20] See Norton's reminiscences of these sessions in *The Annual Report of the Dante Society* (1882) quoted by Samuel Longfellow, *op. cit.,* III, 63-64.

[21] LF&A, p. 182.

[22] *Ibid.,* p. 183.

[23] "Address of William Dean Howells," *Cambridge Historical Society Publications,* II (Feb., 1907), 61. This address, which Howells wrote for the observance of the Longfellow centennial, was read by Bliss Perry. About the same time, it was published (without the reminiscence of the Dante Club quoted here) as "The Art of Longfellow," *North American Review,* CLXXXIV (Mar. 1, 1907), 472-485.

[24] LF&A, p. 184.

the story-telling prowess of Fields or the wit of Longfellow's brother-in-law Tom Appleton came into its own. The supper usually consisted of cold turkey, a haunch of venison, or a brace of grouse which the poet carved in his place at the head of the table. There was also a deep bowl of salad and a plentiful supply of "those elect vintages which Longfellow loved, and which he chose with the inspiration of affection."[25] The effect of these weekly sessions at Craigie House on the assistant editor of the *Atlantic* has best been evaluated by himself. He wrote in 1896:

They [the members of the club] were the men whom of all men living I most honored, and it seemed to be impossible that I at my age should be so perfectly fulfilling the dream of my life in their company. Often the nights were very cold, and as I returned home . . . I was as if soul-borne through the air by my pride and joy . . . I still think that was the richest moment of my life, and I look back at it as the moment in a life not unblessed by chance, which I would most like to live over again. . . .[26]

The acquaintance of Howells and Longfellow, thus begun with a common interest in Dante, ripened into a warm friendship through their mutual liking for all things Italian; and whenever there was an Italian occasion to celebrate, Howells received an invitation to dine with Longfellow. "He always asked me to dinner," Howells wrote, "when his old friend Greene came to visit him, and then we had an Italian time together, with more or less repetition in our talk, of what we had said before of Italian poetry and Italian character."[27] When Larkin Mead and his Venetian wife

[25] *Ibid.*, p. 185.

[26] *Ibid.*, p. 194. First printed as "The White Mr. Longfellow," *Harper's Monthly*, XCIII (Aug., 1896), 327-343. Howells quoted from this passage when he wrote his speech for the celebration of the one hundredth anniversary of Longfellow's birth in 1907.

[27] LF&A, p. 205.

visited the United States in 1874, Howells took his brother-in-law to dine at Craigie House, in honor of which event Longfellow had composed a poem on the Ponte Vecchio in Florence, Mead's adopted city.[28] On still another occasion the poet invited Howells to dinner to meet the actor Tommaso Salvini, but that time Howells had a previous engagement in Boston and reluctantly had to decline.[29]

Howells also was something of an intermediary between Longfellow and his Italian translators. The spring before the poet made a tour of Europe, he transmitted a letter to him from Professor Frattini of Padua addressed to "Mr. Professor Greatest Poet." He is, wrote Howells, "one of your many Italian translators and admirers and one you should meet when you go to Padua."[30] To this the poet replied that he certainly would, if he visited that old university town.[31] Later when the Italian government wanted to decorate Longfellow, the award was suggested by Professor Messadaglia, another translator-friend, whom Howells, for some reason he could not remember in 1896, had put in correspondence with Longfellow.[32] At still another time Brunetta, then a teacher in Verona, wanted authorization to make an interlinear translation of *Evangeline,* and Howells wrote Longfellow to expedite the permission.[33]

The relationship between the poet and the editor of the *Atlantic,* however, was not entirely one-sided. Howells had a chance to pay his dept to Longfellow when Ticknor and Fields brought out a collected edition of the poet's works in 1867. For this event he wrote a warm tribute to the man as well as the poet, concluding: "It is certainly one of the privileges of a beloved poet to have his thoughts so inter-

[28] Samuel Longfellow, *op. cit.,* III, 235-236.
[29] LF&A, p. 205.
[30] Apr. 25, 1868; MS at Craigie House.
[31] Apr. 29, 1868; MS at Harvard.   [32] LF&A, p. 198.
[33] July 21, 1874; MS at Craigie House.

woven with his readers' days, that . . . they [the readers] seem not so much to have read his work as to have lived it. . . ."[34] The same sensitive and affectionate appraisal went into Howells's address prepared for the Longfellow centennial forty years later. In 1881 Longfellow's friend Luigi Monti, prototype of the young Sicilian in the *Tales of a Wayside Inn,* needed work, and the poet enlisted Howells's aid in procuring him a consulship in Italy. "I have written to the Secretary of State," wrote Longfellow, "and if you will write to the President, something may be done."[35] Monti did not receive the consulship, but it is more than likely that Garfield's assassination early in his administration was responsible.

The interest in Dante which Howells found perennial was manifested again when the Dante Society was founded.[36] Norton suggested to some of his students in 1880 that there should be an organization for the purpose of encouraging Dante research and publishing the product of such scholarship. The students picked up the idea and carried it out, persuading Longfellow to act as the first president of the society. The initial meeting was held at his house in the winter of 1880-1881, following which the society flourished. It stimulated scholarly work on the poet by offering an annual prize and built up the Dante collection in the Harvard Library. It is, of course, not surprising

[34] "Henry Wadsworth Longfellow," *North American Review,* CIV (Apr., 1867), 540.

[35] Mar. 14, 1881; MS at Harvard. Monti, a naturalized citizen, had come to America from Italy as a political refugee in 1850, and Longfellow had got him an instructorship in Italian at Harvard. From 1861 until 1873 he was American consul at Palermo, his native city. He returned to the United States in 1873, where he wrote, lectured, and taught during the 1870's and 1880's. In 1893 he again went back to Italy where he died in 1914. See J. Van Schaick, Jr., *The Characters in Tales of a Wayside Inn,* pp. 48-66.

[36] The material in this paragraph is taken from W. R. Thayer's paper on the founding of the society in *The Annual Report of the Dante Society* (1909) as quoted in *Letters of Charles Eliot Norton,* II, 100-106.

that Howells was asked to join the society when it was founded, and the reports of the organization for the years 1881 through 1884 carry his name as one of the members.[37]

Although Howells developed a strong attachment for the poetry of the *Divina Commedia,* he deplored attempts to make a prophet or superman out of the author. One of his first reviews after returning to the United States in 1865 was an attack on the Dante cultists directed specifically at Vincenzo Botta's *Dante as Philosopher, Patriot and Poet,* a volume hastily prepared for the sexcentenary of Dante's birth.[38] He was not so much annoyed at the hodgepodge of ill-digested, secondhand criticism as he was incensed by Botta's attempt to make Dante a seer who had anticipated modern science, modern political institutions, and the Reformation. Howells concluded that the book was worthless—unless it had some purpose which he had not discovered.

Howells believed that the *Divina Commedia* contained moments of great poetry, but he also felt there were many stretches of it which were "dull and tough and dry."[39] Writing in middle age of his study of Dante, he admitted: "I had a deep sense of the majesty and grandeur of Dante's design, [but] many points of its execution bored me."[40] The intermixture of small local fact, neighborhood history, and personalities had detracted from his total enjoyment, but the personality of Dante himself had fascinated him. An example of this interest in Dante's personality may be

[37] I can find no satisfactory reason for Howells's dropping his membership in the society after 1884. He was, however, out of the main current of Cambridge life by that time and perhaps found it hard to attend the meetings. He had quit the *Atlantic* early in 1881, and even before that he had moved from Cambridge to Belmont. After 1882 he lived in Boston, and during one full year that he belonged to the society (July, 1882–July, 1883) he was in Europe.

[38] *Round Table,* N. S. no. 4 (Sept. 30, 1865), pp. 51-52.

[39] MLP, p. 200.   [40] *Ibid.,* pp. 200-201.

observed in Howells's review of a book written in 1887 on
the poet's life and works. In this notice he paraphrased
approvingly Dante's definition of nobility (*Convito* iv. 20)
as not being the possession of inherited wealth but the love
and practice of virtue. "It is very good Americanism for the
thirteenth century," he concluded.[41] This preoccupation
with author and context made Howells's mature critical
point of view of Dante essentially historical. Summarizing
this middle-aged position, he wrote:

What I finally perceived was that his poem came through him
from the heart of Italian life, such as it was in his time, and
whatever it teaches, his poem expresses that life, in all its splendor and squalor, its beauty and deformity, its love and its hate.

Criticism may torment this sense or that sense out of it, but
at the end of the ends the Divine Comedy will stand for the
patriotism of medieval Italy, as far as its ethics is concerned, and
for a profound and lofty ideal of beauty, as far as its aesthetics
is concerned.[42]

During the spring that Howells moved to Cambridge
and began attending the Dante Club he wrote his first criticisms of Dante's translators. As the publication date of
Longfellow's *Divina Commedia* drew near, he sent an essay
to the *Round Table* on "The Coming Translation of Dante,"
an article designed to whet the public appetite.[43] He promised that the translation would be the most scholarly and
faithful yet published; but he feared the public would ignore the poem, and he did not expect the readers who had
been charmed by the "rhetorical sentimentalism" of *Voices
of the Night* to like the translation. In this advance notice
Howells virtually challenged his audience to read the poem
or admit a lack of taste for the exquisite things in poetry.

[41] "Editor's Study," *Harper's Monthly*, LXXV (Nov., 1887), 965. Review
of M. A. Ward's *Dante, and His Life and Works* (Boston, 1887).
[42] MLP, p. 201.   [43] III (May 19, 1866), 305-306.

When the translation subsequently appeared, he reviewed it
for the *Nation*,[44] illustrating at length the simplicity, fidelity, and scholarly rendering of the poem. He displayed
excerpts from six earlier translators, comparing their work
with Longfellow's, to show that "not one of these translators, however free with the original, has won a grace beyond the reach of Mr. Longfellow's fidelity."[45] Howells
gave Longfellow's translation his highest praise: the poem
was indeed Dante. He wrote:

Here at last that much-suffering reader will find Dante's greatness manifest, and not his greatness only, but his grace, his
simplicity, and his affection. Here he will find strength matched
with wonderful sweetness, and dignity with quaintness—Dante
of the thirteenth century and Dante of eternity.[46]

If Howells was completely in sympathy with Longfellow's translation of the *Divina Commedia*,[47] he also was
well satisfied with Norton's rendering of the *Vita Nuova*.
He reviewed the latter for the *Atlantic* and reported that
both Longfellow and Norton used the same principle: to be
literal, so that the end product is Dante and not the translator. But there was a difference: where Longfellow had
used Latinisms to give the flavor of the Italian epic, Norton
had adopted a starkly simple Anglo-Saxon diction in har-
mony with the simplicity of Dante's youthful work. Concluding his notice, Howells paid Norton's work the greatest
compliment he could devise: ". . . it is the fit companion

[44] IV (June 20, 1867), 492-494.

[45] *Ibid.*, p. 493.

[46] *Ibid.*, p. 494.

[47] His only reservation was in the matter of rhyme. He declared in a
review of T. W. Parsons's translation of the *Inferno* (*Atlantic*, XX, Dec., 1867,
759-761) that he thought the problem of translation into *terza rima* was exaggerated, although he had little use for the *abab* quatrains which Parsons used.
Howells tried translating into *terza rima* in the passage he quoted from the
Divina Commedia at the beginning of his essay "Ducal Mantua," but he was
not particularly successful.

of Mr. Longfellow's unmatched version of the *Divina Commedia,* with which it is likewise uniform in faultless mechanical execution."[48] Ten years after Longfellow's death, when Norton published his prose translation of the *Divina Commedia,* Howells declared that such a version "was almost the only word left to say about Dante," and that Norton was offering his translation, "unqualified and as little as possible changed, to such as can receive it only at second hand. . . ."[49]

Although Howells began his post-Italian years condemning the deification of Dante, he ended his career attacking those who underestimated the poet. Reviewing Albert Mordell's *Dante and Other Waning Classics,* he had only scorn for the theory that such masterpieces as the *Divina Commedia* and *Paradise Lost* were being less and less read because medieval scholasticism and seventeenth-century Puritanism were no longer live issues. In this essay Howells stated his final position on Dante, a criticism which had shifted between middle age and old age from the historical to the aesthetic:

. . . the virtue and the vitality of an artist reside in his art, and . . . no classic can wane while this art remains alive with beauty in any part of it. We will cheerfully allow that the scheme of the *Divine Comedy* is tiresome almost beyond endurance, and that it is atrocious and loathsome in certain details; we will allow that the scheme of *Paradise Lost* is preposterous, but while certain strains of their majestic music renew themselves in the soul from time to time like the remembrance of personal experience, there cannot be any question of their waning.[50]

[48] *Atlantic,* XX (Nov., 1867), 639.
[49] "Editor's Study," *Harper's Monthly,* LXXXIV (Feb., 1892), 482.
[50] "Editor's Easy Chair," *Harper's Monthly,* CXXXII (May, 1916), 960.

MODERN POETRY: ESSAYS, LECTURES, TRANSLATIONS

"Write us another on 'Modern Italian Literature,' or anything you like," wrote Lowell in 1864 when he announced that the article on Italian comedy was in print.[1] The combined invitation and suggestion contained in this letter did not need to be repeated, for Howells was ready and able to begin the exploitation of a literary field which American criticism had so far left untouched. In his old age he recalled:

I perceived it was open to me to be a critic. . . . No one else that I knew of was discussing contemporary Italian literature . . . and that kind, that over-kind letter of my *dolce duce* gave me an impulse that was not exhausted till it had eventuated in the studies and versions of the *Modern Italian Poets*. . . .[2]

This "impulse," which was to last twenty-three years, launched him on an intensive reading program in Italian poetry of the late eighteenth and early nineteenth centuries. Poetry was the inevitable choice, since he already had written on the drama and did not care for the historical romances which dominated Italian prose fiction. His studies of the contemporary poets, begun in desultory fashion before 1864, occupied much of his time during his last year in Italy. He made numerous translations from the Italian poets in the weeks before leaving Venice; and the work continued with great success as he took up his editorial duties on the *Atlantic*. During 1866, 1867, and 1868 he kept his place among the contributors to the *North American Review* with an annual article on modern Italian poetry. In 1870 and 1871 he lectured at Harvard and the Lowell Institute on his specialty, and for the following fifteen years occasional articles in the *Atlantic* attested the durability of his interest. The final episode in this long exploitation of

---

[1] *Letters of James Russell Lowell*, I, 338.
[2] "The Turning Point of My Life," p. 165.

Italian poetry, the publication of *Modern Italian Poets* in
1887, occurred a full quarter of a century after he had first
gone to Italy.

In two respects this book supplied a fitting valediction to
the first half of his literary career. Not only was it the last
word of the youthful Romantic poet who once had aped
Heine and Longfellow, but it was also a personal tribute
to the Italian patriots whose struggle for political liberty
he had watched for many years. By the time it came out,
he had transferred his literary allegiance to New York,
where he was already beginning to preach the gospel of
Realism from the "Editor's Study" of *Harper's Monthly*.
After the publication of the book he abandoned modern
Italian poetry as a field for literary criticism, although it
had provided him with a rich vein to mine during the years
he was working towards a literary reputation.

Despite its patriotic fervor—and ever-present Classicism
—Italian poetry in the late eighteenth and early nineteenth
centuries added its voice to the literature of the world-wide
Romantic movement. Howells's studies in this field, therefore, represent a somewhat synthetic interest and are more
a tribute to his affection for things Italian than an intrinsic
pleasure. His twenty-five years as a critic of this literature
overlapped his conversion to Realism, and he was writing
on Italian Romantic poets long after his novels had become
vehicles of studied Realism. In his later years he showed
little interest in the Romantic movement, either in America
or England, and though he included Romanticists individ-
ually among his favorite authors, it is well to note that no
modern Italian poets appear in *My Literary Passions*
(1895).

Political events of the one hundred years before 1861
stirred Howells deeply. In less than three generations
America had won independence, France had overthrown

the Bourbon dynasty, and important beginnings had been made in Italian unification. Everywhere in Europe the desire for political liberty had been quickened by the abortive revolutions of 1848, and nowhere was the awakened political consciousness more apparent than in Italy. When Howells arrived in Venice he found himself at the ringside of the fight for Italian independence. The Province of Venetia was *Italia irredenta* even before the expression had come into current usage, and across the nearby Po River lay the newly created Kingdom of Italy. The *risorgimento* had produced an intellectual rebirth as well as a desire for political self-determination, and writers of all degrees of competence were producing voluminously when Howells, with characteristic enthusiasm, plunged into the study of Italian poetry. He read avidly the work of the poets who reflected their country's national aspirations—particularly those who had been exiled or imprisoned for their writings. His tenacious Americanism aligned him on the side of Mazzini, Garibaldi, and other Italian patriots, and it is small wonder that the spirit of the age tinctured his critical judgments.

Modern Italian Poets should be considered an historical document rather than a lasting contribution to literary criticism. The book began as a series of review articles on contemporary Italian literature and criticism, and Howells was, in effect, engaged in a task of reporting. If all the poets represented in his gallery have not survived, it is because posterity has judged them more severely than their contemporaries did. The very subject matter, the longing for political liberty, was topical and doomed to eclipse when Italian unification was accomplished, although to the extent that patriotism is an enduring theme the poetry of the *risorgimento* has permanent value. Howells was the first to recognize the incompleteness of his book, and he wrote in the introduction: "Possibly I should not offer my book to the public at all if I knew of another work in English studying even with my incoherence the Italian poetry of the time mentioned. . . ."[3]

Despite its limitations the book surveys with more than a little discernment a homogeneous segment of Italian literature in a series of attractive essays illustrated freely with translations. The period Howells covers, the one hundred years prior to 1870, is "unique in the history of literature for the unswerving singleness of its tendency," and "it was, perhaps, more than any other poetry in the world, an incident and an instrument of the political redemption of the people among whom it arose."[4] He does not ignore any of the principal writers of the epoch, but he also treats at length some of the minor figures scarcely mentioned in twentieth-century literary histories. The period begins with Neoclassicism in the saddle and ends with Romanticism trying to dominate the literature, but throughout the book runs the unifying thread of Italian national aspirations.

Modern Italian Poets in its final form sketches the lives and works of eighteen poets, beginning with Parini (1729-1799), who lived all his life in the eighteenth century, and ending with several writers who were alive at the time Howells was in Italy. Three of these poets receive major treatment in chapters of approximately fifty pages: Alfieri (1749-1803) and Manzoni (1785-1873), both, of course, important figures in Italian literature, and Giambattista Niccolini (1782-1861), a second-rate tragedian who already has been forgotten. Eight others are given secondary importance in essays ranging from ten to thirty pages, foremost of whom is Leopardi (1798-1837), perhaps the greatest Italian poet of the nineteenth century and one whose repu-

[3] MIP, p. 2.   [4] *Ibid.*

tation now exceeds Howells's estimate of him. Two of
the eight, Francesco Dall'Ongaro (1810-1873) and Aleardo
Aleardi (1812-1878), have suffered eclipse in twentieth-
century opinion, but they exerted a peculiar fascination,
having been poets militant who were imprisoned and exiled
during the struggle for independence.[5] In addition Dall'-
Ongaro was born in Friuli, educated in Venice, and corresponded with Howells in the late 1860's while Aleardi was
born near Verona and educated in Padua. A photograph
of Aleardi in the Howells family album further testifies
to the author's interest, although there is no evidence that
he ever met him. Except for Foscolo (1778-1827), who still
is a major figure, the five remaining poets of the group
given secondary treatment were properly evaluated and retain only minor importance in Italian literature: Parini,
Monti (1754-1828), Foscolo, Giusti (1809-1850), and Prati
(1815-1884). Prati, however, may be slightly more important than Howells's estimate would indicate. In all events,
he receives only slightly more space than Giovanni Berchet
(1783-1851), a fairly consequential early Romantic poet,
who is discussed in a chapter including also the lesser
figures Silvio Pellico (1789-1854), Tommaso Grossi (1791-
1853), and Luigi Carrer (1801-1850). In another composite
chapter, the last in the book, three more minor writers are
considered briefly: Giulio Carcano (1812-1884), Arnaldo
Fusinato (1817-1888), and Luigi Mercantini (1821-1872).
Only the third member of this trio has eluded oblivion, and
his immortality rests on authorship of the words to the
Garibaldi hymn.

[5] Howells's essay on Dall'Ongaro (*North American Review*, CVI, Jan.,
1868, 26-42) was translated into Italian and published as an introduction to
the poet's *Stornelli politici e non politici* (Milan, 1883). Three of the *stornelli*
which Howells translated in MIP have been reprinted in Rossiter Johnson and
Dora K. Ranous (eds.), *An Anthology of Italian Authors from Cavalcanti to
Fogazzaro*, pp. 275-276.

As we have seen, Howells's study of Italian poetry bore its first fruit in the *North American Review* for October, 1866. Nominally a discussion of six works on Italian literature,[6] all except one comparatively recent, the article actually was an essay on the poems of Monti, Foscolo, and Leopardi. The section devoted to Monti passed almost intact into *Modern Italian Poets,* the pages on Foscolo were revised in part, and the material on Leopardi underwent complete rewriting. During the twenty-one years between periodical and book publication Howells modified his critical opinions somewhat in the light of further study and intellectual growth. The most important force both in recasting and in strengthening his early judgments was Francesco de Sanctis, the most renowned Italian critic of the nineteenth century, whose works he read after leaving Italy.[7]

He did not change his first impressions of Monti, a facile poet whose liberal tendencies ebbed and flowed under the vicissitudes of republicanism in the Napoleonic era. De Sanctis confirmed his opinion that Monti was a clever artist but one lacking in the inner resources of a first-rate poet, and Howells concluded that he was a classic of a type common to all languages—a corpse which retained its form in the coffin but crumbled to dust when exposed to the air. On the other hand, he revised his estimate of Foscolo, perhaps in light of the Italian critic's strong championship.

[6] P. Emiliani-Giudici, *Storia della letteratura italiana* (Florence, 1855), C. Cantù, *Della letteratura italiana* (Turin, 1860), G. Arnaud, *I Poeti patriotici* (Milan, 1862), Marc Monnier, *L'Italie est-elle la terre des morts?* (Paris, 1860), *I Contemporanei italiani* (Turin, 1861) [an Italian men-of-letters series], F. P. Cobbe, *Italics* (London, 1864). Howells finds Emiliani-Giudici, Arnaud, and the men-of-letters series useful, but Cantù's book is the "product of an utterly commonplace mind," Monnier's work an effort to get credit for dicovering modern Italian literature, and Cobbe's volume an attempt to show that there is no modern Italian literature.

[7] Howells's bibliography in MIP, p. [370], lists De Sanctis's *Saggi critici* (Naples, 1869), and *Storia della letteratura italiana* (Naples, 1879).

In the review article Howells had recognized that "I Sepol-
cri" was an important poem and had translated a long
passage from it; but he offered his version with important
qualifications. He considered it hackneyed Classicism and
inferior to either "Thanatopsis" or Gray's "Elegy," to which
it bears an analogous relationship. He further thought
it could not stand close analysis and that it contained a
lame and impotent conclusion. In *Modern Italian Poets,*
although still refusing to give the poem unstinted approval,
he deleted his strictures and quoted from De Sanctis's praise
of Foscolo's masterpiece.

His criticism of Leopardi also underwent a certain
amount of evolution between youth and middle age. The
poet's sickness and unhappiness, combined with his exquisite lyric gift, made him a romantic figure in the eyes of
the young American consul, but as Howells grew older
he acquired a sense of perspective which made his early
attitudes less tenable. His essay on Leopardi, completely
rewritten and greatly expanded, was published in the *Atlantic* in 1885, the last chapter of *Modern Italian Poets* to
be printed serially. Between the early and late versions his
presentation of Leopardi changed from enthusiastic and
uncritical exposition to sympathetic but realistic appraisal,
a shift in viewpoint reflecting perhaps his retreat from Romanticism. Where he at first agreed with many Italians
who counted Leopardi "one of the greatest men of genius
our time has produced,"[8] he later saw him as an important
transitional figure between Classicism and Romanticism,
a poet of marvelous skill but one whose morbidity made
him less attractive than he once had seemed. Again Howells followed De Sanctis in large part, letting the Italian
critic speak for him in nearly half of his critical material
on Leopardi; but where Howells wrote of the poet as "The

[8] "Modern Italian Poets," *North American Review,* CIII (Oct., 1866), 337.

Laureate of Death," De Sanctis, in effect, considered him the laureate of life, finding in his brooding introspection not a negative sort of pessimism but a liberating force which freed Italian literature from the shackles of Neoclassicism.

The poems which the youthful Howells selected for translation from Leopardi, with one exception, were allowed to illustrate the revised essay in 1885, and the accurate and well-contrived blank verse of 1866 remained unchanged.[9] Sacrificing the irregular rhyme to preserve the rhythm of the Italian, he produced translations which often seem more successful than his own original poetry. As we have seen, Howells's verse is largely imitative, but what is a defect in his own versification sometimes becomes a merit in translation. Three samples will serve to illustrate the faithful rendering which he achieved—not only of Leopardi's poetry but in his other Italian translations as well. The first is the opening period of the patriotic "All'Italia," which every Italian schoolboy commits to memory:

> My native land, I see the walls and arches,
> The columns and the statues, and the lonely
> Towers of our ancestors,
> But not their glory, not
> The laurel and the steel of that old time
> Our great forefathers bore. . . .[10]

Compare this with the Italian:

> O patria mia, vedo le mura e gli archi
> E le colonne e i simulacri e l'erme
> Torri degli avi nostri,
> Ma la gloria non vedo,
> Non vedo il lauro e il ferro ond'eran carchi
> I nostri padri antichi. . . .[11]

---

[9] Six poems appear in MIP, pp. 259-271. A seventh, "Imitazione," was not reprinted from the *North American Review*.

[10] MIP, p. 259.

[11] Giuseppe de Robertis (ed.), *Giacomo Leopardi opere*, I, 137.

Whoever attempts to turn Italian poetry into English verse must, of course, reconcile the disparity of the two languages. English contains so many more monosyllables that the translator feels obliged to add words to fill out the lines, and it is difficult to retain the original meter without distorting meaning. In the above example, surprisingly enough, Howells came out with one less word than Leopardi, a feat which he often accomplished, and in one of the two samples which follow he used only one word more than the Italian. But more important than the number of words he used is the success with which he duplicated Leopardi's rhythm, preserving the same number of accents in the successive lines while at the same time keeping a fairly literal translation. For instance, in the first line of Leopardi's poem,

> O patria mia, vedo le mura e gli archi,

there are fifteen syllables but only five accents. Although this line nearly translates itself,

> My native land, I see the walls and arches,

it comes out in English with only eleven syllables while retaining five accents. Howells was able to manage this effect in many of his versions from the Italian poets. In the following illustration, three lines from Leopardi's "Sopra il ritratto di una bella donna," Howells is at his best. Not only does he preserve the rhythm and translate accurately, but he also has created in the English a genuinely poetic expression:

> Mortality! if thou
> Be wholly frail and vile,
> Be only dust and shadow, how canst thou
> So deeply feel? . . .[12]

[12] MIP, p. 268.

And in the original:

> Natura umana, or come
> Se frale in tutto e vile,
> Se polve ed ombra sei, tant'alto senti?[13]

The next illustration shows both Howells's skill and his shortcomings. The poem is eminently Leopardi's in mood and rhythm, but the translation lacks the spontaneity of the original. The passage which follows is the first stanza of "A Silvia":

> Sylvia, dost thou remember
> In this that season of thy mortal being
> When from thine eyes shone beauty,
> And in thy shy glances fugitive and smiling,
> And joyously and pensively the borders
> Of childhood thou did'st traverse?[14]

And the Italian is this:

> Silvia, remembri ancora
> Quel tempo della tua vita mortale,
> Quando beltà splendea
> Negli occhi tuoi ridenti e fuggitivi,
> E tu, lieta e pensosa, il limitare
> Di gioventù salivi?[15]

Because the translation uses the obsolete English second-person-singular to duplicate Leopardi's familiar address, the version suffers from too much literalness. In addition, Howells has added "shy" in the fourth line, though perhaps this padding of the Italian text is not objectionable. The worst offense is in the poorly chosen diction in the last two lines, specifically the translation of "il limitare . . . salivi"

---

[13] De Robertis (ed.), *op. cit.*, I, 233. Howells might better have rendered *alto* as "nobly," suggesting elevation rather than intensity of feeling, but his reading is not incorrect.

[14] MIP, p. 269.

[15] De Robertis (ed.), *op. cit.*, I, 201.

as "the borders . . . thou did'st traverse." The condition described in the original, the transition of the girl from adolescence to womanhood, cannot be rendered as "traverse" and "boundary" without giving the reading too concrete and prosaic an image for the description of a subtle biological process.

The most important recognition of Howells's competence in modern Italian literature was the offer in 1869 of a special Harvard lectureship. The new president of the university, Charles W. Eliot, wrote in June that he was planning a lecture series the following year on contemporary literature. Howells seemed the logical choice to conduct the Italian part of the program, and Eliot wanted him to join with Lowell, Child, and other distinguished teachers to organize this special course of study. It was to be given at the graduate level, and Eliot wanted not so much formal lectures as "talks out of a full mind."[16] The project, he wrote, was somewhat of an experiment and was to be tried with an estimated twenty advanced students.

Despite his extensive studies of Italian literature for more than seven years, Howells had a modest opinion of his scholarly attainments and was awed by the collective dignity of the Harvard faculty. In 1865, slightly incredulously, he had written his wife from New York that "everybody regards me here as having *scholarship*,"[17] and following that letter he had launched with great success his series of articles on Italian poetry in the *North American Review*. Harvard already had given him an honorary degree, and in addition he had turned down a professorship at Union College. But Eliot's offer, nonetheless, made him feel an inadequacy and lack of formal education. He declined the proposal soon after it was made, and not even Lowell, act-

[16] June 9, 1869; MS at Harvard.   [17] LinL, I, 101.

ing as special emissary for the Harvard president, could change his mind. He wrote his wife, then visiting in Vermont, that Lowell had been to see him but had not kept him from writing Eliot again to decline the lectureship. Circumstances, however, conspired against him; and the following morning, before receiving the second letter of refusal, Eliot called in person to urge reconsideration. In the face of such persistence Howells could hold out no longer, and writing his wife of his decision, he concluded: "So I'm a professor in spite of myself. I told him what a superficial fellow I was, and warned him of his risk, but it made no difference."[18]

Howells made his debut at Harvard in a brief series of lectures which did not start until the middle of May, 1870. Soon after the course began he wrote Lowell, then a visiting professor at Cornell, that the series was going well, and in a playful vein described his initial experiences as a teacher:

The base-ball club seduced all the male students away from my class, but the gentlemen who came in on my passes were there, to a martyr. I have bribed the barbarian darky by the way, and now anybody comes that likes. . . . I've an audience of twenty, and the quality is even more distinguished than the quantity. Up to the close of yesterday the lectures had not been received with yells of derision—Mr. Child, for example, did not hiss, once, nor Mr. Longfellow ask to have the lecturer put out....[19]

Although the first lectures, given under the title "New Italian Literature," were few in number, their success was shown by the invitation Howells received to lecture twice during the following academic year.[20] In the late winter

[18] *Ibid.*, p. 139.   [19] *Ibid.*, p. 155.

[20] Eliot wrote Howells on April 20, 1871 (MS at Harvard), hoping that the course could be repeated the following year, but it was not. Perhaps Howells's elevation to the editorship of the *Atlantic* in July, 1871, increased his duties and also made the honorarium from lecturing seem less desirable.

and spring of 1871 at Harvard he expanded the series and gave it a new title, "Modern Italian Poetry and Comedy," but before offering the course a second time at the college, John Amory Lowell asked him to lecture at the Lowell Institute. In this second performance the lectures grew to twelve and were given in the autumn and early winter of 1870 under the title "Italian Poets of Our Century."

The Lowell lectures were a valuable but unnerving experience for a neophyte public speaker. There were some two hundred and fifty people in the audience, and he had to appear before them in evening dress once a week from mid-October until January. On the first night he developed a severe case of "stage-fright" and raced through his speech, but during the following week he worked hard to improve his performance. Declining an invitation to dinner on the night of the second lecture, he wrote Kate Fields, daughter of the publisher: "If I were as old a lecturer as you are, and not afraid of the public, I should accept your courtesy."[21] He added that he was obliged to spend hours wrestling with his manuscript before the talk, and he and Mrs. Howells planned to eat supper alone somewhere near the Lowell Institute. At the second lecture his delivery was greatly improved, and he was able to write his father: ". . . last night I had the severe critical testimony of Elinor in my favor, as well as that of Mr. Lowell, who was kind enough to come in to the lecture, and who declared himself interested and contented with the performance."[22] But after this trial of public lecturing at the Lowell Institute, Howells gave up the business, and it was more than twenty-five years before he was induced to go off on a speaking tour.

By the time Howells gave his first Harvard lecture, he

[21] Oct. 25, 1870; MS at Boston Pub. Lib.
[22] LinL, I, 157. Letter dated Oct. 30, 1870.

already had published a quarter of the material which later went into *Modern Italian Poets*. In the three review articles appearing between 1866 and 1868[23] he had covered, very briefly in some instances, eleven of the eighteen poets represented in the final collection of essays. It seems likely that the first and shortest group of lectures was made up from this early material which gave major attention to Monti, Foscolo, Manzoni, Leopardi, and Prati, all figures of first or second magnitude, plus Dall'Ongaro and Aleardi, in whom Howells had a special interest. Pellico, Grossi, Carrer, and Carcano were mentioned in passing.

In 1872 he published no less than three articles on the Italian poets, the first in the *Atlantic* and the second and third in consecutive issues of the *North American Review*. This rapid publishing sequence would suggest that the essays had been prepared for the lectures of the preceding season, the expanded series which was given both at the Lowell Institute and at Harvard. These papers included a long article on the forgotten tragedian Niccolini and a shorter piece on the Florentine satirist Giuseppe Giusti. The third was a sketch of the Arcadians, who flourished in the late seventeenth and early eighteenth centuries, an essay furnishing illumination and background for the nineteenth-century literature.

Howells's theater attendance and study of Italian comedy in Venice broadened into an interest in poetic drama. In the spring of 1865, much to the disgust of his friend Brunetta, he read and enjoyed Guarini's sixteenth-century pastoral, *Il Pastor Fido*,[24] and went on to Tasso's *Aminta,* the

---

[23] Besides the 1866 article, previously cited, on Monti, Foscolo, and Leopardi, and the 1868 piece on Dall'Ongaro, also cited earlier, the third article was "Modern Italian Poets," *North American Review*, CIV (Apr., 1867), 317-354, in which were discussed Manzoni, Grossi, Pellico, Carrer, Aleardi, and Carcano.

[24] Brunetta wrote from Padua (Mar. 20, 1865; MS at Harvard) advising

model for all such dramas. He derived a great deal of pleasure, he later remembered, from the absolutely unreal shepherds and shepherdesses of Tasso and Guarini with their "Dresden china loves and sorrows" among their "enameled meadows."[25] To Howells the Realist, this indulgence in a most artificial sort of literature was very pleasant if taken in small quantities, like an occasional sugarplum after dinner; but it did not provide the substance for serious study. Passing through the general literary stagnation which plagued Italy in the seventeenth century, Howells found no dramatist who interested him until he came to Alfieri in the century following. Poetic tragedy subsequently assumed an important part of his studies of modern Italian writers, and he proceeded from Alfieri to Manzoni to Niccolini. This interest, moreover, did not end until he had translated an entire tragedy for the American stage, Ippolito D'Aste's *Sansone*. Two-fifths of *Modern Italian Poets* is devoted to these tragedians, and most of his translations of them are taken from their dramas. The essay on Alfieri first appeared in the *Atlantic* in 1875 and two years later as the introductory chapter to Howells's edition of the Italian's best-known work, the autobiography. The essay on Manzoni was completely rewritten from the early *North American Review* article previously cited and never published periodically in its final form.

Not only is Alfieri one of the important poets of modern Italy, but he also was a figure who captured the imagination of his countrymen during the *risorgimento*. Born into the nobility in 1749, he grew up a vociferous hater of kings and tyrants and bellowed his republican sentiments in a score of tragedies. Howells was fascinated by his per-

---

Howells to read modern authors instead of Guarini in order not to learn obsolete Italian.

[25] MLP, p. 217.

sonality as exhibited in his autobiography, a document
which he ranked in a class with Goldoni's memoirs, and he
found him a stimulating figure in his plays. He read widely
among his dramas but never managed to read him completely, and in his old age admitted not having read *Saul*
(1782), often considered Alfieri's greatest tragedy. In the
historical dramas Howells objected to the rigid use of the
Classical unities, which he thought the poet got from French
drama, on grounds that credibility had to be sacrificed
unnecessarily. In addition, the interest in Alfieri's plays,
wrote Howells, came from the situation and action,
and there was no character development in the modern
sense.[26] He liked best the dramas based on Greek mythol-
ogy and translated the entire fifth act of *Oreste* (1777)
plus enough of the earlier action to give the necessary background. This version, he wrote Brander Matthews in 1915,
"is mine-issimo, and Alfieri's too, almost word for word.
I'm very proud of it . . . I wish I had done the whole
play. . . ."[27] On the same occasion he described *Oreste* as
"tremendous," a judgment with which many critics today
will agree, for it unquestionably treats the revenge motif
powerfully, delineates a good tragic figure in the character
of Clytemnestra, and roars courageously the author's hatred
of tyrants.

Howells saw in Manzoni a gifted man of letters whose
patriotism combined with his art to make him a versatile
hero of the *risorgimento*. Although born in Milan in 1784,
he lived long enough to be elected a Senator of the Realm
after the Kingdom of Italy came into being in 1861. Liberal
in his social philosophy and religion, he refused to use the

[26] MIP, p. 67.

[27] LinL, II, 350-351. Matthews was compiling his anthology of *The Chief
European Dramatists* and had asked Howells's advice about what to put in of
Alfieri and Goldoni. Howells offered to let him use his translation of *Oreste,*
but nothing of Alfieri was included. Howells's reference to this play as
"Clytemnestra" is incorrect.

title inherited from his father and was a devout Catholic who opposed strenuously the temporal powers of the Pope. As a man of letters, he wrote the most famous Italian novel of the century, *I Promessi sposi,* and produced an ode on Napoleon's death which is known to every literate Italian, "Il Cinque Maggio." Besides these activities he published a much-admired volume of hymns and two closet tragedies of a patriotic character.[28]

Relying heavily on De Sanctis for critical support, Howells concluded that Manzoni was the chief poet of the Romantic school in Italy. His tragedies, *Il Conte di Carmagnola* (1820) and *Adelchi* (1822), both written in bold defiance of the earlier unities, represented a rejection of the Classicism of Alfieri. Howells translated two scenes from the former, one from the latter, and in addition he turned into English verse a reverberating chorus from Act II of *Il Conte di Carmagnola,* making a booming rendition of a passage still often printed from a play now seldom read. Typical of the plunging rhythm which Howells was able to duplicate from Manzoni are the first four lines:

> On the right hand a trumpet is sounding,
>   On the left hand a trumpet replying,
>   The field upon all sides resounding
>   With the trampling of foot and of horse.[29]

And the Italian:

> S'ode a destra uno squillo di tromba;
>   A sinistra risponde uno squillo:
>   D'ambo i lati calpesto ribomba
>   Da cavalli e da fanti il terren.

---

[28] Howells's brief treatment of Manzoni in the 1867 *North American Review* article dismissed these tragedies as dull and praised his lyrics as his best poetic achievement. The shift in emphasis between the early and late criticism elevates the patriotic strain at the expense of the romantic. I suspect that De Sanctis's high opinion of Manzoni resulted in Howells's re-evaluation and extended treatment of him.

[29] MIP, p. 142.

Niccolini has a secure place in the history of Italian unification, but his tragedies have proved to be ephemeral. He
was more of a political propagandist than an artist, but his
plays served a useful purpose and were rewarded by a tremendous popular following. Howells was stirred by the
bold republican sentiments of the dramas, particularly the
vigorous opposition to the Pope's efforts to maintain his
political powers. If he overrated these tragedies, it was
partly because he lived in Italy in the period when the
Pope was making his last stand against the irresistible
movement of political events. He thought *Arnaldo da
Brescia* (1843) was a magnificent tragedy, and he translated
a condensed version of it, tying together the scenes he rendered with prose summaries of the action.[30] The life of
Arnaldo, a twelfth-century monk who died opposing the
temporal powers of the Pope, furnished material for a
tragedy highly applicable to the nineteenth century. Howells felt so strongly about the issues involved in the drama
that he believed the destruction of temporal power of the
Pope would be "known in history as infinitely the greatest
event of our greatly eventful time"; about the play itself,
he added: ". . . its conception is that of a very great artist,"
and "the execution is no less admirable."[31]

Two years after publishing his condensed version of
Niccolini's tragedy, he was able to broaden his connection
with the drama by translating a play for stage presentation.
Tommaso Salvini, the Italian tragedian, had toured the
United States in 1873, making a brilliant success in the title
role of *Sansone,* a play written especially for him by the
obscure Ippolito D'Aste. The American actor Charles R.

---

[30] This translation with accompanying prose matter is reprinted without
credit in Alfred Bates (ed.), *The Drama,* V, 193-216. Parts of Howells's essay
on, and translations from, Manzoni also are reprinted without credit in this
work, pp. 180-190.

[31] MIP, p. 243.

Pope saw it and wanted an English version for himself. Howells, meantime, had long wanted to make the leap from essayist and critic to playwright, and his ample studies of Italian drama and translations of Italian verse had prepared him for the actor's commission. Clemens, conveniently enough, knew Pope and was the means of bringing the two men together. After arrangements had been made for the work, Howells wrote the humorist: ". . . it is owing to your kindness that I'm thus placed in relation with the stage—a long-coveted opportunity."[32] Pope was delighted with the translation and wrote from St. Louis a few days before the first performance that he was "in love with the part and the play."[33] After the tragedy opened in the Missouri city in early October, 1874, he praised it extravagantly: "I have every reason to believe it will be a permanent success and live in the dramatic literature of the age."[34]

This prediction was wildly exaggerated, of course, but the play did prove an excellent vehicle for an able tragedian, and when Salvini returned to the United States in 1889 he played the role again with as great success as before,[35] using an American cast and Howells's translation for all the parts except his own, which he played in Italian. The play opened his tour on October 10 at Palmer's Theater in New York and was described by one critic as "undoubtedly the most important dramatic event of the season."[36] The ova-

[32] LinL, I, 190; letter dated July 11, 1874. Howells arranged with Pope to make the translation for $400 on acceptance, $100 additional after fifty nights, and one dollar per night thereafter. According to Howells's wishes, Pope deposited a check with Clemens when Howells sent him the play, the idea being that the check would not be passed on to Howells unless Pope was satisfied with the translation. There are eight letters from Pope to Howells about this transaction in the Howells Collection at Harvard.

[33] Sept. 25, 1874; MS at Harvard.

[34] Oct. 9, 1874; MS at Harvard.

[35] See George C. D. Odell, *Annals of the New York Stage*, XIV, 234-235.

[36] "Salvini as Samson," *The Critic*, N. S., XII (Oct. 19, 1889), 191.

tion on the first night was "so intense and demonstrative
that it seemed rather to belong to an assemblage of a Latin
race than . . . Anglo-Saxon."[37] With Salvini playing the
leading role, the translator's success was assured; nevertheless, the lines of D'Aste's play were fashioned into a facile
English blank verse of the type already produced successfully in the translation of Niccolini. One of the New York
reviewers, commenting on Howells's part in the performance, wrote that he had "done his work well and faithfully. . . . His English lines flow smoothly in print and
bear the impress of ripe scholarship."[38] Twenty-one years
after the tragedy was first performed in English, the play
was still being presented, and in 1895 Howells went to a
Bowery theater to see it. The play was then in the hands of
Walter Kennedy, who played it vigorously to a simple-
hearted German-American audience. By this time Howells's modest beginning in the theater had already developed
into a strong subordinate interest from which had resulted
fifteen comedies and farces.

GOLDONI[1] AND REALISM

Criticism so far has discounted or ignored the literary
influence exerted on Howells by the writer whom he called
"one of the greatest realists who has ever lived"—Carlo
Goldoni.[2] There is, however, abundant evidence that the
Venetian dramatist, more than any other writer, turned him

[37] "Salvini at Palmer's Theater," New York *Tribune*, Oct. 11, 1889, p. 6.
[38] "Bene Arrivato, Salvini," New York *Herald*, Oct. 11, 1889, p. 10.

[1] Carlo Goldoni (1707-1793) was born in Venice, the son of a doctor,
and educated in several North Italian cities. Trained for the law, he practiced
in Venice but soon turned to writing plays, the first important one being
L'Uomo di mondo (1738). During the 1750's he was at the peak of his
Venetian career, but in 1762, in order to escape the intense jealousies of rival
playwrights, he went to Paris where he lived for the rest of his life, continuing
to write but with slightly less popular success. At the age of seventy-five he
began dictating his memoirs in French and completed them five years later.
[2] MLP, p. 207.

from Romantic poet into prose Realist. This is not to say
that Howells either abandoned poetry after leaving Italy
or had not written a large quantity of prose before becoming the American consul at Venice, but Goldoni's plays
exerted a powerful and lasting effect on his literary career.
Between 1861 and 1865 the Goldonian drama helped mold
the opinions which later solidified into the Howells doc-
trine of literary Realism. Through Goldoni's eyes Howells
first saw the possibilities of prose fiction based on the commonplace events of contemporary life. Later these plays
provided direct inspiration for his own comedies and farces.
Despite the general failure to recognize this influence, the
American's debt to the Italian is freely acknowledged in his
writings.

Howells the Realist occupies a place somewhere between the unashamed Romanticist and the hard-boiled
Naturalist; but whether his Realism is the result of native
bent or the literary climate of his age is a moot point.
Parrington found Howells's Realism a home-grown product which could best be explained by temperament.[3] Pattee
thought his Realism was the product of twenty years of
gradual retreat from youthful Romanticism.[4] Whatever the
critical point of view, the Italian years have been neglected
—so much so that even the best study scarcely mentions
Goldoni,[5] and a recent critical judgment concludes that the
Italian sojourn "affected him less profoundly than one
might expect."[6]

One of the most candid statements in all of Howells's
delightfully frank literary reminiscences, however, acknowl-

[3] Vernon Louis Parrington, *The Beginnings of Critical Realism in America*,
p. 248.

[4] Fred Lewis Pattee, *A History of American Literature since 1870*, pp. 201-
206.

[5] Oscar W. Firkins, *William Dean Howells: a Study*.

[6] Robert E. Spiller *et al.* (eds.), *Literary History of the United States*, II,
887. The chapter on Howells is by Gordon S. Haight.

edges the influence of the Venetian dramatist. Of all the
Italian authors, he told H. H. Boyesen in the interview
previously cited, the one he delighted in most was Goldoni.[7]
His poetical leanings and his early interest in Tennyson,
Heine, and Longfellow had not prepared him for the
everyday brand of reality he found in the plays of Goldoni
and he remembered thinking he ought not to like the
Italian but did so in spite of himself. His extensive use of
the minutiae of Venetian life was fascinating. It soon became apparent that the dramatist had turned his friends
and neighbors into characters and used the trivial incidents
of their lives for his plots.[8] This brand of Realism, which
was a new experience for Howells, exerted a powerful pull
on his interests. When he discovered that editors would not
print his imitative Romantic verse, the attraction of Goldoni's art became irresistible and drew him into the orbit
of commonplace Realism. The Boyesen interview, which
contains the most articulate expression of Howells's debt
to Goldoni, explains precisely how the dramatist turned him
towards Realism and has the added interest of being a
spontaneous utterance rather than a calculated essay. The
statement follows in part:

. . . I was an idealist in those days [1862]. I was only twenty-
four or twenty-five years old, and I knew the world chiefly
through literature. I was all the time trying to see things as
others had seen them, and I had a notion that, in literature,
persons and things should be nobler and better than they are
in the sordid reality; and this romantic glamour veiled the
world to me, and kept me from seeing things as they are.
But in the lanes and alleys of Venice I found Goldoni everywhere. Scenes from his plays were enacted before my eyes, with

[7] Boyesen, *op. cit.*, p. 7.
[8] Of course, Goldoni's light-hearted comedies are filled with improbable
incidents and invariably end happily, so that the realist of a naturalistic stamp
would see little affinity between his work and Goldoni's.

all the charming Southern vividness of speech and gesture, and I seemed at every turn to have stepped at unawares into one of his comedies. I believe this was the beginning of my revolt. But it was a good while yet before I found my own bearings.[9]

Howells's reading of Goldoni began during his first year in Italy, and his interest in the dramatist lasted throughout his lifetime. During the year 1862 when he was learning Italian, he and his young friend Brunetta spent their evenings together roaming Venice, talking literature, and visiting the theater. Night after night they went to the Malibran Theater, where they saw the plays of Goldoni performed. It was one of Brunetta's theories that Howells could not hear too much spoken Italian, and the theater, always one of the popular forms of entertainment in Venice, was an excellent classroom. *Venetian Life* recalls:

With increasing knowledge of the language, I learned to enjoy best the unmusical theater, and went oftener to the comedy than the opera. It is hardly by any chance that the Italians play ill, and I have seen excellent acting at the Venetian theaters, both in the modern Italian comedy . . . and in the elder plays of Goldoni,—compositions deliciously racy when seen in Venice, where alone their fidelity of drawing and coloring can be perfectly appreciated. The best comedy is usually given to the educated classes at the pretty Teatro Apollo, while a bloodier and louder drama is offered to the populace at Teatro Malibran, where on Sunday night you may see the plebeian life of the city in one of its most entertaining and characteristic phases.[10]

The fascination which the Venetian dramatist held for Howells may be gauged by this statement made in 1894: "It seemed to me at the time that I must have read all his comedies in Venice."[11] Of course, he missed some, he added, but he undoubtedly read scores of the plays, for at

[9] Boyesen, *op. cit.*, p. 7.   [10] I, 93-94.
[11] MLP, p. 209.

least one hundred and fifty of them had been published. He also studied the works of Goldoni attentively enough to master the difficult Venetian dialect in which many of the plays are written. This is a dialect so different from the standard language that even the Italians have to read the plays with a glossary.

Interest in the plays soon created excitement over the dramatist's *Memoirs*. Early in his second year in Venice Howells wrote his father that he had begun "one of the most fascinating autobiographies that I ever read. . . . that of Carlo Goldoni, the Venetian dramatist."[12] He never tired of this extraordinary book, a masterpiece of its type —lively, amusing, redolent with the personality of the genial playwright, and rich in eighteenth-century color. In 1877 he restated this opinion of the work when he edited and wrote an introduction for an edition of the *Memoirs*. In his old age he took comfort in Goldoni's lasting reputation and classed him with Chaucer, Shakespeare, Cervantes, Goldsmith, Lamb, Austen, and Mark Twain, all writers who wanted, as he put it, to be loved as well as respected.[13] It is not difficult to find the reason why Howells found Goldoni attractive. The author of the *Memoirs* is hardly to be distinguished from the protagonists of many of the plays. He is an affable, generous fellow who endears himself to his public and is best described by the Italian word *simpatico*. Howells found him congenial and like himself in temperament. Although Goloni was a serious artist and desired to improve the theater and society, his method was not to reform with ridicule and scorn but to laugh his audiences out of their foibles. His perpetual lightheartedness makes him gay company; his plays are always amiable, and one never feels that there is a sharp edge of bitterness

[12] LinL, I, 65; letter dated Mar. 15, 1863.
[13] "Editor's Easy Chair," *Harper's Monthly*, CXXVIII (Mar., 1914), 634. Review of H. C. Chatfield-Taylor's *Goldoni: a Biography* (New York, 1913).

lying beneath the fun. This ready good humor, however,
has its limitations, making his contribution to the drama
shallower and less substantial than the achievements of the
greatest playwrights. He is a lesser figure than Molière,
to whom he bears the most resemblance, but he is, nonetheless, a great artist and a natural man in a century that
was often artificial.

A reading of the *Memoirs* led to the inevitable visiting
of places in and about Venice connected with Goldoni's life.
In the summer of 1863 when Conway visited the city,
Howells took his guest to Chioggia, twenty miles south of
Venice, where the playwright had spent part of his boyhood and had gathered some of his dramatic materials.
During the trip by gondola across the lagoon Howells
talked enthusiastically about his latest literary passion.[14]
On another occasion during his Italian years the Consul
looked up the house in Venice where Goldoni was born;
he found it "a fine old Gothic palace on a small canal...
just across from a shop of indigestible pastry."[15] Although
his guide attempted to palm off a newly added room as the
dramatist's study, Howells did not mind but rejoiced that
the cicerone knew anything at all about the playwright.

Howells made early use of his reading of Goldoni in
his own literary output, drawing on both the *Memoirs* and
the plays. His article for the *North American Review,* although entitled "Recent Italian Comedy," devoted three
pages to discussing Goldoni's place in the history of the
Italian theater. He condensed from the *Memoirs* the dramatist's struggle to supplant the improvised *commedia dell'arte*
with a written dramatic literature and evaluated the success
with which he accomplished this undertaking. When
Venetian Life was in progress Goldoni made frequent ap-

[14] *Autobiography,* I, 429. Cf. also the account of this trip in VL, I,
240-246.
[15] VL, II, 27.

pearances in its pages, not only in the chapters on theaters and literary landmarks, but also as the authority for Howells's observations on Venetian manners. Whether it was the dining habits of the people, betrothal customs, or the character of the gondoliers, the playwright furnished a ready source of documentation.[16]

During the first four years that Howells occupied the "Editor's Study" of *Harper's Monthly,* the period between 1886 and 1890, he formulated his mature theory of Realism in fiction. In 1891 he skimmed the cream from his monthly essays and published *Criticism and Fiction,* a cogent and detailed statement of his thoughts on the profession of letters at the age of fifty-four. Three years later he serialized the papers which were to be published the following year as *My Literary Passions,* devoting one chapter to his relationship with the writings of Goldoni. It is interesting to note that the discussion of Goldoni's Realism parallels in all essential elements the theory of Realism formulated in the earlier group of essays.[17] It seems entirely possible that the main features of Goldoni's interests and attitudes had impressed themselves so strongly on Howells as a young man that he developed his own theory of Realism under the direct influence of the Italian dramatist. Moreover, one can show by reference to his early writings that his ideas on Realism in literature took shape soon after making the acquaintance of Goldoni's works and long before writing his first novel.

Howells's theory of what Realism is and should be, as

[16] An interesting exhibit, showing how both Goldoni and Howells wrote with an eye on the object, may be seen in comparing *La Putta onorata,* Act II, scene 21, with VL, I, 173-175. Both detail arguments between gondoliers over the right of way, and one passage brings to mind the other.

[17] This relationship was noticed by Angelina La Piana in *La Cultura americana e l'Italia,* pp. 332-333. Miss La Piana is the only commentator on Howells, so far as I know, who has recognized the influence of Goldoni on Howells.

formulated in *Criticism and Fiction,* is basically simple: "Realism is nothing more and nothing less than the truthful treatment of material . . . ," and what he means by truth is illustrated in the second half of the same sentence: ". . . and Jane Austen was the first and the last of the English novelists to treat material with entire truthfulness."[18] He later details his concept of truth by declaring: ". . . let fiction cease to lie about life; let it portray men and women as they are . . . let it leave off painting dolls and working them by springs and wires. . . ."[19] Elaborating on his definition, Howells explains that the material properly belonging in a work of Realistic fiction is found in the everyday, commonplace events of life. Although the public clamors for the strange and unusual, the novelist who is worth his salt will not despise what he sees about him, and the place to gather material for "truthful treatment" is in the city street or the country lane, the home or the business office. This creed of the Realist carries with it further a corollary concerning the effect of fiction written to these specifications. Whether the author's intention is to produce art for art's sake, or to preach, the "finest effect of the 'beautiful' will be ethical and not aesthetic merely. Morality penetrates all things, it is the soul of all things."[20] Hence the artist of the beautiful either creates beauty which will corrupt or beauty which will edify, and he cannot avoid one or the other effect so long as society retains its present character. To sum up, Howells's theory with its various ramifications is something like this: Realism in fiction is the reportorial use of the ordinary, commonplace details of life which the writer knows at first hand and handles in such a manner that his work will be compatible with the ethical standards of his time and place. To put it even more succinctly, this theory rests on (*a*) truthful treatment of (*b*)

[18] C&F, p. 73.   [19] *Ibid.,* p. 104.   [20] *Ibid.,* p. 83.

commonplace material, which produces (*c*) proper moral effect.

We may now consider the application of this theory of Realism to the discussion of Goldoni's art in *My Literary Passions*. In this book Howells not only wrote of the Venetian as "one of the greatest realists who has ever lived" but also labeled him "the first of the realists."[21] By being the first Goldoni produced his comedies in an era when Realism had not yet been named. He handled his dramatic materials truthfully because he possessed an instinctive reaction to artificiality and a great talent for making literary capital out of his surroundings. When Howells went to Italy in 1861 he was just as unconscious of Goldoni's achievement as the Venetian dramatist himself had been one hundred years before. But he remembered:

. . . I had eyes in my head, and I saw that what he had seen in Venice so long before was so true that it was the very life of Venice in my own day; and because I have loved the truth in art above all other things, I fell instantly and lastingly in love with Carlo Goldoni.[22]

The Venetian dramatist recorded the life of his city so faithfully that Howells could not in after years read his plays without a renewed sense of the sights and sounds and silences of Venice. Goldoni drew his materials from the everyday life of his city—from the characters and lives of gondoliers and fishermen, from the personality and the activities of merchants and lawyers. When Howells took down the plays, as he often did after returning from Italy, he was especially conscious of Goldoni's commonplace material:

. . . there is seldom anything more poignant in any of them than there is in the average course of things. The plays are

[21] MLP, pp. 207-208.   [22] *Ibid.*

light and amusing transcripts from life, for the most part, and where at times they deepen into powerful situations, or express strong emotions, they do so with persons so little different from the average of our acquaintance that we do not remember just who the persons are.[23]

Thus did Goldoni work within the bounds of the first two aspects of Realism as Howells defined it: truthful treatment of commonplace material. The ethical effect which he linked to his theory of Realism is also present in this discussion of Goldoni. "I know of none of his plays," wrote Howells, "that is of wrong effect, or that violates the instincts of purity, or insults common sense with the romantic pretense that wrong will be right if you will only paint it rose-color."[24] The wonder of the Venetian's art lay in the skilful manner in which he recorded the life of the eighteenth century without giving offense to the nineteenth. Those who know that period historically, Howells declared, will perceive Goldoni's artfulness: "This is the perpetual miracle of his comedy, that it says so much to experience and worldly wisdom, and so little to inexperience and worldly innocence."[25] It would be difficult to devise a better statement of the ethical effect for which Howells himself strove in his novels.

We have now to examine Howells's observations on Goldoni when the playwright's art was first making its indelible impression on him and to observe the three fundamentals of his Realism in their inchoate form. In 1864, the year of writing "Recent Italian Comedy," he perhaps never had heard the term "Realism" applied to a conscious literary attempt to treat life truthfully. Although Balzac was long since dead, and *Madame Bovary* was no longer a new novel, Zola had yet to make his mark, and local color in America had not begun to retouch the American literary landscape

[23] *Ibid.*, p. 209.   [24] *Ibid.*, p. 210.   [25] *Ibid.*, p. 211.

with its partially Realistic tints. In "Recent Italian Comedy" Howells wrote that Goldoni's plays depicted Venice of the last century, but Venetian life must always remain the same in so many details that the plays "still form a picture of the Venetian life about us."[26] Even though he did not yet have the label "Realism" to pin on Goldoni's art, he recognized that the Venetian dramatist's method was "the truthful treatment of material":

For his pleasant and friendly genius, Comedy lived everywhere in Venice: danced and capered before him through the carnival; walked with him in the gay Piazza; talked with him behind her mask at the Ridotto; sat and gossiped with him at the *café;* beckoned him down the narrow streets, and led him into cool little, many-balconied courts, where the neighbors chatted and disputed from window to window; made the fish wives and lace-makers of Chioggia quarrel for his delight; drew aside secret curtains, and showed him giddy wives and fickle husbands, old-fogy fathers bent on choosing husbands for their daughters, and merry girls laughing with love at locksmiths; pointed him out the lovers whispering at the lattices, and the old women mumbling scandal over their *scaldini.* And with his *perfect fidelity and truth to this various life Goldoni wrote....*[27]

Concluding his analysis of the playwright's work, Howells assumed the moralistic tone which was to become an inseparable part of his literary theorizing:

... Goldoni wrote, in an age of unchaste literature, plays which a girl may read with as little cause to blush as would be given by a novel of Dickens. At a time when in England only the tedious Richardson wrote chaste romances, Goldoni produced plays full of decent laughter, of cleanly humor and amiable morality, in that Venice which we commonly believe to have been Sodomitic in its filth and wickedness.[28]

[26] *"Recent Italian Comedy,"* p. 373.
[27] *Ibid.,* p. 374; italics mine.
[28] *Ibid.*

Truthful treatment, commonplace material, moral effect; all three elements of Howells's mature theory of what Realism is and should be are present in this essay written in Venice when he was twenty-seven years old. Not only did he repeat these characteristics in *Criticism and Fiction* and *My Literary Passions* when in his fifties, but he stated them at even greater length in his 1877 essay on Goldoni and in less space in his 1914 review of Chatfield-Taylor's biography of the Venetian dramatist. It seems reasonable to conclude that Goldoni played an important part in shaping Howells's theory of Realism in fiction, and it is worth considering that Italian literature, as well as English, French, and Russian, may thus have contributed to the literary ground swell which washed up European Realism on the receptive shore of America.

Howells's interest in the drama had its beginning in Venice when he was using the theater as a laboratory for learning a new language. Before going to Europe his acquaintance with the drama was meager, but in Italy he found a well-developed dramatic tradition and abundant opportunity to see plays. After his return he remained an enthusiastic playgoer[29] and subsequently became a dramatist in his own right. Although his fascination for the theater never became a major interest, twenty-four comedies and farces attest the vitality of this attachment. As

[29] Howells was very much interested in the development of a respectable American dramatic literature and in 1886 ("Editor's Study," *Harper's Monthly,* LXXIII, July, 1886, 315-316) praised Edward Harrigan's Irish-American drama, concluding: "The art that sets before us all sorts and conditions of New York Irishmen, from the laborers in the street to the most powerful of the ward politicians . . . is the art of Goldoni—the joyous yet conscientious art of the true dramatist in all times who loves the life he observes."

Further comments by Howells on Goldoni occur in a review of Eleonora Duse's interpretation of the dramatist's *Pamela (Harper's Weekly,* XL, Apr. 4, 1896, 318-319), in which he laments the inclusion of only two Goldonian comedies in her American repertoire.

we have seen, his theater attendance led to the study both of Goldoni and of the entire field of dramatic literature in nineteenth-century Italy.

Commentators on Howells invariably note his gift for writing clever, incisive, realistic dialogue. The observation that "one may turn pages and chapters of his novels into dramatic form by supplying to the dialogue the names of the speakers"[30] is an accurate judgment, both recognizing a source of strength in his fiction and suggesting its possible origin. His first book after making Goldoni's acquaintance, *Venetian Life,* contains significant bits of dialogue; and the succeeding work, *Italian Journeys,* has in it extended conversations. Skill in dramatic technique becomes more and more apparent in his progress from sketch-writer to novelist. The fact seems inescapable that the Italian theater, represented most characteristically by Goldoni, provided the laboratory in which Howells studied the construction of sparkling dialogue.

Goldoni's guiding genius was even more apparent when Howells turned from novel-writing to try his hand at the drama, for it is difficult to see a more logical or direct influence on his farces and comedies than the Venetian dramatist. This indebtedness has been persistently overlooked by American critics, although it was immediately apparent to Miss La Piana:

Yet it is enough to read the many little comedies and farces which Howells wrote during his long life, to be convinced that he adapted Goldonian methods, ideas, and situations to the special circumstances of American life which he wished to portray. . . . they [Howells's plays] testify to a special infatuation, which may be explained by the unforgettable Goldonian reminiscences which never ceased to delight him. . . .[31]

[30] Pattee, *op. cit.,* p. 213.
[31] *Op. cit.,* p. 335; translation mine.

The similarity between the Goldonian theater and Howells's more modest collection of comedies and farces is hardly accidental. The common tone of lightheartedness and amiability is at once apparent, and the plays of both authors range from broad farce to subtle comedy of manners. The transference of the scene from eighteenth-century Venice to nineteenth-century Boston precludes the possibility of exact parallels, but in so far as the limitations of time and place may be reconciled the likeness is striking.

Both Howells and Goldoni made extensive use of the same farcical devices: mistaken identity, practical jokes, intrigue, fortuitous complications, and slapstick comedy.[32] The mistaking of a stranger for a long-separated brother in *The Sleeping Car* (1883), for example, recalls a similar failure of mutual recognition between a father and son in *La Putta onorata* (1749); and in *The Albany Depot* (1892), *The Garroters* (1889), *Un Curioso accidente* (1755), and *Il Bugiardo* (1750), to name only two plays by each author, the humor derives from mistaken identity. In both *Le Morbinose* (1758) and *The Mouse Trap* (1886) a practical joke is used to initiate the action, although in the former the heroine has the fun at the expense of her lover and in the latter the reverse situation prevails. Intrigue, which Goldoni used more frequently than Howells, is present in *A Likely Story* (1888) and *Le Morbinose,* both farces in which a chain reaction of ludicrous incident is set off by the

[32] These are the same contrivances, of course, that writers of comedy always have employed—from Plautus and Terence to Ben Jonson and Molière. But Howells almost certainly derived his inspiration from the Venetian. He wrote in 1895 (MLP, p. 235) that he never had been "a great reader of the drama," and among his literary passions only two dramatists, Shakespeare and Goldoni, figure prominently. He devoured Shakespeare as a boy, enjoying most the histories, *Macbeth,* and *Hamlet.* He did not read Molière until after he had formed a taste for Goldoni, and there is no mention of Ben Jonson in his early writings. In fact, he says, without explaining just what playwrights he means: "The taste for the old English dramatists I believe I have never formed" (MLP, p. 235).

sending of a letter. A multitude of complications stemming from an accidental happening provides the fun in *The Elevator* (1885) and *Il Ventaglio* (1785). Howells stumbled badly when he attempted to follow Goldoni into the realm of slapstick comedy, for the treatment of the feuds of the peasants of Chioggia found a suitable vehicle in *Le Baruffe Chiozzote* (1762), whereas the handling of a summer-morning scuffle among the proper Bostonians misses fire in *A Masterpiece of Diplomacy* (1894). In Howells's play the dramatis personae clown in a manner more appropriate to Goldoni's fishwives than to characters who on other occasions sparkle in drawing rooms on Beacon Hill.

These approximate parallels of situation and incident in the farces carry over into the plays or parts of plays which reach the level of social comedy. Howells's happiest moment in this type of drama is *The Unexpected Guests* (1893), in which the delightful Mrs. Campbell proves master of an embarrassing social situation. The subtle treatment of feminine psychology and the effective use of dramatic irony combine to produce an exquisite comedy of manners. Possibly cognate might be Goldoni's best-known play, *La Locandiera* (1753), usually translated as *The Mistress of the Inn*. In this comedy a subtle feminine character also displays complete control over a difficult situation, circumstances under which she holds off two suitors while captivating a woman-hating third. Furthermore, the play is full of bright dialogue between Mistress Mirandolina and her male pursuers, an aspect which recalls many scenes from Howells's comedies in which the plot is the familiar boy-gets-girl. Another type of two-person dialogue, this time repartee between husband and wife, was frequently employed by both Goldoni and Howells, and good examples are found in the opening scenes of *La Putta onorata* and *Evening Dress* (1893). In the former the conversation takes place between a preoccupied husband and wife preparing to go out, while in the latter the dialogue opens with the wife giving a tired husband instructions for following her to a musicale. Although *La Putta onorata* develops into a drama of intrigue and *Evening Dress* degenerates into broad farce, both give promise of social comedy in their opening scenes. A slightly different type of social situation, the dinner party, furnishes another occasion for comparing both writers. In *The Garroters* and *The Unexpected Guests,* for example, the action takes place as the guests assemble for dinner, and the lighthearted banter in these plays is the same sort of repartee bandied about by the dinner guests in *Le Morbinose.*

Examples of the similarities between the plays of Goldoni and Howells might be multiplied many times without mentioning the long list of comedies which Howells must have read with profit but which cannot be equated with any of his own. A play such as *L'Impressario delle Smirne* (1761) contains a great deal of brisk dialogue in the development of a situation which could not be adapted to the American scene—the competition of three unemployed prima donnas for the leading place in a new opera company. Here the devious and wily maneuverings of these volatile Italian singers, motivated by jealousy and need, are artfully neutralized by another delightful character, the perfect foil for these conniving artists, Count Lasca, who achieves the near-impossible in getting the refractory ladies to work together. This amusing play has the mood and tone of a Howells farce, and no doubt the former consul captured the spirit of Goldonian comedy from this and similar plays.

Another aspect of the Venetian dramatist's potential influence may be found in the recurrent use of the same characters. Goldoni wrote when the *commedia dell'arte* still retained a popular following, and he used the stock characters of the older improvised drama for his own purposes. He retained, among others, Pantalone, the rich Venetian merchant, Il Dottore, the Bolognese doctor, Brighella, the roguish servant, and Arlecchino, the dull and foolish scapegoat. He used the stock figures in about half of his one hundred and fifty comedies, but he handled them with skill and variety, so that the type characters took on a measure of individualty. Howells wrote that he preferred among all the comedies those which followed this pattern adapted from the earlier *commedia dell'arte*.[33]

This predilection for stock characters was reflected in Howells's own plays. In twelve of his twenty-four farces and comedies he chronicles the lighter moments in the lives of a certain set of engaging Bostonians. Chief among these is the Roberts-Campbell quartet. Mrs. Roberts, a woman of amazing volubility, is matched by her timid, absent-minded husband, while Mrs. Campbell, a witty conversationalist and charming hostess, is paired with Willis Campbell, a jovial, masculine individual who represents more or less the norm. The activities of these couples on Pullman cars, in elevators, at teas, and in the country run the gamut from slapstick farce to sophisticated comedy. Not only did Howells like best the recurrent characters of Goldoni, but he gave his own brightest efforts to detailing the antics of the Roberts and the Campbell quartet. His repeated use of these figures is thoroughly Goldonian in spirit, and in view of his demonstrable debt to the Italian dramatist his stock figures too may be considered Goldonian in inspiration.

THE ITALIAN NOVEL

Despite his fondness for Italian poetry and drama, Italian fiction held little interest for Howells—with one notable

[33] *Memoirs of Carlo Goldoni,* Introduction, p. 23. He liked the *commedia dell'arte* so well that in creating his utopian society in *Through the Eye of the Needle* (1907), p. 161, he patterned the Altrurian theater after this old Italian comedy.

exception—until long after he had returned to America. "I found that the Italians had no novels which treated of their contemporary life; that they had no modern fiction but the historical romance," he wrote reminiscently of his days in Venice,[1] and his friend Brunetta's efforts to kindle his enthusiasm for this literature met with indifference. He dutifully read the novels of Guerrazzi, Grossi, D'Azeglio, and Cantù, as part of his Italian education, but he was interested in these works only so far as they reflected the political ferment of the *risorgimento*. Having already taken a dislike to Scott, Howells did not find pleasure in that novelist's Italian imitators.[2]

Even though he did not care for their writings, Howells honored the Italian nineteenth-century novelists as men and patriots. When D'Azeglio died in 1866, he paid high tribute to his patriotism and political acumen, declaring in an obituary that the Piedmontese novelist occupied a place second only to Cavour in the history of Italian statesmanship.[3] He also recognized the propaganda value in the novels of the day and approved of political action as the disguised purpose of historical romance. He quoted approvingly Guerrazzi's opinion of his own work:

"When I write it is because I have something *to do;* my books are not productions, but deeds. . . . When we have not the sword, we must take the pen. . . . To write slowly, coldly, of our times and of our country, with the set purpose of creating a *chef-d'œuvre,* would be almost an impiety. . . . I begin a

[1] MLP, p. 207.

[2] In C&F, pp. 21-22, Howells writes that Scott's style is cumbrous and diffuse, his character development long-winded and static, his dialogue artificial, his exposition tiresomely descriptive. "In the beginning of any art even the most gifted worker must be crude," concluded Howells. In MLP, p. 41, Howells recalls reading all of Scott's novels in rapid succession during Oct., 1861, the month before leaving for Venice.

[3] *Nation,* II (Feb. 15, 1866), 202-204. He liked at least one of D'Azeglio's characters, Fanfulla in *Niccolò de' Lapi,* whom he called "one of the most enjoyable and original creations of fiction" (*ibid.,* p. 203).

story to draw the crowd; when I feel that I have caught its ear, I say what I have to say ... my works of siege will be destroyed after the war ... but what does it matter?"[4]

As long as Romanticism was in the saddle, Howells found high praise for only one Italian novel, Manzoni's *I Promessi sposi,* which is perhaps the best known of all Italian works of fiction. His opinion of this novel did not change from the age of thirty to the age of seventy-three, for in 1867 he was tempted to place it "above all other historical novels"[5] and in 1910 he included it in a list of his favorite novels.[6] Manzoni's romance held its lofty place in his esteem even after he had read Tolstoy, and he placed the Italian below the Russian only because Manzoni wrote in the infancy of his art, while Tolstoy wrote in its maturity. "Both are coeval in the inspiration of their work," he added categorically, going on to find a common bond of social consciousness in the two writers, a common pity for the poor, the oppressed, and the lonely, and abhorrence of violence and pride.[7]

Three years after equating Manzoni and Tolstoy, Howells read the work of Giovanni Verga (1840-1922) and immediately mustered the Sicilian novelist into the ranks of De Forest, Turgenev, Bjornson, Hardy, Zola, Valdes, and other Realists whom he had previously championed as literary pioneers. Howells discovered Verga in 1886, announcing his find in a review of *I Malavoglia* (1881) in the "Editor's Study" of *Harper's Monthly.* He hailed the Italian as a writer with "an incomparable grasp of Italian actualities" and his book as one "eminently worthy of translation."[8] Four years later Harpers brought out an English

[4] MIP, p. 3. As reported by the Swiss critic Marc Monnier.
[5] "Modern Italian Poets," p. 318.
[6] *Imaginary Interviews,* p. 233. Also included is Verga's *I Malavoglia,* the only other Italian selection.
[7] "Editor's Study," *Harper's Monthly,* LXXVIII (May, 1889), 984.
[8] LXXIII (Nov., 1886), 964.

version under the title *The House by the Medlar-Tree,* and Howells eagerly accepted a chance to write the introduction. Again he gave his apostolic blessing to the first Italian convert to Realism, praising Verga's book as one of the most perfect pieces of literature he knew and a contribution to the modern trend towards reality. It was, he wrote, a sincere treatment of commonplace life in a Sicilian fishing village, and he added: "Anyone who . . . feels the tie binding us all together in the helplessness of our human life, and running from the lowliest as well as the highest to the Mystery immeasurably above the whole earth, must find a rare and tender pleasure in this simple story. . . ."[9] Several years later he again spoke of this novel, calling it a "story of infinite beauty, tenderness and truth,"[10] and it remained one of his favorite works of fiction throughout his life.

[9] Giovanni Verga, *The House by the Medlar-Tree,* p. iii.
[10] MLP, pp. 245-246.

IV. Italian Life

HOWELLS maintained that literature cannot be divorced from life, and the truth of that statement is apparent in his own career. As we have seen, he spent his four consular years diligently recording his Italian impressions and observations and preparing himself for a career in letters. He cut his critical teeth on Italian comedy while in Venice and made himself an authority on Italian poetry in the years after returning to America. The faint woodland notes of his poetic youth were often warbled under Venetian skies, but the finest product of his literary apprenticeship was the travel book, a type of writing to which he returned many times and out of which developed his novels. When he turned to the composition of prose fiction in 1868, he drew inspiration from the well of his Italian experience, and the first important invention was a long short story laid in Venice. It was 1871 before he found time to write a novel, but once he had adopted that form of literary expression, he leaned heavily on his Italian residence in three out of his first seven novels. In his earliest fiction he used Venetians for the leading characters, but as his foreign sojourn receded into the past, he switched to American protagonists and showed them against the background of Italian life.

The first English edition of *Venetian Life* was scarcely off the press before Howells began to plot a fictional exploitation of his Italian residence. He wrote his sister on June 17, 1866: "I'm thinking now about commencing a romance—the scene of it to be laid in Italy, or Venice rather

—but I have ever so much work begun which I must finish first."[1] It is entirely possible that this was the story which ultimately became *A Foregone Conclusion*,[2] but the pressure of other duties kept him from following up the plan. There was no further hint of a novel until eighteen months later when he notified Hurd: "I'm at work on the novel when I can get a moment. . . ." He was forced to add, however: ". . . it's slow business, and may turn out a failure."[3] His fears were prophetic, and he seems to have put off writing long fiction indefinitely in favor of sketches of the type already mastered. Six years then elapsed before he finally completed a novel laid in Venice.

In 1867 Howells apparently was not capable of writing a novel, and he was forced to backtrack for an additional period of apprenticeship. Disregarding his abortive effort in 1867, one can perhaps discern an orderly pattern in his development from a clever writer of travel sketches to a skilled novelist. He laid aside the Venetian romance which he could not handle and contented himself the following year with composing the short story "Tonelli's Marriage," a semifictional sketch. He next planned a biography, settling on Lucrezia Borgia,[4] but six months later had to admit that the lady "would not be wooed in any Boston library."[5] A similar disappointment occurred in an attempt to write on American history. Early in 1869 Howells wanted badly to put together a new book to capitalize on the success of his Italian travels, and he considered making a volume out of his essays on Italian poetry in the *North American Review* but concluded that such a book would not

[1] LinL, I, 113.
[2] This is asserted in the annotations to LinL (I, 111), but there is no supporting evidence.
[3] LinL, I, 125; Dec. 15, 1867.
[4] *Ibid.*, p. 129; Howells to William Cooper Howells, May 25, 1868.
[5] *Ibid.*, p. 138; Howells to C. E. Norton, Nov. 12, 1868.

sell.[6] In the end he continued the papers already begun on contemporary topics and appearing in the *Atlantic,* sketches such as "Mrs. Johnson," and the result was *Suburban Sketches* (1871), a group of essays on people and places in and near Cambridge. As we have noted earlier, *Suburban Sketches* did for Cambridge what *Venetian Life* had done for Venice, and if Howells could not yet write a novel laid in Italy, he at least could describe Mrs. Johnson, the cook, as he had done Giovanna, the handmaid, and he could relate conversations with the Italian scissors-grinders and chestnut-roasters of Cambridge, as he had reported his parleyings with the gondoliers and *facchini* of Venice.[7]

Howells took a long step forward in 1870-1871 in his advance from sketch-writer to novelist. After visiting Niagara Falls and Canada on a summer vacation trip, he returned home with the idea of recording his travels in fiction. Accordingly, he produced *Their Wedding Journey* (1872), a book in which the characters Basil and Isabel March follow the same route he had followed with his wife. The volume passes for a novel, but actually it is a fictionalized travelogue—the sort of book *Italian Journeys* might have been if its characters had been invented. While he was writing this transitional work, he wrote his father: "If I succeed in this—and I believe I shall—I see clear before me a path in literature which no one else has tried. . . ."[8] The novel was a success, and Howells immediately repeated the formula in *A Chance Acquaintance* (1873), this time taking a set of different characters from Quebec to the Saguenay River and back. He injected a "love interest" and also created a pert, attractive heroine in Kitty Ellison. Two aspects of the story are important, the rejection of

[6] *Ibid.,* pp. 153-154; Howells to M. M. Hurd, Feb. 4, 1869.

[7] See "Doorstep Acquaintance," *Atlantic,* XXIII (Apr., 1869), 484-493; reprinted in *Suburban Sketches.*

[8] LinL, I, 162; undated.

Arbuton's proposal and the contrast in manners of the Western girl and the Bostonian, for both features occur again with a different application in his third novel.

By the time he had written three books of sketches and two rudimentary romances, Howells was capable of producing a well-integrated novel, and he picked up the abandoned Venetian romance. Writing Henry James on March 10, 1873, he reported that he had already finished thirty pages of his new story, in which "the hero is a Venetian priest in love with an American girl."[9] The writing went along steadily during 1873, and in December he again wrote James to report that the tale was nearing its end and he was impatient to "get it all once fairly on paper, so that I can . . . clean it up a bit."[10] The narrative, which he called *A Foregone Conclusion,* was serialized in the *Atlantic* in the last half of 1874 and appeared in book form in time for the Christmas trade. It was an instantaneous success, and seventeen days after publication Osgood had sold three thousand copies. "It hasn't had one adverse notice yet," Howells wrote his father gleefully on December 20.[11]

At last Howells had written a book which neither depended on the travel device to give it movement nor used Mr. and Mrs. Howells as the thinly disguised protagonists. For the first time he had managed to create a respectable plot in which complicated characters enacted their story in a severely restricted locale. The advance in his technique was apparent to his friends and commented on most articulately by Stedman, who wrote four days after the book appeared:

. . . I have read the closing chapters of *A Foregone Conclusion,* having followed it along the *Atlantic,* and like it the best of all your books. Indeed it has been of curious interest to me to see

[9] *Ibid.,* p. 175.   [10] *Ibid.,* p. 181.   [11] *Ibid.,* p. 199.

your *gradual* but steady progress in *construction*—invention of plot and management of separate characters. . . . Each of your books has had a little more *story* to it, and this is a story throughout and therefore the best of all. Of course you had nothing to gain in style or insight of character.[12]

To this warm praise Howells returned his thanks and added humbly: "No man ever felt his way more anxiously, doubtfully, self-distrustfully than I to the work I'm now doing."[13]

He had indeed profited from the novels and sketches which had preceded *A Foregone Conclusion,* and the lessons thus learned helped make that story a popular and continued success. From *Venetian Life* had come many background details and the character of the American consul Ferris, who in many respects is a self-portrait. From *Their Wedding Journey* had come the fictional use of travel, for to the extent that the Vervains are tourists in Venice the travel motif is re-used. From *A Chance Acquaintance* had come the heroine (Kitty Ellison and Florida Vervain are at least first cousins) and the idea of contrasting the manners of different geographic localities. Don Ippolito, the Venetian priest, alone had not been suggested by any earlier books but was largely drawn from life.

While it marks a great advance on his previous novels, *A Foregone Conclusion* contains a weak ending. Howells recognized as one of its shortcomings the dénouement which destroys the pace and unity—the sop which he threw to the magazine public by marrying Ferris to Florida, speeding up the passage of time, and shifting the scene from Venice to America and back again.[14] He wrote Norton

[12] Laura Stedman and George M. Gould (eds.), *Life and Letters of Edmund Clarence Stedman,* I, 526.

[13] LinL, I, 197.

[14] Henry James picked out this weakness as the only flaw in an otherwise superb novel. See "Review of *A Foregone Conclusion,*" *North American Review,* CXX (Jan., 1875), 207-214.

apologetically: "If I had been perfectly my own master—
it's a little droll but true, that even in such a matter one
isn't—the story would have ended with Don Ippolito's rejection. But I suppose that it is well to work for others in
some measure. . . ."[15] Apparently contemporary taste de-
manded a happy ending, and an editor of the *Atlantic* was
not one to go against the wishes of his readers. He seems
guilty of rationalizing, however, when he adds: ". . . I
feel pretty sure that I deepened the shadows by going on,
and achieved a completer verity, also."[16]

Despite the concession to the magazine public in the
matrimonial ending, Howells did not hesitate to use the
novel as a forum for criticizing the Catholic church. He
had observed at first hand the corruption of the clergy in
Italy, and he blamed for at least part of its rottenness the
priestly vow of celibacy. He thought it both morally wrong
and unnatural, and had written in the New York *Times*
soon after returning from Venice:

It would be scarcely useful to rehearse here the evils which
intelligent Italians believe to result from the celibacy of their
priesthood, or to define the anomalous position which the priest,
isolated from mankind by an ascetic superstition of the middle
ages, holds in the ameliorated society of this day. The reader
. . . can understand how impossible it must be for the celibacy
of the priesthood to continue in a State like new Italy.[17]

With more ardor than perspicacity Howells deplored the
widespread immorality resulting from this vow and strenuously advocated marriage for the priesthood. Eight years
later, when he wrote *A Foregone Conclusion,* he attributed
the tragedy of Don Ippolito to the tradition of celibacy which
prevented a priest's participation in normal social relation-

---

[15] LinL, I, 198; Dec. 12, 1874.
[16] *Ibid.*
[17] "Marriage among the Italian Priesthood," p. 4.

ships. His outspoken attack on this phase of Catholicism is of a piece with the scattered criticisms of the Church in his travel books, and it did not go unchallenged. At least one prominent Catholic, John Boyle O'Reilly, then editor of the Boston *Pilot,* entered a formal protest against the reflection cast on the priesthood by Don Ippolito,[18] but Howells never softened his portrait of that melancholy and frustrated priest.

Don Ippolito, however, was the first full-length study which Howells had managed to chisel in the round—"a real creation," James called him;[19] and his friends were enthusiastic in their praise of the characterization. Longfellow thought the priest powerfully drawn,[20] and Child wrote that he did not "grudge some sniffling over Don I . . . his story is so tragic."[21] John Hay declared: "Your priest is the best thing of the sort that has been done";[22] while Robert Dale Owen, who had been minister to Italy, wrote that Don Ippolito was "an admirable portrait, tenderly sketched and true to the best Italian nature."[23]

Perhaps the most interesting problem connected with *A Foregone Conclusion* lies in the identification of Don Ippolito with one of Howells's Italian friends. The problem is complicated at the outset by an error which Mildred Howells made in her annotation of the letters.[24] She named as the model for the Venetian priest Padre Giacomo Issaverdenz, a brother in the Armenian convent at San Lazzaro and a lifelong friend of the Howells family. Actually the prototype was another priest whom the Consul knew in the

[18] J. B. O'Reilly to Howells, Sept. 23, 1874; MS at Harvard.
[19] "Review of *A Foregone Conclusion,*" p. 210.
[20] Samuel Longfellow, *op. cit.,* III, 240; letter to G. W. Greene dated Dec. 7, 1874.
[21] Nov., [1875]; MS at Harvard.
[22] Dec. 10, 1875; MS at Harvard.
[23] Nov. 24, 1874; MS at Harvard.
[24] LinL, I, 192.

city of Venice, the same priest who led his faltering steps through Dante's *Divina Commedia*. The search for the correct identification contains all the elements of a detective story, beginning with the false clue planted by an editor who presumably should have known the facts. The trail leads through various scattered writings and an interview and ends with unmistakable proof in the Howells family album.

Starting with the preconceived notion that Don Ippolito was drawn from Padre Giacomo, one reads *A Foregone Conclusion* and *Venetian Life* to compare the characterization of the priest in the novel with the chapter on the Armenians in the travel book. It soon becomes clear that something is wrong with the supposed identification, for Howells levels severe criticism at the Catholic church through the portrayal of Don Ippolito, depicting a man who is a priest by mistake, a man who admits he is living a lie, and a man who wants to renounce his vows. Furthermore, the priest is a frustrated inventor who wishes to leave Italy as well as the priesthood and to go to America. On the other hand, Howells's attitude towards Padre Giacomo and the Armenians is quite different. Their branch of the Church, he feels, holds fast to the ideals of Catholicism and is untouched by the religious corruption of the age. Moreover, the entire relationship between Howells and Padre Giacomo, as developed from a reading of the five letters from the priest to Howells now in the Harvard Library, makes the identification seem impossible.

The first clue to the existence of a second candidate for the original of Don Ippolito occurs in "A Year in a Venetian Palace," the essay Howells wrote in 1870 describing the last fourteen months that he lived in Venice, a sort of sequel to *Venetian Life*. In this article there is one paragraph about his friend Padre L——, an inventor whose

living quarters are cluttered with his inventions, just as
Don Ippolito's rooms are littered in *A Foregone Conclusion*.[25] When Consul Ferris visits the priest in the novel,
he sees the same anteroom frescoed to resemble a grape
arbor that Consul Howells describes, and he sees the identi-
cal piano hooked to a melodeon for one-man duets. There
is also the oratory converted into a forge, the miscellaneous
assortment of chemical apparatus, and the multitude of inventions, both fantastic and practical. In every detail Padre
L——'s apartment matches Don Ippolito's, and the reader
concludes immediately that this priest supplied at least the
scientific side of the good Don's character.

In searching for more information about Padre L——,
the investigator turns back to a letter written in October,
1863, to Charles Hale[26] at the time the *Atlantic* rejected the
Venetian sketches. In offering this work to his second
choice, the Boston *Advertiser,* Howells enumerated the titles
of the papers on hand in addition to those previously submitted to the magazine. Among the articles listed was one
called "My Priest, the Inventor," but unfortunately this
turns out to be the only essay of the group never to appear
in the newspaper.

After this false scent gives out, the trail does not become
warm again until another reference to the anonymous
priest-inventor turns up in *Italian Journeys.* The Howells
family had been visiting Possagno, birthplace of Canova,
and they had seen a replica of the Pantheon built by the
sculptor as a church for his home town. The building reminded them of certain parallels between paganism and
Christianity, and Howells wrote: "I remembered how
Padre L—— had said to me in Venice, 'Our saints are only
the old gods baptized and christened anew.' "[27] Here, then,

[25] Cf. AFC, pp. 47-50, with VL, II, 279-280.
[26] LinL, I, 78.   [27] IJs, p. 282.

is another clue, one which presently will assume considerable importance; for the priest is not only an inventor but also a religious skeptic, and Don Ippolito fits this description exactly.

The next reference to Padre L—— occurs in a completely unexpected place, the interview which H. H. Boyesen held with Howells in 1893. The younger novelist had been questioning his senior about the Italian sojourn and literary studies in that period. Howells had volunteered the information that he remembered studying Dante with a Venetian priest, and he added: "This priest in certain ways suggested Don Ippolito . . . what interested me most about him was his religious skepticism. He used to say, 'The saints are the gods baptized.' Then he was a baffled inventor; though whether his inventions had the least merit I was unable to determine."[28]

This casual remark is the last important link in the chain of accumulating evidence, and it is now possible to establish beyond doubt that Padre L—— is the priest on whom Don Ippolito is modeled. Although he is not designated by name or initial in Boyesen's interview, we can apply the elementary geometric theorem that things equal to the same thing are equal to each other. Padre L—— was an inventor and skeptic, and such an inventor and skeptic was the prototype of Don Ippolito. *Ergo:* Padre L—— and Don Ippolito, the Venetian priest in *A Foregone Conclusion,* are the same person.

The discovery of the priest's real name comes as an anticlimax, but to make the picture complete, this last piece of information appears in the cramped handwriting of Howells's old age under a photograph of a Venetian priest in the family album previously cited. Here the priest is cryptically identified as Padre Libera, the original of Don Ippolito in *A Foregone Conclusion.*

[28] Boyesen, *op. cit.,* p. 6.

Although Padre Giacomo did not sit for the portrait of Don Ippolito, he appears in *A Foregone Conclusion* in a a photographic likeness retouched only with an assumed name. He is the Padre Girolamo of chapter ii, who conducts the Vervains and Consul Ferris through the Armenian convent at San Lazzaro, a function which he enacted in real life whenever English-speaking visitors called at the island in the Venetian lagoon. In 1874, a month after Howells had given Warner a letter of introduction to Padre Giacomo, the priest thanked him for sending his friend to visit him, adding delightedly that he had just read a recent instalment of the novel in the *Atlantic*. "I saw that you remember very well of my own description," he wrote, "as in your words I found all myself."[29] And he signed the letter: "Padre Giacomo . . . otherwise P. Girolamo."

The use of the Armenian convent for local color is a typical illustration of the manner in which Howells adapted his experiences to the use of fiction. The visit to San Lazzaro in *A Foregone Conclusion* is merely a reworking of the factual description of the Armenians contained in *Venetian Life*.[30] There are so many other similarities between the two books that it is necessary to refer constantly to the sources to be certain which incidents occur in the travel book and which in the novel. Although Howells called his novel a romance, it is filled with authentic background, and the exoticism of the setting should not be allowed to obscure the realism of detail. The subordinate character of Ferris, the American consul, to cite another example, gives Howells a chance to work in much material from his Venetian experiences, and the details in the novel concerned with the Consul's dealings with Italians and his ministrations to

[29] Oct. 26, 1874; MS at Harvard.
[30] Cf. AFC, pp. 25-30, with VL, I, 247-257.

traveling Americans are taken from life. The story, moreover, takes place during the first year of the Civil War. The quarters occupied by Ferris are placed at the precise corner of Venice where the Howells family lived in Casa Falier, and the apartment which Mrs. Vervain rents recalls many details from Palazzo Giustiniani, which housed the Consul and his family during their last year in Venice.[31]

A Foregone Conclusion was the most popular of Howells's early fictions as well as his first real novel. It was a source of income for most of his life as well as a means of introduction to a new generation of readers. Fourteen printings appeared in thirteen years, and the book was reissued as late as 1916. In 1879 the novel found its way into a Tauchnitz edition for continental Europe,[32] after being translated in 1876 into German as *Voreilige Schlüsse;*[33] and in 1882 Howells was asked for permission to publish a Danish translation.[34] The novel was dramatized and produced both in London and New York in 1885 and 1886,[35] but the play never became a hit. "It is liked by the front-seat people," wrote the London producer, "but the somber character of the story is not just now to the taste of the multitude. . . ."[36] However, the tale was popular in England, and John Hay reported to Howells in 1882 that he

[31] Cf. also the accounts of the Corpus Christi Day parades in both books, AFC, pp. 161-169, and VL, II, 90-96.

[32] LinL, I, 275-276.

[33] *Ibid.,* p. 220.

[34] See letter dated Copenhagen, Jan. 23, 1882 (MS at Harvard), from C. L. Hertz to Howells. The translation had been made and permission to publish was requested. This was unnecessary, of course, since the American international copyright act was not yet in existence, but the book is not listed in *Dansk Bogfortegnelse, 1881-1892* (Copenhagen, 1893-1894).

[35] See LinL, I, 367, and II, 63. Also see Arthur H. Quinn, *A History of the American Drama: from the Civil War to the Present Day,* I, 74, and Odell, *op. cit.,* XIII, 218.

[36] William Pole to Howells, Aug. 20, 1885; MS at Harvard. There are several letters in the Howells Collection from Pole pertaining to this dramatization.

had seen a thumb-worn copy of the book on the drawing-room table in the Prime Minister's house, and "the Prime Ministress [Mrs. Gladstone] authorized and requested me to say to you how much she liked it."[37]

"I don't know when I have had such a good time over a story," wrote Sara Orne Jewett after rereading "Tonelli's Marriage" in 1881.[38] As a competent judge of the short story, she recognized the subtle shadings and local color which went into this Venetian piece, Howells's first fictional use of his consular years. The story, written in the spring of 1868,[39] not only is interesting for its use of the Italian scene but also illustrates the close relationship between the author's life and his art. As we have seen in chapter i, the characters are nearly all drawn from life: the middle-aged bachelor Tonelli, the patriotic young girl, the compromised advocate Cenarotti, the girl's mother, and Tonelli's young friend Pennellini. These people formed a circle of acquaintance which Howells cultivated zealously during his Italian years. The only person in the story who cannot be identified from surviving records of the author's Venetian friends is Carlotta, the woman who marries Tonelli. But even she may have a basis in fact. Tonelli was probably the unidentified friend in *Venetian Life* (chap. xix) who confessed to the Consul one day that he was in love with a modestly dowered blonde from the mainland—a description which fits Signorina Carlotta. Perhaps also the verses which Howells wrote for the Zeni-Foratti nuptials celebrated the marriage of Tommaso Tonelli. Whether or not the courtship

[37] W. R. Thayer, *The Life and Letters of John Hay*, I, 409.

[38] July 26, [1881]; MS at Harvard. Miss Jewett wrote that she had seen the story before but on second reading it seemed new and "perfectly delightful." The story was originally published in the *Atlantic*, XXII (July, 1868), 96-110, and later reprinted in AFR, pp. 211-255.

[39] LinL, I, 129. He wrote his father in May that he had been hard at work for some time on the story.

of these Venetians actually took place, it furnished a plot
device by which Howells could chronicle the gradual alien-
ation of Tonelli and his old friends, the Cenarotti family,
as the result of his falling in love.

The characters in "Tonelli's Marriage" are placed against
the setting already sketched vividly in *Venetian Life,* and
in the words of the witness who previously has given expert
testimony: ". . . it is an episode of Venetian life of true and
appropriate Goldonian color."[40] This is to say, it is the
thing itself. The story captures faithfully the atmosphere
of the city, the economic conditions under the Austrian
occupation, the social customs of the people, the gossiping
in the cafés, and the suppressed patriotism of the *irredentisti.*
It is sketched with deft, bold strokes and charged with exquisite humor—humor too refined for the multitude, wrote
Lowell, "but which the knowers will prize at its true worth,
and after them the many."[41]

We may obtain a further insight into Howells's creative
process by comparing this early story with his first travel
book, for the documentation of the fiction exists in ample
measure in *Venetian Life.* The chapter on "Venetian Dinners and Diners," for example, provides an extensive factual
account of the customs from which the details of Tonelli's
gastronomical habits are drawn, and it is obvious that the
Consul's experience in eating in Venetian restaurants found
its way into his fiction as well as into his sketches. Similarly, the elaborate social protocol surrounding Italian courtship and marriage forms an important part of the local
color in the short story. Howells had watched young men
casting furtive glances at heavily chaperoned young ladies;
he had seen Venetian love-making reported faithfully on
the stage in Goldoni's *Il Bugiardo;* and he was, moreover,

---

[40] La Piana, *op. cit.,* p. 339; translation mine.
[41] M. A. DeW Howe (ed.), *New Letters of James Russell Lowell,* p. 129.

a man whose brother-in-law had wooed a Venetian beauty. Hence he was well qualified to write about the marriage customs of the Venetians, and he used this material both in *Venetian Life* and in "Tonelli's Marriage."[42]

Howells returned in part to his theme of the American girl in Europe, creating Lydia Blood, the lady of the *Aroostook,* in the same year James limned her more famous cousin Daisy Miller.[43] In *A Foregone Conclusion* he already had contrasted American and European manners, and after trying a summer boarding house locale in *Private Theatricals* (1875-1876), he once more packed his characters off for Venice. Four years had elapsed, however, between the composition of the Venetian romance and of *The Lady of the Aroostook,* and in that period Howells had performed a wide variety of editorial tasks, writing a campaign biography of Rutherford B. Hayes, three comedies, and editing seven autobiographies. When he turned to fiction again, he was able to produce in Lydia Blood a convincing portrait which bears a family resemblance to Kitty Ellison and Florida Vervain but goes beyond anything he had previously accomplished.

Howells devotes almost three-quarters of this novel to getting the ship *Aroostook* to Europe, subordinating the contrast of international manners in an Italian setting to the display of opposing American types—the country girl against two young Bostonians. Once in Venice, however, South Bradfield, Massachusetts, meets a cross section of European society—expatriated Englishmen and worldly wise Venetians—under the chaperonage of a parvenu Amer-

[42] Cf. VL, I, 107-118, with AFR, pp. 213-214; also cf. VL, II, 130-136, with AFR, pp. 229-231, 233, 246.
[43] James's story was serialized in the *Cornhill Magazine* in June and July, while Howells's novel began in the November *Atlantic*. They were both written in the first half of 1878.

ican aunt. *The Lady of the Aroostook* lacks the subtlety of
Daisy Miller, but Lydia Blood is more American than
James's heroine. In this novel Howells abandons the attempt to create Italian character and concentrates on
American types. The foreign milieu has become largely
stage-setting, but it is scenery which he always shifts *con
amore.*

   The Lady of the Aroostook had its genesis fourteen
years before Howells actually wrote the story. When Samuel P. Langley and his brother visited Venice during the
last year of the Civil War, they reported what had seemed
an unusual situation in their Atlantic crossing. A New
England girl on the way to visit an aunt who lived in Italy
had traveled with them as the only woman on board the
ship. For the novelist of manners this incident had interesting possibilities, not only for contrasting the American
girl's small-town background with European society, but
also for exposing her naïveté to the sophistication of well-
bred Bostonian shipmates. Howells remembered the incident and in 1878 worked it up for the plot of his fifth
novel. Langley was in Florence when he read the first
chapters of the story and was inspired to call on the girl's
aunt, who still lived in that city, to renew an old acquaintance. He reported to Howells later that Lydia Blood's post-
Italian history had been considerably more romantic than
her original's. "But the living Miss ——— is still Miss—
Blood," he wrote, "and she still is a school-teacher. I
wonder if she reads the *Atlantic!*"[44]

   The realistic detail of Venice, so abundant in *A Foregone Conclusion,* is less conspicuous in this novel, though
a certain amount of local color is used with good effect.
There are moments in *The Lady of the Aroostook* which
recall scenes and descriptions from *Venetian Life*—such

   [44] LinL, I, 266; S. P. Langley to Howells, Mar. 23, 1879.

bits as the trip from Venice station through the canals in the early morning, which is condensed from Howells's account of his own arrival in 1861, and Miss Blood's bedroom in her uncle's palace on the Grand Canal, which is drawn from the author's bedroom in Palazzo Giustiniani.[45] The ocean voyage itself, while not a part of the Italian backdrop, is taken from the author's own crossing in the 1860's, and the ship-life aboard the *Aroostook,* even though a sailing vessel, is much like the daily round of activity Howells remembered from the *City of Glasgow.*[46] The characterization of the satirized Englishman in the uncle, Henshaw Erwin, is worth a brief comment, for he may have been suggested by one of Howells's early friends in Italy, a Captain Tubbs, formerly of the East India Company's service, with whom the Consul had held joint ownership of a gondola.[47] The Indian background and the singular gondola-rowing of the fictitious Erwin suggest the parallel with this Englishman Howells had known.

The Lady of the Aroostook was another popular success, and letters of praise came from all directions. Stedman, for example, read the book at a sitting and was amazed at Howells's continued development as a novelist. "This tale is absolutely *realistic,"* he wrote.[48] William Wetmore Story reported from Venice that his household, including Robert Browning, who was staying with them,[49] was reading the

---

[45] Cf. LofA, pp. 243-244, with VL, I, 35-38; also cf. LofA, p. 244, with VL, II, 249.

[46] The character of Hicks, the dipsomaniac, may have been inspired by a passenger on the *City of Glasgow.* Howells remembered in "Overland to Venice," p. 839 (though it is doubtful how reliable that reminiscence is), that there had been such a character on board and that he had put him into a sea novel "with much imaginary detail, rounded out from nature's sketch by my invention."

[47] There is a picture of Capt. Tubbs and his wife in the previously cited family album at Harvard.

[48] *Life and Letters of Stedman,* II, 338.

[49] Oct. 7, 1879; MS at Harvard.

book with great delight, and Lowell, Hay, and Clemens were in their usual places among the chorus of admirers.[50] As a commercial venture, the novel was so popular that Canadian publishers pirated five editions,[51] Tauchnitz put it into his "British" library,[52] and Houghton Mifflin reprinted it as recently as 1921.[53]

The year 1881 marks a turning point in the career of Howells the editor and Howells the novelist. Shortly before his forty-fourth birthday, when the burden of managing the *Atlantic* became insupportable, he stepped down from the editorship he had held for ten years to devote full time to writing. Already he had produced six novels, two travel books, and a wide variety of lesser works, but he was only approaching his ripest creative years. As soon as he had relinquished his editorial responsibilities, he began work on *A Modern Instance,* his most important work up to this time and one of the novels on which his reputation is most likely to rest.

In this transitional year he also wrote the last chapter of his youthful, idyllic Venetian sojourn in *A Fearful Responsibility*. This slight story, which was serialized in only two instalments of *Scribner's,* cost an undue effort. He wrote Clemens in April: "My difficulty in finishing the two-number story that I've just ended has given me a scare about loading up with more work till I see my way through the novel [*A Modern Instance*]."[54] Evidently he had nearly ex-

[50] *Letters of James Russell Lowell,* II, 240; LinL, I, 259, 264-265.

[51] LinL, I, 268-269, 276.

[52] *Ibid.,* pp. 275-276. Many of Howells's novels, in addition to VL, IJs, and TCs, were put into Tauchnitz editions. See the appropriate volumes of *Kayser's Bücher Lexicon* for the period 1870-1900.

[53] A French translation, *La Passagère de Aroostook* (Paris, 1884), is listed in the *Catalogue général des libres imprimés de la Bibliothèque Nationale* (Paris, 1929), LXXIV, 70.

[54] LinL, I, 296. The "more work" referred to was Clemens's plan to enlist Howells's assistance in editing his *Library of Humor.*

hausted his Italian experiences, and with this final exploitation of his Venetian consulship Howells dropped his Italian
settings until he had refilled the reservoir by a return visit
in 1882-1883.

A Fearful Responsibility attempts to combine successful
features from both A Foregone Conclusion and The Lady
of the Aroostook. Like the former, it is laid in Venice during the Civil War and is well supplied with palaces, canals,
and Austrian occupation troops. It provides another obliging American consul in Clay Hoskins, a sculptor, who suc-
ceeds Henry Ferris, the painter; but the poetry of Howells's
youth, which gives the earlier novel great charm, is missing from this story written sixteen years later. In the image
of Lydia Blood, the author has created Lily Mayhew, a
small-town American girl who travels to Italy to visit
friends, and through whom American and European manners are again contrasted; but the portrait is slighter, and
the reader feels that Howells already has done it better.
One also is tempted to see the influence of Daisy Miller,
for Miss Mayhew, deficient in Miss Blood's unbending New
England rectitude, becomes involved in a social indiscretion
through the innocence of her unsophisticated American
heart.

The most interesting thing about A Fearful Responsibility, however, is the autobiographical content. Once again
Howells drew on his own experiences, for Lily Mayhew is
taken from Mary Mead, the author's sister-in-law, who
visited Venice in 1864 and 1865. Mildred Howells writes:

There is, in her sister's [Mrs. Howells's] sketch book, a
drawing of her [Mary Mead] standing upon the balcony of the
Palazzo Giustiniani beside a somewhat drooping young man;
their backs are turned towards the artist and their figures are
framed in the open window against the Grand Canal. It was
afterwards discovered by the unsuspecting artist to have been

the unconscious portrait of a rejected proposal, and it long
served in the family as an example of the fearfulness of the
responsibility."[55]

The proposal described here becomes in the novel the second of three offers made to Lily Mayhew during her visit,
that of a young Englishman who subsequently takes his
broken heart to India; but it is hardly likely that Mary
Mead's eligibility caused Consul Howells as much anguish
as Lily Mayhew causes Professor Elmore. The professor's
headache results chiefly from the girl's indiscretion in making a railroad-trip acquaintance with an Austrian officer and
the officer's interpretation of Upstate New York camaraderie
as an invitation to matrimony.

The novel gives a faithful picture of Italian life in Venice during the last years of the Austrian occupation, showing at the same time the inevitable social retirement forced
on an American couple living in the city in that period.
Howells's early Anglophobia again is displayed here as well
as his sympathy for Italian national aspirations. The stu-
dious Professor Elmore, who went to Venice during the
Civil War to write a history of the city, is something of a
self-portrait, and Mrs. Elmore bears more than a superficial
relationship to Mrs. Howells. In the creation of this hus-
band-and-wife team the novelist is in effect reverting to the
Basil-and-Isabel March combination he already had used
and was to repeat several more times.

Another significant aspect of this novel is the attitude of
the author towards military service in the Civil War. Written sixteen years after the conflict ended, it expresses, more
articulately than Howells ever before had phrased it, re-
morse over not having been in the fight. This sentiment is
voiced both by Consul Hoskins and Professor Elmore. The
former, who has been wounded in action and discharged

[55] *Ibid.*, p. 75. Cf. AFR, pp. 93-94.

earlier in the war, hopes to capture the Confederate privateer *Alabama,* which has been sighted in the Adriatic,
so that he can "stop that infernal clatter inside about going
over and taking a hand again."[56] The Professor, who has
been advised by his doctor not to enlist, has rationalized at
the outset the propriety of his leaving America during the
war, but when Lily Mayhew describes the return home of
maimed war veterans, he exclaims: "I can never forgive
myself for not going to war. . . ."[57] Whether Howells actually regretted his own foreign residence during the Civil
War cannot be demonstrated, but the sentiments expressed
in this novel show clearly that the author had thought
deeply on the subject.

ITALY REVISITED

After Howells gave up the editorship of the *Atlantic,*
there was nothing to prevent his fulfilling a long-sup-
pressed wish to revisit the scene of his most memorable
four years of early manhood. His new business arrangements, under which Osgood became both literary agent
and publisher, began auspiciously with the serialization of
A Modern Instance in the *Century.* In seventeen years he
had climbed to an enviable position in American letters
and no longer feared that foreign residence would jeopard-
ize his literary reputation. Family considerations, in addition, made a winter in Italy desirable. His daughter Winifred had been seriously ill in the summer of 1881, and for
seven weeks at the end of the year Howells himself was
down with "some sort of fever";[1] hence both father and
daughter needed a change, and Europe seemed an ideal
place to recuperate.

On several occasions between 1865 and 1882 Howells
betrayed nostalgia for his pleasant years in Venice. "We

---

[56] AFR, p. 22.   [57] *Ibid.,* p. 26.   [1] LinL, I, 303.

often sigh for the renewal of our own vague life there," he publicly admitted in 1870, but hastened to add that the longing was only momentary.[2] In his private letters, however, he wrote less guardedly, and when James visited Italy in 1872-1873, he dropped all restraint, exclaiming on one occasion: ". . . O my lagoons of Venice, and the seaweedy smell of the shallows! . . . *Ricorditi di me*—when you lie there in your boat, and at least say, Poor Howells, he liked Venice. . . ."[3] Several months later he repeated this sentiment even more emphatically, outlining a plan which he could not carry out for a decade, and then only partially:

At times the longing is almost intolerable with me, and if I could see any way of keeping the bird in the hand while I clutched at those in the bush, I should go. I have a scheme for work some day in Italy which I hope to carry out. It would take me there just about the time the children should be studying French and music and keep me there five years.[4]

Howells was not merely disturbed by the financial hazards of giving up his editorship to go abroad, but he never really wanted to become an expatriate. When the round of social obligations in Cambridge began disrupting his family life and proving too heavy a strain on Mrs. Howells's health, he considered a sojourn in Europe as a means of reducing the fraction of life. He recognized that he could live abroad inexpensively and that the children would profit by the experience; "but one at my time of life," he told his father, "loses a vast deal of indefinable, essential something, by living out of one's own country, and I'm afraid to risk it."[5] The dilemma in this case was resolved by building a house in rural Belmont, the township beyond

[2] "A Year in a Venetian Palace," p. 6. Reprinted in VL, II, 257 ff.
[3] LinL, I, 173.
[4] *Ibid.*, pp. 176-177.
[5] *Ibid.*, p. 217.

Cambridge, and two years later he told Clemens that he had outlived all longing for Europe.[6]

Howells was neither temperamentally nor pecuniarily able to spend a year abroad solely resting and absorbing impressions for later literary use. He could not stop writing unless flat on his back, and the desire to support his family in the manner of Boston's upper middle class made his prodigious efforts necessary. In the interval between his daughter's illness and his own sickness Howells suggested to Osgood a project which would take him to Italy for an extended tour of the northern cities.[7] He wanted to write a series of papers on thirteen Italian cities: Bologna, Parma, Modena, Verona, Brescia, Vicenza, Ferrara, Lucca, Bergamo, Padua, Trento, Pisa, and Siena, four of which he had never visited and only half of which he had written about before. He explained to Osgood:

My notion is to treat them [the cities] as I did "Ducal Mantua" in *Italian Journeys,* sketching the history of each with contemporary light and incident, and making each study as attractive as possible with anecdote and adventure. I should seek rather interest than thoroughness, and I believe I should succeed and make some sketches which people would like. It is the ground I know, and I should work con amore.[8]

The publisher was delighted with the proposal and began negotiations with the Century Company to place the articles. By the end of March an agreement had been drawn up,[9] and Howells was ready to go abroad.

[6] *Ibid.,* p. 256.

[7] He actually had talked with Osgood about a similar plan eighteen months before (see letter to Osgood dated Apr. 17, 1880; MS at Harvard), going so far as to authorize Osgood to enter into an agreement on the basis of $25.00 a page for magazine rights (approximately what the subsequent agreement gave him), but he insisted that the arrangement be made conditionally upon his "being able to do the work at all." The project seems to have been dropped until the fall of 1881.

[8] Nov. 6, 1881; MS at Boston Pub. Lib.

[9] There is a copy of this agreement dated Mar. 30, 1882, in the Howells

His departure for Europe in 1882[10] bore little resemblance to his dismal autumnal sailing from New York in
1861. The former consul, now critic and novelist, left from
Quebec on a bright summer day with his wife, three children ranging in age from nine to eighteen, and his brother-
in-law, William Rutherford Mead, the architect. He had
booked passage from the Canadian port not only because he
was a poor sea-traveler, but also because he wished to visit his
father, then American consul at Toronto, and his sister
Anne, who had married a Canadian and lived in Quebec.
The steamer *Parisian,* carrying the Howells family, slipped
away from the "mural-crowned and castled rock"[11] of the
city and started down the St. Lawrence on July 22 to begin
its voyage to Europe. The crossing was both faster and
pleasanter than the fourteen stormy days in 1861 and was
accomplished without seasickness in eight days. It was "as
comfortable as a sea voyage could be," reported Howells,
adding that "the ship was extraordinarily steady . . . did
not roll and scarcely pitched."[12]

The first stop-over was London, where James looked
after the travelers as long as they remained in England.
Howells wrote Osgood contentedly two days after arriving:
"We are here in a very charming lodging, which James
had taken for us, and in which we sat down to a dinner
that was cooking for us on our way up from Liverpool."[13]
The stay in England was delightful; Howells was wined
and dined by English artists and writers, and, significantly,
his letters of this period reflect no trace of his former Anglo-

---

Collection at Harvard, showing that Howells was to receive $2,500 for the
serial rights to a series of from ten to twelve papers of from ten to twelve pages
each.

[10] See LinL, I, 313-315.

[11] *A Chance Acqaintance,* p. 27. See this source for the description of a
trip down the St. Lawrence River from Quebec made in 1870.

[12] LinL, I, 315-316.

[13] *Ibid.*

phobia. He found British hospitality so time-consuming that he was obliged to cut short his visit and move on to Switzerland in order to work. Before leaving, however, he had managed to finish an article on "Niagara Revisited,"[14] and to produce one hundred pages of his new novel, *A Woman's Reason* (1883)—all in addition to showing his family the standard tourist attractions of London and its environs.

On September 18 the Howells family boarded the train for Dover, crossed to Calais, and rode all night across France in a *wagon-lit*. They awoke at the border and soon were established within a stone's throw of Lake Geneva and within two minutes' walk of the Castle of Chillon.[15] There they stayed for nearly ten weeks, living in a *pension* in the quiet little town of Villeneuve near Montreux. After a month Howells wrote Clemens: "We are having a good, dull, wholesome time . . . and we have not spoken to an American soul, and to but one English. . . ."[16] The surroundings were conducive to work, and he plunged with characteristic energy into learning spoken French. "I trample accent and syntax into one common pulp," he told his father after a week in Switzerland,[17] but seven weeks later he reported that he was getting on very well with the language: ". . . it is a comfort to go about and talk with people," he wrote his father, "and I pry bits of information out of a great many who don't suspect it. I have a note book quite full."[18]

Work on the novel, however, was progressing slowly,

---

[14] Osgood placed the article with the *Atlantic* (LI, May, 1883, 598-610) and Howells later reprinted it as the last chapter of *Their Wedding Journey*. The article also was printed without authorization as a railroad advertisement in 1884 and suppressed by Howells. See Gibson and Arms, *op. cit.*, p. 31.

[15] LinL, I, 322.   [16] *Ibid.*, p. 325.   [17] *Ibid.*, p. 323.

[18] *Ibid.*, p. 326. Since Howells wasted none of his experiences, this material found its way ultimately into *A Little Swiss Sojourn*, after being serialized in *Harper's Monthly*, LXXVI (Feb., Mar., 1888), 452-467, 572-587.

and in November Howells wrote Roswell Smith, president
of the Century Company, that he hoped he could finish it
by January in Italy. But he was sufficiently worried about
not completing the manuscript on schedule to suggest a
stand-by plan for modifying the series of articles on North
Italian cities. Proposing a less ambitious project, which
would require only short side trips from Florence, he asked:
". . . how would you like, instead of the Minor City series,
a series of semi-historical studies of Florence and the formerly dependent cities of Pisa, Siena, etc.?"[19] He added
that such a group of papers might have more continuous
interest than the others. Smith replied promptly that he
would prefer the new scheme and in a follow-up letter
urged him to carry it out, writing: "This brings the whole
thing up on a higher plane than simple sketches of the
minor Italian cities, and introduces the historical element
which we think you will do most admirably."[20] By the
time Howells received this letter, he was eager to alter his
early plan, and the result was the series of articles which
became *Tuscan Cities* (1886).

By the middle of November winter was fast approaching
in Switzerland. Almost daily the snow line crept farther
down the mountain sides, and the nights turned cold,
though the days remained mild and roses still bloomed in
the valleys. In the last week of November Howells moved
southward with his family to take up winter residence in
Florence. Except for three weeks in Siena in the late winter,
he remained in the Tuscan capital until the end of March.
In April there were side trips to Pisa and Lucca followed
by a four- to six-weeks' stay in Venice.

Howells's apprehensions over the novel were groundless,

[19] *Ibid.*, p. 329.
[20] Dec. 6, 1882; MS at Harvard. The follow-up letter is dated Jan. 15,
1883; MS at Harvard.

for he finished it soon after moving his family to Florence. But the difficulty of writing fiction abroad was more than he cared to put up with, and he dropped additional plans for a novel to be laid in "Venice at the time of the decadence."[21] He told Osgood: "I find the strain of working out plots and characters amidst new and distracting scenes is awful. . . ."[22] Consequently, he turned towards his work on *Tuscan Cities,* and before that task was completed, he took his family home. His next novel, *The Rise of Silas Lapham,* was written after returning to the United States, and the novel which derives its background entirely from the winter spent in Florence, *Indian Summer* (1886), was not written until the Italian experiences were cold.

Italy had grown older and dingier in the interval between Howells's consulship and his return in 1882. His affection for the country remained unshaken, but he was unable to recapture the youthful charm; gone was the golden sunshine which had lighted the Italy of the young American consul. Switzerland, whose canny mountaineers and rugged terrain reminded him of New England, was more to his taste at the age of forty-five than Italy was, and if he had to live anywhere in Europe, he wrote Lowell, he would settle there.[23] Howells relived his youth in Italy in the delight which his children experienced there,[24] and

[21] LinL, I, 328. In the same letter in which he suggested the change in plans for the travel series (Nov. 19, 1882) Howells broached two new plans. One was a history of Venice, which will be considered separately later, and the other was this novel.

[22] Dec. 16, 1882; MS at Harvard.   [23] LinL, I, 335.

[24] Tangible evidence of this is *A Little Girl among the Old Masters,* a collection of juvenile drawings made by Mildred Howells in Italy and put together with commentary by her father—perhaps his first literary work after returning home. In the commentary, dated Aug. 21, 1883, Howells says that the drawings "are simply the reflection in a child's soul, of the sweetness and loveliness of early Italian art; and they have been reproduced here with the hope that at least their utter sincerity and unconsciousness may please" (p. 3). He seems to have felt that ten-year-old Mildred had captured something of the poetry of Italy which he once had known.

he realized that Italy was now only a valued part of his
irretrievable past. He summed up his disappointment a
month after reaching Florence:

> We are here in Italy again, in the old soft air, under the same
> mild old sky, out of which all snap and sharpness have gone . . .
> I don't know whether the old charm is here or not; it is by brief
> surprises, and all sorts of indirection, I suppose. At least there
> is something that faces me afar, and flits and comes again in the
> distance. But I perceive that it will no longer be intimate and
> constant; perhaps it finds me rude and cross.[25]

Two and a half months later, when he was preparing to
write his papers on the cities of Tuscany, he explained to
Thomas Sergeant Perry: "I have been turning over a good
many books, and putting myself in rapport with Italy again.
But I'm not sure that it pays. After all, *we* have the country
of the present and the future."[26]

In mid-April Howells took his family to Venice, although he must have dreaded the visit after the failure of
Florence to match his expectations. Nevertheless, he wanted
to show his older daughter where she was born, look up old
friends and former haunts, and to roam the *calle* and canals
of the city where he once had been "more intensely at home
than in any other, even Boston itself."[27] When he stepped
from the train it seemed as though he never had been away,
but his second impression found Venice strangely shrunken.
There were steamers on the Grand Canal, contributing to
the effect of shrinkage, and the churches and palaces were
somehow meaner and shabbier than he had remembered.
St. Mark's Square was outwardly unchanged except for
new lampposts and the absence of Austrian troops, but the
Calle Lunga San Moisè, the street he had traveled daily

[25] LinL, I, 335.
[26] *Ibid.*, p. 338.
[27] VL (1907 ed.), p. 406.

between Casa Falier and the Square, had been renamed
Calle Ventidue Marzo for an unfamiliar patriotic event.
One day he took his son John for a walk back of the Rialto
and was dismayed by the misery and squalor apparent
everywhere. Winifred, however, was enraptured by the
romantic beauty of the city, and Howells wrote his father
that he did not let her get far from St. Mark's Square,
where there was a little "galvanic gaiety." At the same time
he added: "But I would not live here again for four years
on hardly any conditions short of ownership of the city—
and then I should be afraid it would fall on my hands."[28]

Howells had broken ground on the sketches of the
Tuscan cities in March,[29] but the writing he had planned to
continue in Venice was interrupted by an unexpected round
of social activities. He had gone, of course, to see Padre
Giacomo, Brunetta had come from Verona to see him, and
he had visited Tortorini at Monselice; but the city which
once had been devoid of society was filled with tourists of
all nationalities, as well as hospitable Italians, who wanted
to lionize the author of *Venetian Life*. After he had been to
see the Crown Prince and Princess of Germany, he confessed to his father that he found himself unable to write:
". . . my head has stopped like a watch that's been dropped;
and we shall perhaps hurry away a little sooner, to England,
on that account. . . . I find that I can't write while shifting
about so much, and there is no happiness for me in anything else."[30]

His failure to report immediately on Venice revisited
deserves special comment, for he had planned an essay on
the city prior to leaving America. The fact is that James
wrote an article on Venice for the November, 1882, issue of

[28] Apr. 22, 1883; MS at Harvard.
[29] See letter from Howells to J. R. Osgood dated Mar. 28, 1883; MS at
Boston Pub. Lib.
[30] LinL, I, 341-342.

the *Century,* thus killing the subject for anyone else. Howells had informed Osgood the previous October: "I certainly don't want to follow James on the subject. . . . My
first mind about Venice was not to touch it at all . . . ," and
he added that he was "doubtful about the wisdom of going
over that old ground again."[31] Accordingly, Howells made
no use of this material until he added a final chapter to the
revised edition of *Venetian Life* in 1907.

After leaving Venice for the last time, Howells retraced
his steps across northern Italy towards England. On May
20 he was in Verona, where he visited Brunetta for two
weeks, and by early June he was back in London. He hoped
to continue work on the Tuscan cities, but once again the
round of social engagements made him "acutely miser-
able."[32] Lady A invited him one day, Lady B the next,
and the Lord Chancellor's daughter on the third. Lowell,
for whose diplomatic career Howells had been responsible,[33] took him to a reception at the house of the Prime
Minister and the following week invited a roomful of titles
to dinner to meet him. Altogether he was greatly relieved
to board the steamer *Parisian* once more for the return trip
to Quebec, and he landed in Canada on July 13 after an
absence of nine days less than a year. He had searched
unsuccessfully in Italy for the fountain of youth.

Tuscan Cities, the book which Howells planned as a
series of semihistorical studies, might aptly be called an
apotheosis of travel literature. Certainly it raised the guidebook genre to a higher level by blending history and contemporary reporting as successfully as one imagines these

---

[31] Oct. 4, 1882; MS at Harvard.   [32] LinL, I, 345.

[33] Lowell, then Minister to England, had first been appointed Minister to
Spain in 1877 by President Hayes through the efforts of Howells, who had
written a campaign biography and was distantly related by marriage to the
President.

types of writing can be combined. The pristine charm of
Venetian Life is gone, but there is no trace of middle-aged
disillusionment in *Tuscan Cities*. Howells's ability to record
accurate, observed detail is nowhere better displayed than
here, and to those who find history dull the Tuscan past is
brought to life in a manner which a professional historian
might envy. The book shows careful workmanship, and
the two-year interval between the experience and serialization suggests that little of the material actually had been
written in Europe.[34] The editor of the *Century*, Richard
W. Gilder, wrote enthusiastically after reading proof on
the second instalment of the Florentine material: "The old
and ever-new Florence are blended here as they are in
reality. . . ."[35]

"I can't find anything in less than ten or twelve volumes," complained Mrs. Bowen in *Indian Summer* as she
hunted a short, painless way of absorbing the history of
Florence.[36] This was Howells's own experience when he
was preparing notes on the city, and in 1901 he stated flatly
that "there is nowhere, to my knowledge, so compendious
a sketch of all Florentine history as in my book, *Tuscan
Cities*. I tried in vain for such a sketch before I wrote it."[37]
Consequently, he prepared the section called "A Florentine
Mosaic," which occupies half of the book, to fill a need, and
he followed the same pattern, though more briefly, in treating Siena, Pisa, and Lucca. When Howells came to write

[34] The book was serialized in the *Century*, XXIX, XXX (Feb., Apr., June,
Aug., Sept., Oct., 1885), 483-501, 803-819, 199-219, 534-549, 659-673, 890-
910.

[35] Jan. 23, 1885; MS at Harvard.

[36] IS, p. 19.

[37] As quoted in preface, "A Word from the Director," in *Florence in Art
and Literature*, published as *Course X* of the Booklovers Reading Club. This
book, to which Howells was asked to contribute a supplemental reading list
on Florentine art, literature, and history, is further evidence of his reputation
as an authority on things Italian. TCs was used as one of the textbooks for
this course.

his first travel book in nearly two decades, he approached his material with a definite theory of such literature. At the outset he stated the controlling idea of the volume:

At home, in the closet, one may read history, but one can realize it, as if it were something personally experienced, only on the spot where it was lived. This seems to me the prime use of travel; and to create the reader a partner in the enterprise and a sharer in its realization seems the sole excuse for books of travel, now when modern facilities have abolished hardship and danger and adventure, and nothing is more likely to happen to one in Florence than in Fitchburg.[38]

The technique he developed for carrying out this plan is a further refinement of his early travel sketches. In "A Florentine Mosaic," for example, he begins with a report of the sights and sounds of the city from his hotel window, establishing immediately the atmosphere of the modern scene. Then he tours leisurely the points of interest and projects himself back into the historical epoch connected with the landmark under consideration. Finally he concludes his study with an analysis of present-day Florentine society. Although the bulk of the material is historical, it is constantly aerated by the current of life flowing by the author in his rambles; and one is not permitted to witness the deathbed scene of Lorenzo de' Medici without shivering in the modern unheated halls of the Villa Careggi, or visit the church where Dante was married without examining the nineteenth-century sacristan.

The evidence of Howells's extensive wanderings through the source material on the cities of Tuscany is plainly visible in the pages of this book. His reading was wide, though perhaps eclectic, and ranged from the Middle Ages to the late nineteenth century. He quotes from Machiavelli and Vasari, alludes to the *Divina Commedia* and Boccaccio, cites

[38] TCs, pp. 17-18.

James Howell's epistles and Mary Shelley's reminiscences, and refers often to writers among his contemporaries such as Pasquale Villari, the biographer of Savonarola. The authorities cited are unobtrusively worked into the narrative, and the sources are dutifully acknowledged. Once again Howells refrains from describing the pictures and statues he has seen, leaving that type of information to the more conventional guidebooks.

The most important product of Howells's return to Italy was *Indian Summer,* a novel laid entirely in Florence at the time he was there and making use of American characters living abroad. He wrote it probably in 1884 after completing *Tuscan Cities,* which had been started abroad, and *The Rise of Silas Lapham.*[39] The novel is noteworthy in one minor aspect of its publication, for it was Howells's first work serialized in *Harper's Monthly,* and thus it began a publishing relationship which was to last for thirty-five years.[40] The first instalment appeared in July, 1885, and the story ran concurrently with the serialization of *Tuscan Cities* in the *Century.*

Howells was disappointed in the critical recognition *Indian Summer* received, because he thought it one of his most mature and artistic creations. He remembered in his old age that J. W. Harper had been somewhat dismayed to receive a manuscript which opened on the Ponte Vecchio in Florence when he had expected to get a Boston story.[41] Many years later William Lyon Phelps praised the novel, and Howells replied gratefully: "So few people know how good *Indian Summer* is, and I am glad and proud to have Mrs. Phelps and you of that little band."[42] He had reached

[39] The evidence is not conclusive, but the serialization dates suggest this. *Indian Summer* has been reprinted in the Everyman's Library with an introduction by William M. Gibson (E. P. Dutton & Co., 1951).

[40] He had, of course, already published four poems in *Harper's Monthly.*

[41] *The House of Harper,* p. 320.   [42] Apr. 1, 1906; MS at Yale.

the conclusion at the time of publication that the public did not want its novels laid on foreign ground, and he expressed this opinion to Professor T. R. Lounsbury of Yale, also adding: "I enjoyed doing it better than anything since *A Foregone Conclusion*. But . . . I shall hardly venture abroad again in fiction."[43] Although he used foreign travel often in his later novels, he never again placed a story entirely in a foreign setting.

Indian Summer is a minor masterpiece which deserves not to be forgotten, even though it is unrepresentative of Howells's best-known work. It belongs among the ablest international novels in American literature, along with James's *The Ambassadors* (1903), with which it has a common theme of the middle-aged American in Europe. The story is a neatly plotted study of a forty-one year old American who falls in love in Florence. It has excellent unity of time, place, and character, and creates a singleness of effect which is not always present in Howells's novels. The foreign setting, which he valued as a means of segregating his characters and studying them at leisure, provides an effective background for sharpening the outline of American character and making subtle details stand out more distinctly.

In limning the protagonist Colville, Howells once more drew on his own Italian experience and Midwestern background. A former newspaper editor from Indiana who had traveled in Italy as a young man, Colville goes back to Europe after seventeen years' absence. Settling down in Florence, where he plans to write a history on the order of *Tuscan Cities,* he meets Imogene Graham and Mrs. Bowen, her sponsor, and falls in love with each in turn. Only three years younger than Howells himself at the time of the story, Colville is superficially a projection of the author, and his experiences, other than those pertaining to his

[43] Nov. 22, 1885; MS at Yale.

romance, parallel events in the life of the author in the winter of 1882-1883. The other characters are less interesting; Imogene Graham is another vivacious Howells ingénue of a type already familiar, and Mrs. Bowen is a well-drawn portrait of a middle-aged widow, sensitive, sensible, and intelligent. No doubt Howells had seen such women as she among the expatriates encountered during his winter in Florence.

The comparison which we have made before between Howells's travel books and his novels is again pertinent. There are many parallel passages in *Indian Summer* and *Tuscan Cities* which emphasize the continued correlation between his literature and life.[44] Colville, for example, describes the Church of Santa Maria Novella to Imogene over the tea table, drawing on the same details which Howells put into his travel book,[45] and on another occasion discusses with a minor character the life of Savonarola and Villari's treatment of it.[46] Both the fictional character and the author browse among the shops on the Ponte Vecchio,[47] and they also make use of Vieusseux's Circulating Library.[48] The climactic episode of the novel takes place during a one-day excursion by carriage to near-by Fiesole in April, a trip that the Howells family made in the same manner and at the same time of year.[49]

[44] In this connection Joseph Pennell's "Adventures of an Illustrator—with Howells in Italy," *Century*, CIV (May, 1922), 135-141, supplies added background for a study of IS. Pennell was commissioned to go to Italy to make the illustrations for TCs at the same time Howells went abroad, and from his reminiscences one learns that the painters known in the novel as the Inglehart boys were in real life the Duveneck boys. There are other similarities worth noting, such as the *trattoria* where Pennell ate and which Colville visits (cf. IS, pp. 104-105), and there is the suggestion of a prototype for the clergyman Walters among the Americans the illustrator met in Florence.

[45] Cf. IS, p. 60, with TCs, pp 12-13.
[46] Cf. IS, pp. 87-88, with TCs, pp. 49-52.
[47] Cf. IS, p. 1, with TCs, p. 17.
[48] Cf. IS, p. 19, with TCs, p. 21.
[49] Cf. IS, pp. 336-356, with TCs, pp. 247-251.

INVETERATE ITALOPHILE

In the foregoing pages we have traced Howells's life in
Italy as a young man, returned with him in middle age,
evaluated the influence of its literature and society, and
surveyed his use of his impressions and experiences. When
he was fifty the Italianate interests which strongly tinctured
the first half of his literary life had become less pronounced,
and in his later thinking and writing the Russian influence
began to supply the more important coloring. Italy, however, had been a vital part of his first half century, and it
remained a permanent part of his later life. As long as he
lived, he continued to exploit his Italian experiences on a
reduced scale, and at the time of his death he was at work
on the memoirs of his consular years. For the quarter of a
century between 1874 and 1900 he planned, but never wrote,
a history of Venice; at the age of seventy-one he produced
a volume of Italian travels; he filled his later novels with
characters who had traveled, lived, and studied in Italy;
and in his periodical essays he employed his Italian experiences again and again.

Howells's major exploitation of Italy ended, with the
exception of one late fictional blossom, in 1887, the year
Modern Italian Poets was published and the year after
Indian Summer and *Tuscan Cities* appeared. After he had
written these books, representing his activities in criticism,
fiction, and travel, the reservoir of Italian experience was
again nearly dry, and he turned to novels laid in New
York, where he went to live in 1888. Nevertheless, the
Italian interests of twenty-six years were so deeply in-
grained that his subsequent novels often picked up, perhaps unconsciously, elements of Italian background and
color. This deep dye of Italy is visible, for example, in ten
of the twelve volumes of prose fiction written between

1888 and 1899 which Howells called novels.[1] Three of them make Italy an integral part of the plot; four more use it incidentally; and the last three employ Italian color and background in New York settings. *Annie Kilburn* (1889) begins in Rome, where the heroine has lived eleven years, and after its immediate shift to Massachusetts contrasts Italian and American character. *An Imperative Duty* (1892) brings an expatriated American doctor home from Europe, marries him to a woman one-sixteenth Negro, and takes the couple off to Rome to live. *April Hopes* (1888) begins soon after the self-exiled Pasmer family returns to Boston from a long residence in France and Italy, and Italian immigrant laborers are subsequently used as one of the New England properties in the novel's staging. At the end of *The Quality of Mercy* (1892) the author disposes of one set of minor characters, the Hilarys, by having them plan to spend the winter in Rome. In *The Landlord at Lion's Head* (1897) the Vostrands have lived in Florence before the story opens and return there during the course of the novel. Jeff Durgin, the hero, winters in Florence and the artist Westover also has studied in Italy.[2] *Their Silver Wedding Journey* (1899), although based on Howells's 1897 visit to Germany, gives the Marches frequent opportunities, which they make the most of, to compare things German and Italian. *A Hazard of New Fortunes* (1890) finds the Marches living in New York at an earlier period. They see immigrants who remind them of their Italian days, delight in eating in Italian restaurants, and often buy favorite delicacies in Italian grocery stores. In *The World of Chance* (1893) the first person Shelley Ray

---

[1] In the last two decades of his life Howells worked occasional Italian details into these novels: *The Kentons, The Son of Royal Langbrith, Through the Eye of the Needle, The Vacation of the Kelwyns.*

[2] Bromfield Cory, too, in *The Rise of Silas Lapham* (1885) and *The Minister's Charge* (1887) had studied art in Rome as a young man.

meets upon detraining in New York is an Italian bootblack, and in *The Coast of Bohemia* (1893) Cornelia Saun-
ders, arriving in New York to study art, immediately meets
Charmian Maybough, who has lived in Italy and has friends
who have traveled there.

Thirteen years after vowing never again to venture
abroad in fiction, Howells granted visas to another set of
American characters for travel in Italy. The story in which
he returned to the international novel was *Ragged Lady,*
serialized in *Harper's Bazar* in 1898 and published in book
form the following year. Once again he used the Lydia
Blood-Daisy Miller theme, this time taking a New England
village girl, Clementina Claxon, to Italy to meet her future
husband, the homespun American George Hinkle. The
novel, however, runs the first third of its course in a White
Mountain summer hotel where the heroine has the ques-
tionable fortune of meeting the neurotic, semi-invalid Mrs.
Lander, who takes her to Venice and there dies.

This novel ranks low in order of excellence among
Howells's works, having a poor plot and little form, but it
testifies to his unquenchable enthusiasm for Italian settings.
It has the added interest of a delayed reaction to Howells's
return visit to Italy in 1882-1883, for it is laid approximately
at the time he went back to Italy, and the characters spend
a winter in Florence, as the author did, before traveling on
to Venice in April, the same month that Howells and his
family went north. There is, moreover, a certain similarity
to *Indian Summer.* The relationship between Imogene
Graham and Mrs. Bowen, for example, is roughly analogous to that of Clementina Claxon and Mrs. Lander, though
Miss Claxon is more of a rough diamond than Miss Graham
and the pampered hypochondriac Mrs. Lander is far less
attractive than the charming Mrs. Bowen. Hinkle, however, reminds one of Colville, even though he is younger,
more unsophisticated, and plays a less important part.

The long lapse between Howells's return to Italy and
the writing of *Ragged Lady* no doubt accounts for the absence of his earlier lavish foreign background. He confines
the setting to a few properties, enough to make the locale
definitely Florentine or Venetian, but he uses far less
scenery than he had employed when writing fresh from his
experience. Details of hotel rooms and housekeeping, a
Russian nihilist and a brilliant American woman expatriate
give color to the Florentine scene, while the aquatic character of Venice, Florian's Café, and the Lido beach supply
the inevitable setting in that city. This novel also is
equipped with the familiar American consul—this time actually a vice-consul—who takes care of funeral and business
arrangements for the heroine when Mrs. Lander dies. This
individual, curiously enough, is approximately the age
Howells would have been if he had remained on duty in
Venice through the years.

The vitality of the Italian influence on Howells in his
old age is nowhere better demonstrated than in a survey
of three volumes of collected essays: *Impressions and Experiences* (1896), *Literature and Life* (1902), and *Imaginary
Interviews* (1910). These books contain seventy-three essays
written, with one exception, between 1893 and 1910 and for
the most part published originally in departments of *Harper's Weekly* ("Life and Letters") and *Harper's Monthly*
("Editor's Easy Chair"). Twenty-three of these essays contain significant use of Howells's Italian memories and interests, largely references to places visited, scenes remembered, and experiences encountered. There also are frequent allusions to, or discussions of, Italian literature. For
anyone statistically minded, these figures might suggest that
every third time Howells sat down to write an essay some
recollection of Italy was likely to embellish his page. But,
putting the figures aside, let us glance briefly at some typical

illustrations. When he visits Bermuda the island-dotted
waters remind him of the lagoon at Venice,[3] and when
night falls on the boat basin near his summer home at
Kittery Point, Maine, he thinks of the basin of St. Mark's.[4]
On still another occasion the steps of a public building
glimpsed on the way to the Bronx Zoo recall the Spanish
Steps in Rome.[5] At Rockaway Beach, Long Island, Howells smells frying sea food and is immediately transported
to the Riva at Venice,[6] and, similarly, an article on circuses
takes him back to the amphitheater at Verona where he
once had witnessed a performance.[7] L'Elisir d'amore at
the Metropolitan Opera House in New York inevitably
brings to mind his Venetian sojourn, when he saw his first
production of Donizetti's opera.[8] Tourist that he was, Howells could be counted on for frequent observations on the
ways and means of foreign travel, and in an essay discussing European railroads the badness of the state railroads in
"poor, dear Italy" is exhibit A.[9]

For more than a quarter of a century Howells wanted
to write a history of Venice,[10] and at least three times between 1874 and 1901 the project went far enough to be
recorded in his correspondence. The first definite reference
occurs in 1874 when Warner informed him that the Hart-
ford publisher Elisha Bliss wanted the "social-romantic"
history of Venice that "you had in mind," and he added
that Bliss thinks "it will sell well if you make it light and

[3] *Literature and Life*, pp. 79-80.   [4] *Ibid.*, p. 253.
[5] *Imaginary Interviews*, p. 351.   [6] *Literature and Life*, p. 168.
[7] *Ibid.*, pp. 187-192.   [8] *Imaginary Interviews*, pp. 44-56.
[9] *Ibid.*, p. 151.
[10] When Howells wrote MLP (1895) it seemed to him that he had always
wanted to write a history of Venice. He recalled that he had gone to Italy in
1861 with this in mind (p. 199), but there is no evidence of it either in his
published or unpublished letters. Perhaps by middle age he had identified
himself with Professor Elmore in AFR, who did go to Venice for that purpose.

not too heavy historically."[11] It seems likely that Warner's letter belongs to the period referred to by Howells eight years later when he recalled: "The work was something that I wished very much to do for the *Atlantic* at one time; I even collected some material for it, but I found that I had not the time to read for it, and edit the magazine, and so I gave it up."[12]

The history was proposed again in 1882 when Howells was revisiting Europe. He asked Roswell Smith at that time if he would be interested in a "popular history of Venice from the Bostonia [*sic*]-Chicago-New York point of view."[13] He thought he could make a new thing in history, something that would be thoroughly interesting and intelligible to all the *Century* readers. Smith replied promptly: "Let us have the History of Venice by all means";[14] but he was unwilling to discuss the "grand cash" which Howells wanted for such an undertaking until the author returned home.

In 1900 plans for the history progressed as far as an outline and contract, but once again the proposal was dropped—this time for good. Howells opened the final negotiations in the fall of 1899 with a proposal to write "A Heroic History of Venice," treating the city as a sort of medieval Chicago. H. M. Alden, editor of *Harper's Monthly,* replied cordially that he wished he had thought of the idea first. He added that "such work from your pen is quite sure to awaken the enthusiastic interest of thoughtful readers who know the quality of work already done by you in the field of Italian history and literature."[15] Later the same month Alden began to talk terms and outlined his editorial requirements.[16] He wanted one hundred

[11] Mar. 26, 1874; MS at Harvard.　　[12] LinL, I, 329.
[13] *Ibid.,* p. 328.　　[14] Dec. 6, 1882; MS at Harvard.
[15] Oct. 3, 1899; MS at Harvard.
[16] Oct. 26, 1899; MS at Harvard. Howells simultaneously proposed a work

thousand words for serialization in the magazine not later
than 1903, to be followed by book publication. He offered
ten thousand dollars for magazine rights and a ten per cent
royalty on the book. Howells waited until January to accept
these terms,[17] and at the same time submitted an outline of
his proposed history.[18] He hoped to go to Venice for a
long sojourn to study the locality once more and to gather
material, but he made it clear that his agreement must not
bind him to a trip abroad. Alden then drew up a contract
for the history, but the record of these dealings ends
abruptly, and there is no apparent reason for the abandon-
ment of the plan.

After returning to Europe in his mid-forties, Howells
did not venture abroad again for a dozen years, but in his
old age he became a frequent transatlantic traveler. Between 1894 and the summer of 1913, when he was seventy-
six, Howells revisited Europe eight times, traveling ex-
tensively through England, Scotland, Germany, Holland,
France, Spain, and Italy. On two occasions he spent the
winter abroad, once at San Remo and another time at
Rome, and on an earlier trip to the Continent in 1897 he
cancelled plans for wintering in Italy, having worn himself
out traveling in Germany. During the last seven years of
his life he contented himself with journeys to Bermuda
and Florida.

In the autumn of 1903, when Clemens was about to
leave for Italy, Howells wrote his sister speculatively: "If
it could be managed I should like to spend the rest of my

---

of 200,000 to 250,000 words, taking two years to write, for which he would
receive $25,000 for serial rights and 5 per cent royalty on the book. See copy
of outline for the history dated Oct. 26, 1899, in the Howells Collection at
Harvard.

[17] See letter to Alden dated Jan. 6, 1900 (LinL, II, 122).

[18] The outline drawn up after Howells accepted Alden's terms is reprinted
in LinL, II, 122-124.

winters at Florence or Rome. . . ."[19] The following March he went abroad for his longest sojourn since the visit in 1882-1883, and after a summer in England, which included the bestowal of a Litt. D. degree by Oxford, he drifted southward towards Italy, planning to settle down for the winter on the Italian Riviera, where he hoped the mild climate would benefit his wife's health. After his arrival at San Remo in mid-October, he took an apartment for the winter, and then wrote his sister: "It is a joy to be in Italy again, and this is so much more tropical than Venice that it seems as if I had never been in Italy before."[20] Less than a month later, however, he wrote his son that the season promised to be dull, but he hoped more people would soon arrive.[21] The situation did not improve much, although in January he told Perry that he had found one literary man with whom he could talk, the novelist Henry Harland, then dying of tuberculosis.[22] Howells's chief occupation that winter was the writing of two English travel books, *London Films* (1906) and *Certain Delightful English Towns* (1906), and in March he returned home.

His visit to San Remo resulted in three items of literary interest, a short story, a travel sketch, and an essay for "The Editor's Easy Chair," all of which found their way eventually into the Harper publications. The story, "A Sleep and a Forgetting," published in 1906-1907, is a slight study of abnormal psychology, in which a doctor marries his patient after her recovery from amnesia. The background of San Remo is not at all essential to the story, although it contributes an exotic condiment which the author had never before used to season his fiction. The travel sketch and Easy Chair article were among the last things he published, and appeared in *Harper's Monthly* in February, 1920, only three months before he died.

[19] LinL, II, 178.   [20] *Ibid.*, p. 202.   [21] *Ibid.*, p. 203.   [22] *Ibid.*, p. 205.

At the age of seventy Howells recaptured his youthful
ideal of Italy—the ideal which had coyly eluded his search
in 1882. Returning to Europe for the most important of
all his old-age junkets, he revisited Rome after an absence
of forty-four years. Instead of a city still under the temporal
rule of the Pope, as he remembered it in 1864, modern
Rome was the prosperous, busy capital of the Kingdom of
Italy. He must have felt like an ancient Roman returning
from the wars to receive the conqueror's laurel. Social engagements of all sorts were pressed on him, including invi-
tations to tour the city with the mayor and the American
ambassador and to attend the theater in a princess's box.
To climax the homage, Victor Emmanuel III was pleased
to grant the author a private audience. Soon after leaving
Rome, Howells wrote Norton: "We had ten or twelve
weeks of constantly decreasing disappointment in Rome,
till we left the glorious town with a full sense of its greatness and wonderfulness. . . . I missed no remembered
charm in her, and I found a thousand new ones."[23]

Howells's long and productive literary career turned full
cycle between his early and later travel books, and *Roman
Holidays and Others* (1908) could be aptly named "Italian
Journeys *Rediviva*." In this book, as well as in others of
the same vintage, Howells acknowledged that he had renewed the practice of his youth, "for I was a traveler long
before I was a noveler, and I had mounted somewhat
timidly to the threshold of fiction from the high-roads and
by-roads where I had studied manners and men. I am
not yet sure which branch of the art I prefer."[24] When his
Roman travel papers began running in the Sunday New
York *Sun*, he discovered with no little delight that he had
regained the touch which had brought him acclaim as a

[23] *Ibid.*, p. 254.
[24] *The House of Harper*, p. 326.

young man. In the midst of preparing the articles for a book, he wrote James that the sketches had been much liked and their "success has brought back my sense of success in the *Venetian Life* letters printed forty odd years ago in the Boston *Advertiser*."[25]

The return of Howells's youthful zest for Italy was a source of wonder both to James and to Norton. The former congratulated him on his achievement, declaring himself envious of "your being moved to-day to Roman utterance . . . in presence of the so bedrenched and vulgarized . . . City . . . of our current time."[26] And James added that there was nothing he could have done less easily than write of Rome when he had been there fifteen months before. Norton, for his part, could not believe that the charm of Rome was as great as it had been fifty years before, "and yet my dear old friend Howells," he wrote Meta Gaskell, daughter of the novelist, "has fallen under the spell of its charm as completely as if it were the same delightful Rome that we knew so well."[27] Howells himself was surprised and amused to find that he had once more adopted "the old point of view."[28]

There is a marked similarity both in plan and execution between *Italian Journeys* and *Roman Holidays*. The latter seems patterned after the former, even though it does not cover as much Italian ground and begins with chapters on Madeira and Gibraltar. But once the Italian material begins, the 1908 book follows closely the itinerary of the earlier volume. Both travelogues record brief stops at Genoa, sightseeing in Naples, visits to Pompeii, and a long stopover in Rome. Although the bulk of both volumes is laid in the Italian capital, before the author leaves Italy he travels

[25] LinL, II, 256.
[26] Percy Lubbock (ed.), *The Letters of Henry James*, II, 100.
[27] *Letters of Charles Eliot Norton*, II, 410.
[28] LinL, II, 256.

northward to Leghorn, sidesteps into Pisa, and continues towards Genoa. Once again the early method of treating the subject is revived, using the anecdotal, reportorial technique with its wealth of well-chosen incident and shrewd observation of people and places instead of the semihistorical sketch of his middle years. The old enthusiasm for sight-seeing is present once more, and the whole collection of sketches is diffused with a mellow light of old age which is not unlike the sunshine of youth.

Many of Howells's old attitudes are unchanged, but the wisdom of age has softened some of his judgments—at the expense of *élan*—and his deepened humanity has made him more tolerant and understanding. In Naples he finds the teeming old city with its "joyful Neapolitan noises" as charming as he remembered, and in Rome the *corsi* and piazzas, gardens and fountains are as enchanting as they were in 1864. Moreover, the baroque churches still are ugly and the Roman ruins remain a disappointment. But at the same time, Howells rejoices over the face lifting the ancient city has undergone since his first visit, and he roundly scolds the tourist who mourns the demolition of the Ghetto and the passing of the picturesque mud flats which went with the construction of the Tiber embankments. His earlier hostility towards the Catholic church, of course, has vanished, and along with it has disappeared his youthful impatience with the dullness and vulgarity of his fellow tourists. But, unfortunately, in place of the spice and impetuosity of the earlier book there is substituted a certain prosaic quality and a greater preoccupation with details of sight-seeing, travel accommodations, and creature comforts.

In the twilight of old age Howells's memory carried him from the first World War, then raging, back to the days of the Civil War when he had been a young man in Venice.

After completing his last novel and the first part of his autobiography, he suggested to Thomas B. Wells, editor of *Harper's Monthly,* a series of articles on his Italian days.[29] The following year he wrote three reminiscent essays, "Overland to Venice," "An Old Venetian Friend," and "A Young Venetian Friend," all referred to here in earlier chapters. These papers are rich recollections that show surprisingly clear faculties in their octogenarian author. The sketches, however, were not written entirely from memory but composed after re-reading the letters which his brother and sisters had saved. Earlier he had given up half of his work for Harpers, intending no longer to write so much, but the habit seemed inveterate.

The reminiscences of Howells's Venetian friends Tortorini and Brunetta are the most valuable of the series, and the facts check with the surviving letters of his consular days. The account of the Atlantic crossing on the *City of Glasgow,* however, is of less certain historical value, for it introduces several details of that trip which cannot be corroborated. Private letters describing this voyage have not survived, and there is no substantiation from the newspaper letters which Howells sent to the *Ohio State Journal* upon arriving in Italy. Not having any contemporary records available, Howells may have refreshed his memory for "Overland to Venice" from a semifictitious account of the journey he had written in 1910.[30] There are several suspicious details in this 1910 Easy Chair article, all previously unreported in his many autobiographical sketches—details which turn up again in the memoir of 1918.

Howells went on from these reminiscent sketches to plan another instalment of his autobiography, and less than a year before his death he was at work on a project which

[29] See Wells's reply dated Nov. 17, 1916; MS at Harvard.
[30] "Editor's Easy Chair," *Harper's Monthly,* CXXII (Dec., 1910), 149-151.

would have chronicled his life from 1861 to perhaps the
end of his *Atlantic* editorship. He sent Wells an outline of
the memoir, saying he would call it "Years of My Middle
Life," and added: "I have put down a few heads from each
of which many tails would dangle."[31] Unfortunately, he
never lived to finish the work, and although he had already
written much about his years on the *Atlantic,* his recollections of the Venetian sojourn would have chinked a gap in
an otherwise rather extensive but incomplete record. Certainly it is significant that Howells ended his life at work
on the Italian material from which he had made his literary
start. In the course of nearly six decades he had moved in
the orbit of his literary career, under the powerful attraction
of Italy, from perihelion to perihelion.

[31] LinL, II, 387. The outline is reprinted following the letter to Wells.

Conclusion

HOWELLS was conspicuous among the many American Italophiles who edited the newspapers and wrote for the magazines during the decades which followed the Civil War. Known among his contemporaries as a warm friend of Italy, he was considered an authority on things Italian, and both friends and strangers drew upon this special competence. Soon after returning from Europe, for example, he was invited, in the capacity of former consul at Venice, to attend the celebration in New York of Italian unification;[1] subsequently, during his long career he often was called upon to recommend Italian books for friends, to assist Italian refugees and scholars, and to aid in various Italian causes. Even in the twilight of old age during the first World War his help was solicited in the verbal battle against German propaganda which sought to drive a wedge between Italy and America. Throughout his life, whether he was discussing Italian authors in private correspondence, checking Italian background in the work of brother writers, or proclaiming publicly his affection for Italy, his inclination in that direction was constant.

Statistically, the Italian content of Howells's work tells a convincing story. Gibson and Arms in their bibliography list approximately two hundred books which he wrote wholly or in part during his vastly productive lifetime, and

[1] See *The Unity of Italy: the American Celebration of the Unity of Italy, at the Academy of Music, New York, Jan. 12, 1871, with Addresses, Letters, and Comments of the Press*, p. 76. Howells could not attend the meeting but wrote the committee in charge: "The liberation of Italy is a fact that all real Americans will celebrate with you . . . since the citizen of every free country loves Italy next to his own land, and feels her prosperous fortune to be the advantage of civilization."

fifty of these titles, or one-quarter of the total, have supplied the primary sources for this study. Among the one hundred novels, poems, plays, travelogues, etc., of which Howells was the sole author, the concentration of Italian material is still heavier; for of this group thirty-five, or more than one-third, exploit the Italian experience in varying degrees. If one breaks down the figures further, to consider his most characteristic literary product—the novel, the ratio climbs to an even more impressive level. Between 1871 and 1916 he wrote three dozen novels, five being laid wholly or in large part in Italy, fifteen making minor use of Italian background, either in setting or character, or in a combination of both, and all but a scant half dozen of the rest containing at least a passing reference to Italian travel, people, politics, art, literature, etc. His predilection for Italy also is strongly shown in his travel books, for out of the ten such volumes he wrote, four were on Italy and the rest divided among England, Switzerland, Spain, and Germany. And so it goes throughout the various literary forms he employed.

As the foregoing chapters have shown, Howells's perennial fondness for Italy, deriving from the rich, fruitful years of his Venetian consulship and lasting through a lifetime of intense literary activity, forms a significant phase of his career as writer and editor. We have seen the youthful author residing in Italy during the Civil War, and we have assessed the impact of those formative days when he was absorbing Italian culture. We have surveyed his literary apprenticeship when the Italian experience was fresh, traced his mature use of this powerful interest, and suggested the depth of the Italian influence.

Since it is thus clear that Howells's Italian interests bulk large in his total accomplishment, it seems inescapable that an attraction of such strength represents a major force in the orientation of his life and work. The extent to which this interest was transmitted to others is, of course, open to speculation; but there can be no doubt that it was communicated significantly; and since Howells occupied a central position in American literary life for half a century, he no doubt played a vital part in fostering the cultural affinity which existed between the United States and Italy during his lifetime. If this tie binding the two countries again seems strong and enduring, having survived the tragedy of Fascism and the Italian debacle in the recent war, Howells's abiding friendship and affection for Italy may have been in some small measure responsible.

Bibliography

MANUSCRIPT SOURCES

Boston Public Library: Letters from Howells to J. R. Osgood, Kate Fields, and John Swinton.

Columbia University Library: Letters from Howells to M. D. Conway, E. C. Stedman, Brander Matthews, and J. R. Osgood.

Cornell University Library: Letters from Howells to Bayard Taylor.

Craigie House, Cambridge, Mass.: Letters from Howells to H. W. Longfellow.

Harvard University Library: The Howells Collection in the Houghton Library contains about three thousand manuscript letters written to Howells between 1855 and 1919 by American and English literary men, also notebooks, photographs, clippings, reviews, and other miscellaneous items. There are approximately five hundred available Howells letters to various correspondents in this collection and in other Harvard manuscript holdings.

Huntington Library, San Marino, California: Letters from Howells to James T. Fields, Mrs. Fields, C. W. Stoddard, C. E. Norton, S. Baxter, W. H. Rideing, and others.

National Archives, Washington, D. C.: Howells's consular correspondence with the State Department is contained in "Consular Dispatches, Venice," Vols. II and III. Among the appointment papers of the department there are seven letters from various correspondents recommending Howells for appointment as consul at Munich.

New York Public Library: Letters from Howells to R. H. Stoddard and M. D. Conway.

Ohio State Archaeological and Historical Society, Columbus,

Ohio: Letters from Howells to W. H. Smith, S. M. Smith, and J. M. Comly.

Historical Society of Pennsylvania, Philadelphia, Pa.: Letters from Howells to S. P. Chase and H. W. Longfellow.

Yale University Library: Letters from Howells to J. R. Osgood, E. P. Whipple, T. R. Lounsbury, W. L. Phelps, and others.

PRIMARY SOURCES

Books

The following list, which is arranged in chronological order, contains books written wholly or in part by Howells. Only first editions are given unless later issues included new material or substantial revisions. Items listed inside brackets I have been unable to locate.

Letter of the Secretary of State, Transmitting a Report on the Commercial Relations of the United States with Foreign Countries, for the Year Ended September 30, 1862. Washington, D. C., 1863. Pp. 376-380.

[Poem for Zeni-Foratti Nuptials. Padua, 1863.] See LinL, I, 76.

[Guide to Venice. Translated from German. Venice, 1863.] See VL (1907 ed.), p. 419; LinL, II, 136.

Letter of the Secretary of State, Transmitting a Report on the Commercial Relations of the United States with Foreign Countries, for the Year Ended September 30, 1863. Washington, D. C., 1865. Pp. 360-362.

Letter of the Secretary of State, Transmitting a Report on the Commercial Relations of the United States with Foreign Countries, for the Year Ended September 30, 1864. Washington, D. C., 1865. Pp. 462-467.

Venetian Life. London, 1866.

Venetian Life. New York, 1866.

Venetian Life. 2d ed.; New York, 1867.

Italian Journeys. New York, 1867.

No Love Lost, a Romance of Travel. New York, 1869.

Suburban Sketches. Boston, 1871.

The Unity of Italy: the American Celebration of the Unity of

Italy, at the Academy of Music, New York, Jan. 12, 1871, with the Addresses, Letters, and Comments of the Press. New York, 1871. P. 76.

Their Wedding Journey. Boston, 1872.

Italian Journeys. New and enlarged ed.; Boston, 1872.

Venetian Life. New and enlarged ed.; Boston, 1872.

A Chance Acquaintance. Boston, 1873.

A Foregone Conclusion. Boston, 1875.

Life of Vittorio Alfieri. Introduction by W. D. Howells. Boston, 1877. Pp. 5-51.

Memoirs of Carlo Goldoni. Translated by John Black. Ed. and with Introduction by W. D. Howells. Boston, 1877. Pp. 4-29.

The Lady of the Aroostook. Boston, 1879.

A Fearful Responsibility and Other Stories. Boston, 1881.

A Little Girl among the Old Masters. Introduction and comment by W. D. Howells. Boston, 1884.

The Rise of Silas Lapham. Boston, 1885.

Tuscan Cities. Boston, 1886.

Poems. Boston, 1886.

Indian Summer. Boston, 1886.

The Minister's Charge. Boston, 1887.

Modern Italian Poets. New York, 1887.

April Hopes. New York, 1888.

Annie Kilburn. New York, 1889.

D'Aste, Ippolito. *Samson.* Translated by W. D. Howells. New York, 1889.

A Hazard of New Fortunes. 2 vols. New York, 1890.

Verga, Giovanni. *The House by the Medlar-Tree.* Translated by M. A. Craig. Introduction by W. D. Howells. New York, 1890. Pp. iii-vii.

Criticism and Fiction. New York, 1891.

Venetian Life. 2 vols. Boston, 1892.

An Imperative Duty. New York, 1892.

The Quality of Mercy. New York, 1892.

A Little Swiss Sojourn. New York, 1892.

The World of Chance. New York, 1893.

The Coast of Bohemia. New York, 1893.
Tuscan Cities. Boston, 1894.
My Literary Passions. New York, 1895.
Impressions and Experiences. New York, 1896.
The Landlord at Lion's Head. New York, 1897.
Ragged Lady. New York, 1899.
Their Silver Wedding Journey. 2 vols. New York, 1899.
"The Mulberries in Pay's Garden," *The Hesperian Tree, a Souvenir of the Ohio Valley,* ed. John J. Piatt. Cincinnati, [1900]. Pp. 431-436.
Literary Friends and Acquaintance. New York, 1900.
Italian Journeys. Boston, 1901.
"Supplemental Books Recommended for This Course by William Dean Howells," *Florence in Art and Literature, Course X:* Booklovers Reading Club. Philadelphia, [1901]. Pp. 113-114.
The Kentons. New York, 1902.
Literature and Life. New York, 1902.
"Awaiting His Exequatur," *The Hesperian Tree, an Annual of the Ohio Valley,* ed. John J. Piatt. Columbus, 1903. Pp. 425-429.
The Son of Royal Langbrith. New York, 1904.
Between the Dark and the Daylight. New York, 1907.
Through the Eye of the Needle. New York, 1907.
Venetian Life. Boston, 1907.
The Mulberries in Pay's Garden. Cincinnati, [1907].
Roman Holidays and Others. New York, 1908.
Imaginary Interviews. New York, 1910.
Harper, J. Henry. *The House of Harper.* New York, 1912. Pp. 319-327.
Years of My Youth. New York, [1916].
The Vacation of the Kelwyns. New York, 1920.
Howells, Mildred (ed.). *Life in Letters of William Dean Howells.* 2 vols. Garden City, N. Y., 1928.
NOTE: The recently issued *William Dean Howells: Representative Selections,* with Introduction, Bibliography, and Notes by Clara Marburg Kirk and Rudolf Kirk ("American Writers

Series"; New York: American Book Co., 1950) is a useful
one-volume anthology with critical apparatus.

Articles

The Boston *Advertiser* letters listed below include only those
which were not reprinted in *Venetian Life* or which were reprinted but omitted significant material.

"Letters from Europe," Ashtabula *Sentinel*, Jan. 22, 1862, p. 1.
    First printed in the *Ohio State Journal*, Jan. 9, 1862, p. 2.
"Letters from Europe," Ashtabula *Sentinel*, Feb. 5, 1862, p. 1.
    First printed in the *Ohio State Journal*, Jan. 30, 1862, p. 1.
"Letters from Europe," Ashtabula *Sentinel*, Feb. 12, 1862, p. 1.
    First printed in the *Ohio State Journal*, Jan. 31, 1862, p. 1.
"Letter from Europe," Ashtabula *Sentinel*, May 14, 1862, p. 1.
"From Europe," Ashtabula *Sentinel*, July 30, 1862, p. 1.
"Louis Lebeau's Conversion," *Atlantic*, X (Nov., 1862), 534-538.
"Letters from Venice," Boston *Advertiser*, March 27, 1863, p. 2.
"By the Sea," *Commonwealth*, I (May 1, 1863), 1.
"The Revival of Mosaic Painting in Venice," Boston *Advertiser*,
    May 2, 1863, p. 2.
"From Venice to Florence and Back Again," Boston *Advertiser*,
    May 25, 1863, p. 2.
"Letters from Venice," Boston *Advertiser*, July 28, 1863, p. 2.
"Letters from Venice," Boston *Advertiser*, Sept. 11, 1863, p. 2.
"Letters from Venice," Boston *Advertiser*, Nov. 21, 1863, p. 2
"Letters from Venice," Boston *Advertiser*, Nov. 26, 1863, p. 2.
"St. Christopher," *Harper's Monthly*, XXVIII (Dec., 1863), 1-2.
"Letters from Venice," Boston *Advertiser*, Mar. 12, 1864, p. 2.
"Recent Italian Comedy," *North American Review*, XCIX
    (Oct., 1864), 364-401.
["The Faithful of the Gonzaga," New York *Ledger*, [winter-
    spring?], 1865.]
"The Road to Rome and Home Again," Boston *Advertiser*,
    Mar. 4, 1865, p. 2; Apr. 13, 1865, p. 1; May 3, 1865, p. 2.
    Reprinted in the Ashtabula *Sentinel*, Mar. 15, 1865, p. 1;
    May 3, 1865, p. 1; May 17, 1865, p. 1.

"Italian Brigandage," *North American Review*, CI (July, 1865). 162-189.

"Spanish-Italian Amity," New York *Times*, Sept. 23, 1865, p. 4.

"Proposed Purchase of Venetia," New York *Times*, Sept. 29, 1865, p. 4.

"Dante as Philosopher, Patriot, and Poet," *Round Table*, N. S., no. 4 (Sept. 30, 1865), pp. 51-52.

"A Day in Pompeii," *Nation*, I (Oct. 5, 1865), 430-432.

"A Visit to the Cimbri," *Nation*, I (Oct. 19, 1865), 495-497.

"Marriage among the Italian Priesthood," New York *Times*, Oct. 19, 1865, p. 4.

"Our Consuls in China and Elsewhere," *Nation*, I (Nov. 2, 1865), 551-552.

"A Pilgrimage to Petrarch's House at Arquà," *Nation*, I (Nov. 30, 1865), 685-688.

"Ducal Mantua," *North American Review*, CII (Jan., 1866), 48-100.

"A Little German Capital," *Nation*, II (Jan. 4, 1866), 11-13.

"Certain Things in Naples," *Nation*, II (Jan. 25, 1866), 108-110.

"Sweet Clover," *Harper's Monthly*, XXXII (Feb., 1866), 322.

"Men and Manners on the Way from Ferrara to Genoa," *Nation*, II (Feb. 15, 1866), 205-207.

"Massimo d'Azeglio," *Nation*, II (Feb. 15, 1866), 202-204.

"A Half-hour at Herculaneum," *Nation*, II (Apr. 5, 1866), 429-430.

"The Coming Translation of Dante," *Round Table*, III (May 19, 1866), 305-306.

"Capri and Capriotes," *Nation*, III (July 5, 12, 1866), 14-15, 33-34.

"Roman Pearls," *Nation*, III (Sept. 27, Nov. 29, Dec. 27, 1866), 253-254, 433-435, 523-525.

"Modern Italian Poets," *North American Review*, CIII (Oct., 1866), 313-345.

"Forza Maggiore," *Atlantic*, XIX (Feb., 1867), 220-227.

"A Glimpse of Genoa," *Atlantic*, XIX (Mar., 1867), 359-363.

"Modern Italian Poets," *North American Review*, CIV (Apr., 1867), 317-354.

"Henry Wadsworth Longfellow," *North American Review,* CIV (Apr., 1867), 531-540.

"Mr. Longfellow's Translation of the Divine Comedy," *Nation,* IV (June 20, 1867), 492-494.

"At Padua," *Atlantic,* XX (July, 1867), 25-32.

"Minor Italian Travels," *Atlantic,* XX (Sept., 1867), 337-348.

"Review of *The New Life of Dante Alighieri,* translated by C. E. Norton," *Atlantic,* XX (Nov., 1867), 638-639.

"Review of *The First Canticle of the Divine Comedy of Dante Alighieri,* translated by T. W. Parsons," *Atlantic,* XX (Dec., 1867), 759-761.

"Mrs. Johnson," *Atlantic,* XXI (Jan., 1868), 97-106.

"Reviews of Francesco Dall'Ongaro's *Stornelli italiani; Fantasie drammatiche e liriche;* and *Poesie,*" *North American Review,* CVI (Jan., 1868), 26-42.

"Tonelli's Marriage," *Atlantic,* XXII (July, 1868), 96-110.

"No Love Lost, a Romance of Travel," *Putnam's Magazine,* N. S., II (Dec., 1868), 641-651.

"Doorstep Acquaintance," *Atlantic,* XXIII (Apr., 1869), 484-493.

"A Year in a Venetian Palace," *Atlantic,* XXVII (Jan., 1871), 1-14.

"The Mulberries," *Atlantic,* XXVII (Mar., 1871), 377-379.

"Some Arcadian Shepherds," *Atlantic,* XXIX (Jan., 1872), 84-89.

"The Florentine Satirist, Giusti," *North American Review,* CXV (July, 1872), 31-47.

"Niccolini's Anti-Papal Tragedy," *North American Review,* CXV (Oct., 1872), 333-366.

"Alfieri," *Atlantic,* XXXV (May, 1875), 533-549.

"An Obsolete Fine Gentleman," *Atlantic,* XXXVI (July, 1875), 98-106.

"At the Sign of the Savage," *Atlantic,* XL (July, 1877), 36-48. (Reprinted in AFR, pp. 167-207.)

"Carlo Goldoni," *Atlantic,* XL (Nov., 1877), 601-613.

"Pordenone," *Harper's Monthly,* LXV (Nov., 1882), 829-835.

"The Laureate of Death," *Atlantic,* LVI (Sept., 1885), 311-322.

"Editor's Study," *Harper's Monthly,* LXXIII (July, 1886), 314-319. (Edward Harrigan compared with Goldoni.)

"Editor's Study," *Harper's Monthly*, LXXIII (Nov., 1886), 961-967. (Review of Verga's *I Malavoglia*.)

"Editor's Study," *Harper's Monthly*, LXXV (Nov., 1887), 962-967. (Review of M. A. Ward's *Dante, and His Life and Works*.)

"Editor's Study," *Harper's Monthly*, LXXVIII (May, 1889), 982-987. (Manzoni and Tolstoy compared.)

"Editor's Study," *Harper's Monthly*, LXXXI (Oct., 1890), 800-804. (Review of Verga's *The House by the Medlar-Tree*.)

"Editor's Study," *Harper's Monthly*, LXXXIV (Feb., 1892), 478-482. (Review of C. E. Norton's translation of the *Divine Comedy*.)

Boyesen, H. H., "Real Conversations—a Dialogue between William Dean Howells and Hjalmar Hjorth Boyesen," *Mc-Clure's*, I (June, 1893), 3-11.

"Roundabout to Boston," *Harper's Monthly*, XCI (Aug., 1895), 427-438.

"Life and Letters," *Harper's Weekly*, XL (Apr. 4, 1896), 318-319. (Review of Duse's performance in Goldoni's *Pamela*.)

"The White Mr. Longfellow," *Harper's Monthly*, XCIII (Aug., 1896), 327-343.

"Life and Letters," *Harper's Weekly*, XL (Oct. 3, 1896), 966. (Recollection of circus at Verona.)

"A Sleep and a Forgetting," *Harper's Weekly*, L, LI (Dec. 15, 22, 29, 1906, Jan. 5, 1907), 1781-1784, 1805, 1862-1865, 1899-1901, 24-27. (Reprinted in *Between the Dark and the Daylight*.)

"Address of William Dean Howells," *Cambridge Historical Society Publications*, II (Feb., 1907), 60-72.

"The Art of Longfellow," *North American Review*, CLXXXIV (Mar. 1, 1907), 472-485.

"The Turning Point of My Life," *Harper's Bazar*, XLIV (Mar., 1910), 165-166.

"Editor's Easy Chair," *Harper's Monthly*, CXXII (Dec., 1910), 149-151. (Sailing for Venice.)

"Editor's Easy Chair," *Harper's Monthly*, CXXVIII (Mar.,

1914), 634-637. (Review of H. C. Chatfield-Taylor's *Life of Goldoni.*)

"Editor's Easy Chair," *Harper's Monthly,* CXXXII (May, 1916), 958-961. (Review of A. Mordell's *Dante and Other Waning Classics.*)

"Overland to Venice," *Harper's Monthly,* CXXXVII (Nov., 1918), 837-845.

"An Old Venetian Friend," *Harper's Monthly,* CXXXVIII (Apr., 1919), 634-640.

"A Young Venetian Friend," *Harper's Monthly,* CXXXVIII (May, 1919), 827-833.

"A Memory of San Remo," *Harper's Monthly,* CXL (Feb., 1920), 321-327.

"Editor's Easy Chair," *Harper's Monthly,* CXL (Feb., 1920), 422-424. (San Remo sketch.)

Secondary Sources

Books

Aldrich, Mrs. T. B. [Lilian Woodman]. *Crowding Memories.* Boston, [1920].

Bates, Alfred. *The Drama.* Vol. V. London and New York, [1903].

Conway, Moncure D. *Autobiography, Memories and Experiences of Moncure D. Conway.* 2 vols. Boston, 1904.

Curtis, George W. (ed.). *The Correspondence of John Lothrop Motley.* 2 vols. New York, 1889.

De Robertis, Giuseppe (ed.). *Giacomo Leopardi opere.* 2 vols. Milan, [1937].

De Sanctis, Francesco. *The History of Italian Literature.* 2 vols. Translated by Joan Redfern. New York, [1931].

Firkins, Oscar W. *William Dean Howells: a Study.* Cambridge, Mass., 1924.

Fiske, Ethel F. (ed.). *The Letters of John Fiske.* New York, 1940.

Gibson, W. M., and George Arms. *A Bibliography of William Dean Howells.* New York, 1948.

Howe, M. A. DeW. (ed.). *New Letters of James Russell Lowell.* New York, 1932.

Johnson, Rossiter, and Dora K. Ranous (eds.). *An Anthology of Italian Authors from Cavalcanti to Fogazzaro.* [New York, 1907.] *(The Literature of Italy.* 16 unnumbered vols.)

La Piana, Angelina. *La Cultura americana e l'Italia.* Turin, 1938.

Longfellow, Samuel. *Life of Henry Wadsworth Longfellow.* 3 vols. Boston, 1899.

Lubbock, Percy (ed.). *The Letters of Henry James.* 2 vols. New York, 1920.

Merriam, G. S. *The Life and Times of Samuel Bowles.* 2 vols. New York, 1885.

Mildmay, Herbert, and Susan [Motley] St. John Mildmay (eds.). *John Lothrop Motley and His Family.* London, 1910.

Momigliano, Attilio. *Storia della letteratura italiana.* Milan, 1946.

Norton, Charles Eliot (ed.). *Letters of James Russell Lowell.* 2 vols. New York, [1893].

Norton, Sara, and M. A. DeW. Howe (eds.). *Letters of Charles Eliot Norton.* 2 vols. Boston, 1913.

Odell, G. C. D. *Annals of the New York Stage.* Vol. XIV. New York, 1945.

Ortolani, Giuseppi (ed.). *Tutte le opere di Carlo Goldoni.* Milan, [1935].

Parrington, Vernon L. *The Beginnings of Critical Realism in America.* New York, 1930.

Pattee, Fred L. *A History of American Literature since 1870.* New York, 1915.

Quinn, Arthur H. *A History of the American Drama: from the Civil War to the Present Day.* 2 vols. New York, 1927.

Spiller, Robert E., *et al.* (eds.). *Literary History of the United States.* 3 vols. New York, 1948.

Stedman, Laura, and George M. Gould (eds.). *Life and Letters of Edmund Clarence Stedman.* 2 vols. New York, 1910.

Stillman, W. J. *The Autobiography of a Journalist*. 2 vols. Boston, 1901.

Thayer, W. R. *The Life and Letters of John Hay*. 2 vols. Boston, [1915].

Van Schaick, J., Jr. *The Characters in Tales of a Wayside Inn*. Boston, 1939.

Articles

Anonymous, "Bene Arrivato, Salvini," New York *Herald,* Oct. 11, 1889, p. 10.

────── "Howells's *Italian Journeys,*" *Nation,* VI (Jan. 2, 1868), 11.

────── "Literary Notices," *Harper's Monthly,* XXXVI (May, 1868), 815. (Review of *Italian Journeys.*)

────── "Politics, Sociology, Voyages, Travels," *Westminster Review,* XXX (July, 1866), 236. (Review of *Venetian Life.*)

────── "Review of *Venetian Life,*" *Athenaeum,* no. 2014 (June 2, 1866), 734.

────── "Review of *Venetian Life,*" *Contemporary Review,* II (Aug., 1866), 594-595.

────── "Review of *Venetian Life,*" *Round Table,* IV (Sept. 8, 1866), 90.

────── "Salvini as Samson," *The Critic,* N. S., XII (Oct. 19, 1889), 191.

────── "Salvini at Palmer's Theater," New York *Tribune,* Oct. 11, 1889, p. 6.

────── "*Venetian Life*—from the *Spectator,*" *Littell's Living Age,* 4th Ser., II (Sept. 22, 1866), 758-761.

Booth, Bradford A., "Bret Harte Goes East: Some Unpublished Letters," *American Literature,* XIX (Jan., 1948), 318-335.

[Curtis, George W.], "Editor's Easy Chair," *Harper's Monthly,* XXXIII (Oct., 1866), 668. (Review of *Venetian Life.*)

[James, Henry], "Review of *Italian Journeys,*" *North American Review,* CVI (Jan., 1868), 336-339.

[James, Henry], "Review of *A Foregone Conclusion,*" *North American Review,* CXX (Jan., 1875), 207-214.

[Lowell, James R.], "Review of *Venetian Life,*" *North American Review,* CIII (Oct., 1866), 610-613.

[Norton, C. E.], *"Venetian Life,"* *Nation,* III (Sept. 6, 1866), 189.

Pennell, Joseph, "Adventures of an Illustrator—with Howells in Italy," *Century,* CIV (May, 1922), 135-141.

[Perry, T. S.], "William Dean Howells," *Century,* XXIII (Mar., 1882), 680-685.

Index

Agassiz, Louis, 104
Akers, Paul L., 103
Alabama, Confederate privateer, 171
Albany Depot, The, 144
Alden, H. M., 91, 191, 192
Aldrich, Mrs. T. B., 24
Aleardi, Aleardo, 116, 125, 125 n.
Alexandria, Egypt, 40 n., 76 '
Alfieri, Vittorio, 115, 126-127, 128;
   Saul, 127; *Oreste,* 127, 127 n.
Annie Kilburn, 187
Appleton, Thomas G., 105
April Hopes, 187
Aretino, Pietro, 90
Ariosto, Ludovico, 99 n.; *Orlando Furioso,* 99
Armenian Monastery, 25, 161
Arquà, 29, 32, 33, 33 n., 67, 99
Arrighi, Bartolomeo, *Mantova e sua provincia,* 95
Ashtabula *Sentinel,* 42; Howells's contributions to, 5, 6, 16, 38 n., 51, 67, 74-75, 80, 85
Asia (steamship), 49, 55
Athenæum, 57
Atlantic Monthly, Howells's rejections by, 27, 32, 33, 52, 79, 84 n., 86, 87, 159; assistant editorship of, 92; editorial duties on, 112, 123 n; resignation from, 168, 171; reminiscences of, 198; contributions to, 7 n., 22, 27, 59, 65, 67, 68, 68 n., 69, 78, 80, 81, 85, 126, 153, 154, 161, 163 n., 165 n., 175 n.
"At the Sign of the Savage," 7 n.
Austen, Jane, 135, 138
"Awaiting His Exequatur," 4, 6, 7 n., 13

Barozzi (Venetian scholar), 21
Bassano, 43, 67
Beckford, William, 58
Beecher, Henry Ward, 32

Belmont, Mass., 172
Berchet, Giovanni, 116
Bergamo, 173
Bermuda, 190, 192
Berni, Francesco, 99
Bliss, Elisha, 190
Boccaccio, Giovanni, 182
Boiardo, Matteo Maria, 99 n.
Bologna, 29, 44, 173
Bonner, Robert, 86, 86 n.
Borgia, Lucrezia, 152
Boston *Advertiser,* Howells's Venetian sketches offered, 33; unpublished Italian sketches, 68; contributions to, 13, 27, 28, 29, 31, 32, 34, 40, 45, 52, 67, 79, 101, 195
Boston *Pilot,* 157
Botta, Vicenzo, *Dante as Philosopher, Patriot and Poet,* 108
Boulogne, 6
Bowles, Benjamin, 25
Bowles, Samuel, 25, 25 n.
Boyesen, H. H., 8, 50, 133, 160
Bremen, 6 n.
Brescia, 173
Browning, Robert, 29, 85, 85 n., 167
Brunetta, Eugenio, 18-19, 106, 125 n., 148, 179, 180, 197
"By Horse-car to Boston," 12
Byron, Lord, 25 n., 62, 89
"By the Sea," 82

Calais, 175
Cambridge, Mass., 64, 92, 98, 153, 172
Campo San Bartolomeo, 15
Cantù, Cesare, 148
Capri, 44, 96
Carcano, Giulio, 116, 125, 125 n.
Carducci, Giosuè, 73
Carrer, Luigi, 116, 125, 125 n.
Casa Falier, 18 n., 26, 28, 30, 31, 34, 35, 38, 162, 179
Castle of Chillon, 175

Century Company, 173, 176
Century Magazine, 171, 180, 181, 181 n.,
    183, 191
Certain Delightful English Towns, 193
Chance Acquaintance, A, 153, 155,
    174 n.
Chase, Salmon P., 13 n., 52
Chatfield-Taylor, H. C., *Goldoni: a
    Biography,* 135 n., 142
Child, Francis, 61, 122, 123, 157
Chile, travelogue of, 50
Ciconi, Teobaldo, 93
Cimbrian mountaineers, 43
Cincinnati *Gazette,* 50
City of Glasgow (steamship), 3, 5, 78,
    167, 167 n., 197
Città Vecchia, 45
Clemens, S. L., 89, 130, 130 n., 135,
    168, 168 n., 173, 175, 192
Coast of Bohemia, The, 188
"Coming," 79
"The Coming Translation of Dante,"
    109
Comly, J. M., 87
Commedia dell'arte, 93, 136, 146, 147,
    147 n.
Commonwealth, 82
Contemporary Review, 57
Conway, M. D., 24 n., 28 n., 30, 33
    n., 35, 37 n., 79, 84, 85, 85 n.;
    visits Venice, 30-31; Howells's let-
    ters to, 52, 57 n., 82 n., 84 n.
Criticism and Fiction, 137-138, 142,
    148 n.
Curtis, George W., 58

Da Benvenuti, Marietta, 18 n.
Dall'Ongaro, Francesco, 76, 93, 94,
    95, 95 n., 116, 125; *Stornelli po-
    litici e non politici,* 116 n.
Dante Alighieri, 98, 99, 105; *Divina
    Commedia,* 84, 96, 100-104, 108-
    111, 158, 182; *Convito,* 109; *Vita
    Nuova,* 110
Dante Club, 102-105
Dante Society, 107-108
D'Aste, Ippolito, *Sansone,* 126, 129-131
Davidson, Lucretia Maria, 94, 94 n.
Dayly, John, 11 n.

D'Azeglio, Massimo, 97, 148; *Niccolò
    de' Lapi,* 148 n.
De Bauernfeind, Vincenzo, 11, 21,
    21 n.
De Sanctis, Francesco, 117, 117 n.,
    118, 119, 128, 128 n.
Dickens, Charles, 18, 141; *David Cop-
    perfield,* 5
"Disillusion," *see also No Love Lost,*
    35, 79, 83, 84, 87-89
Divina Commedia, see Dante Alighieri
Donizetti, Gaetano, *L'Elisir d'amore,*
    190
"Doorstep Acquaintance," 153 n.
Douglas, David, 66 n.
Dover, 175
"Drowsihed," 79 n.
"Ducal Mantua," 36 n., 39, 45, 85,
    95, 96, 101 n., 110 n., 173
Duse, Eleonora, 142 n.
Duveneck, Frank, 185 n.

Elba, Island of, 44
"Elegy on John Butler Howells," 38,
    38 n., 85
Elevator, The, 145
Eliot, Charles W., 122, 123, 123 n.
Evening Dress, 145, 146

"Faithful of the Gonzaga, The," 85-86
Fearful Responsibility, A, 4, 168-171
Ferrara, 29, 44, 67, 99, 173
Ferrari, Paolo, 93
Fields, James T., 68, 79, 87, 103, 104
Fields, Kate, 124
Fiesole, 185
Firkins, Oscar W., 132
Fiske, John, 73, 99
Florence, 29, 44, 100-101, 106, 176,
    177, 178, 181, 182, 183, 184, 185,
    187 n., 188
Florence in Art and Literature, 181 n.
Florida, 192
Flying Dutchman, 76, 77
Folkestone, 6
Follett and Foster, publishers, 50
Foratti, *see* Zeni-Foratti

Foregone Conclusion, A, 11, 12, 64, 97, 100, 152, 154-163, 184; debt to earlier novels, 155-156; identification of Don Ippolito, 157-160; publishing history of, 162; translations of, 162, 162 n.; dramatization of, 162, 162 n.

Fortnightly Review, 57 n.

Foscolo, Ugo, 116, 117, 118, 125

Foster, Frank, 31, 35, 48, 79, 83, 84 n., 87, 88

Fra Diavolo, 97

Frattini, Professor, 32, 82, 106

French Revolution, 98

"From Venice to Florence and Back Again," 29, 29 n., 67, 101

Fusinato, Arnaldo, 116

Garroters, The, 144, 146

Gaskell, Meta, 195

Genoa, 6, 44, 45, 67, 70, 74, 195, 196

German art, Howells's opinion of, 7

Germany, 6

Gibraltar, 195

Gilder, Richard W., 181

Giacometti, Paolo, 94, 94 n.

Giovanna, Howells's servant, 28-29

Giusti, Giuseppe, 116, 125

Godkin, E. L., 67

Goethe, Johann Wolfgang von, *Faust,* 98

Golden Cross Hotel, 5

Goldoni, Carlo, 18, 27, 63, 93, 127 n., 131-137; career, 131 n.; performance of plays, 134; birthplace and boyhood home of, 136; *Memoirs,* 127, 135, 136; *L'Uomo di mondo,* 131 n; *La Putta onorata,* 137 n., 144, 145, 146; *Pamela,* 142 n.; *Il Bugiardo,* 144, 164; *Un Curioso accidente,* 144; *Le Morbinose,* 144, 146; *Le Baruffe Chiozzote,* 145; *La Locandiera (The Mistress of the Inn),* 145; *Il Ventaglio,* 145; *L'Impressario delle Smirne,* 146

Goldonian theater, 93, 144

Gonzaga, House of, 96

Graham, James Lorrimer, 25

Gray, Thomas, 63; "Elegy Written in a Country Churchyard," 118

Greene, G. W., 104, 105, 157 n.

Grossetto, 45, 74

Grossi, Tommaso, 116, 125, 125 n., 148

Gualtieri, Luigi, 93

Guarini, Giambattista, 126, 126 n.; *Il Pastor Fido,* 99, 125

Guerrazzi, Francesco, 148-149

Haight, Gordon S., 132

Hale, Charles, 20, 27, 33, 34 n., 39, 39 n., 40, 53 n., 86, 159

Hale, Charles, & Co., 86

Hale, Edward Everett, 20, 86, 86 n.

Harland, Henry, 193

Harper, J. W., 183

Harper & Brothers, 197

Harper's Bazar, Howells's contributions to, 42, 188

Harper's Monthly, 72; Howells's unreported MSS, 48; "Editor's Study," 113, 137, 142 n., 149; "Editor's Easy Chair," 189, 193, 197; other contributions to, 5, 14, 18, 32, 41, 81, 83, 91, 175 n., 183

Harper's Weekly, Howells's contributions to, 36 n., 142 n., 189

Harrigan, Edward, 142 n.

Harte, Bret, 72

Harvard University, 112, 122, 124, 125

Hawthorne, Nathaniel, 29, 71

Hay, John, 157, 162, 168

Hayes, Rutherford B., 165, 180 n.

Hazard of New Fortunes, A, 187

Heine, Heinrich, 78, 79

Heinemann, William, 70

"Heroic History of Venice, A," 191

Hertz, C. L., 162 n.

Hildreth, Richard, 9, 11, 15-16; *Archie Moore,* 15

Hillard, George S., *Six Months in Italy,* 72

Holmes, O. W., 20, 104

Holmes, O. W., Jr., 4, 98

Hotel Danieli, 8

Houghton, *see* Hurd & Houghton

Houghton Mifflin, 64, 65, 70, 168
Howell, James, 183
Howells, Anne T., 83, 174
Howells, Aurelia H., 29, 192, 193
Howells, Edward, 43
Howells, Elinor Mead, proposal to,
  23; marriage of, 24-25; sketching
  of, 26, 32, 169; pregnancy of, 29;
  effect of Italian climate on, 47; at-
  tendance at Lowell lectures, 124;
  Howells's letters to, 87, 122-123
Howells, John Butler, 37-38
Howells, John M., 179, 193
Howells, Joseph A., 38, 42, 48, 55
Howells, Mary Dean (Mrs. William
  Cooper), 26, 29, 43, 69, 124
Howells, Mildred, annotation of Life
  in Letters, 18 n., 23, 24 n., 157,
  169; A Little Girl among the Old
  Masters, 177 n.
Howells, Samuel D., 42
Howells, Victoria M., Howells's letters to, 4, 6, 13, 17, 50 n., 51, 81,
  151
Howells, William Cooper, writes of
  family problems, 42; urges renewal
  of consulship, 43; tentatively plans
  to publish Venetian Life, 55; cor-
  rects "Louis Lebeau's Conversion,"
  81; receives Zeni-Foratti poem, 83;
  holds Toronto consulship, 174; Howells's letters to, 41, 62 n., 64 n., 95,
  135, 152 n., 154, 163 n., 176, 179
Howells, William Dean (books and
  articles listed separately), departs
  for Venice, 3; appointed consul, 3;
  writes biography of Lincoln, 3;
  on service in Civil War, 3-4, 170-
  171; reaches England, 4; visits London, 5; crosses France, 6; visits
  Stuttgart, 6; visits Austria, 7;
  reaches Venice, 8; duties as consul,
  10-12; learns Italian, 13; illnesses
  of, 14, 38, 171; visits Trieste, 15-
  16; observes Venetian society, 17-
  20; entertains Americans, 20; is
  married, 24-25, 82; translates
  guidebook, 27; visits Florence, 29;
  visits Arquà, 32-33; space rates in

Advertiser, 34 n.; visits Bassano,
  43; plans articles on Italian cities,
  43; visits Rome and Naples, 44-
  45; asks for leave, 46; visits Monselice, 47-48; plans postwar em-
  ployment, 48; receives leave of absence, 48; lands in Boston, 49; attends Dante Club, 102-105; joins
  Dante Society, 107-108; reviews Dante
  translations, 109-111; visits Goldoni's birthplace, 136; theory of
  realism, 138; writes plays, 142-147;
  visits Canada and Niagara Falls,
  153; criticizes Catholic church, 156-
  157; resigns from Atlantic, 168;
  goes abroad in 1882, 174-180; visits
  England, 174-175, 180; visits Switzerland, 175-176; winters in Florence, 176-178; revisits Venice, 178-
  180; proposes history of Venice,
  190-192; old-age travels, 192-194;
  receives honorary degree from Oxford, 193; revisits Rome, 194
Howells, Winifred, 18, 26, 34, 171,
  179
Hunt, Leigh, Autobiography, 98;
  Stories from the Italian Poets, 99
Hurd, M. M., 22 n., 54, 58 n., 60,
  64 n., 68-69, 72, 87, 88, 152
Hurd & Houghton, publishers, 55, 64,
  69 n.

Imaginary Interviews, 99 n., 149 n.,
  189
Imperative Duty, An, 187
Impressions and Experiences, 189
Indian Summer, 177, 181, 183-185,
  186, 188
Issaverdenz, Padre Giacomo, 25-26,
  157, 158, 161, 179
"Italian Brigandage," 45, 95, 96-97
Italian Journeys, 14, 22, 32, 33, 33 n.,
  36, 37, 43, 44, 56, 173; preparation for writing, 66; "A Day in
  Pompeii," 67; "The Ferrara Road,"
  67, 70; "From Venice to Florence
  and Back Again," 67; "The Road
  to Rome and Home Again," 67;
  "Forza Maggiore," 68, 74; "A

Glimpse of Genoa," 68; "Minor Italian Travels," 68; "At Padua," 68; picking title of, 68-69; "Capri and Capriotes," 68 n.; "Roman Pearls," 68 n.; publishing history of, 69-70; revisions of, 70-71; critical reception of, 71-73; critique of, 73-78; "Minor Travels," 74-78; compared with *Their Wedding Journey*, 153; quotes Padre Libera, 159; compared with *Roman Holidays*, 195-196

Italian language, 13, 13 n.

"Italian Poets of Our Century," 124

Jackson, Mrs. Jennie, 95 n.

James, Henry, 71, 74, 154, 155 n., 172, 174, 179, 180, 195; *Daisy Miller*, 165, 166, 169, 188; *The Ambassadors*, 184

Jewett, Sarah Orne, 163, 163 n.

Jonson, Ben, 144 n.

Kellog, Miner, 35

Kennedy, Walter, 131

Kentons, The, 187 n.

Kittery Point, Maine, 190

Lady of the Aroostook, The, 165-168; compared with *Venetian Life*, 166-167; publishing history of, 168, 168 n.

Landlord at Lion's Head, The, 187

Langley, Samuel P., 166

La Piana, Angelina, *La Cultura americana e l'Italia*, 137 n., 143, 164

Leghorn, 45, 68, 196

Leopardi, Giacomo, 115, 117, 118-122, 125; "All'Italia," 119; "Imatazione," 119 n.; "Sopra il ritratto di una bella donna," 120-121; "A Silvia," 121-122

"Letter from Europe," 16

Letter of the Secretary of State . . . 1862, 10-11

Letter of the Secretary of State . . . 1863, 10

Letter of the Secretary of State . . . 1864, 64-65

"Letters from Europe," 5, 6

"Letters from Venice," 13, 27, 31, 32, 34

Libera, Padre, 158-160

Lido di Venezia, 51

Likely Story, A, 144

Lincoln, Abraham, Howells's campaign biography of, 3, 24 n; assassination of, 47, 47 n.

Literature and Life, 36 n., 189

Literary Friends and Acquaintance, 11, 15, 16, 20, 22, 24 n., 41, 54, 79, 86, 102, 106

"Little German Capital, A," 7

"Little Swiss Sojourn, A," 175 n.

Liverpool, 5, 174

London, 5, 48, 49, 174, 175, 180

London Films, 193

Longfellow, Henry Wadsworth, 20, 32, 60, 78, 80, 92, 123, 157; meets Howells, 102; translates Dante, 103-104; dines with Howells, 105-106; works reviewed by Howells, 106-107, 109-110; first president of Dante Society, 107-108; Howells's address at Longfellow centennial, 104 n., 105 n., 107; asked permission to translate *Evangeline*, 106

"Louis Lebeau's Conversion," 27, 80, 85

Lounsbury, T. R., 184

Lowell, James Russell, 20, 41, 42, 45, 67-68, 78, 79, 86, 91, 92, 101 n., 102, 103, 112, 122, 124, 168, 177, 180, 180 n.; praises Venetian letters, 40; opinion of *Venetian Life*, 50; reviews *Venetian Life*, 58-60; writes Howells, 58 n., 95 n.; opinion of "Tonelli's Marriage," 164; Howells's letters to, 46, 53, 54, 123

Lowell, John Amory, 124

Lowell Institute, 112, 124, 125

Lucca, 173, 176, 181

Machiavelli, Niccolò, 182

Madeira, 195

Malibran Theater, 18, 134

Malmocco, 51

Mantua, 36 n., 37, 39, 95, 101

Manzoni, Alessandro, 115, 125, 125 n., 126, 127-128, 128 n., 129 n.; *I Promessi sposi*, 128, 149; "Il Cinque Maggio," 128; *Il Conte di Carmagnola*, 128; *Adelchi*, 128
Marbach, 7
Mark Twain, *see* Clemens, S. L.
"Marriage among the Italian Priesthood," 97, 156
Marseilles, 6
Mason, J. M., 3, 30
Masterpiece of Diplomacy, A, 145
Matthews, Brander, 127, 127 n.
Mead, Larkin G., 23
Mead, Larkin G., Jr., 18, 23, 25, 29, 44, 49 n., 62 n., 105, 106
Mead, Mary, 29, 34-35, 44, 49, 169
Mead, William Rutherford, 174
Medici, Lorenzo de', 182
Mercantini, Luigi, 116
Messadaglia, Angelo, 27, 32, 106
Milan, 22
Milton, John, 98; *Paradise Lost*, 16, 111
Minister's Charge, The, 11 n., 187 n.
Miramare, 16
Modena, 36 n., 37, 39, 173
Modern Instance, A, 168, 171
"Modern Italian Poetry and Comedy," 124
Modern Italian Poets, 112-122, 125, 126, 186
"Modern Italian Poets," 125 n.
Molière, 136, 144 n.
Monnier, Marc, 149 n.
Monselice, 14, 15, 47, 179
Monti, Luigi, 107, 107 n., 116, 117, 125
Mordell, Albert, *Dante and Other Waning Classics*, 111
Motley, J. L., 12 n., 20-21, 43, 46, 47
Mouse Trap, The, 144
"Mrs. Johnson," 153
"Mulberries, The," 90
"Mulberries in Pay's Garden, The," 90
Munich, 4 n., 7, 46, 49
Mutinelli (Venetian historian), 63

My Literary Passions, 113, 137, 139-140
"My Priest, the Inventor," 159

Naples, 44, 67, 70, 74, 97, 195-196
Nation, 58, 58 n., 71; Howells's contributions to, 7, 10, 33, 67, 68, 68 n., 97, 110
Neal, David D., 46, 49
"New Italian Literature," 123
New York *Ledger*, 86
New York *Sun*, 194
New York *Times*, 34 n., 97, 156
Niagara Falls, 153
"Niagara Revisited," 175
Niccolini, Giambattista, 115, 125, 126; *Arnaldo da Brescia*, 129
No Love Lost, see "Disillusion," 31, 31 n., 88
North American Review, 71; Howells's contributions to, 36 n., 37, 40, 45, 59, 69, 91, 95, 96, 112, 116 n., 117, 122, 125 n., 128 n., 136, 152
Norton, Charles Eliot, 40, 58, 92, 95 n., 102, 103, 110-111, 195; Howells's letters to, 152 n., 155-156, 194
Nourse, Miss (Cincinnati teacher), 24 n.

Ohio State Journal, 98; Howells's contributions to, 5, 6, 50, 51, 197
"Old Venetian Friend, An," 14, 47, 197
Ombrone River, 45, 74
"Ordeals," 84
O'Reilly, John Boyle, 157
Osgood, James R., 64, 65, 69, 154, 171, 173, 173 n., 174, 175 n., 179 n.
"Our Consuls in China and Elsewhere," 10
"Overland to Venice," 5, 7 n., 167 n., 197
Owen, Robert Dale, 157

Padua, 29, 39, 70, 106, 173
Padua, University of, 82
Palazzo Giustiniani, 38, 162, 167
Pall Mall Gazette, 57 n.

Palmer's Theater, 130
Parini, Giuseppe, 115, 116
Paris, 6, 24-25
Parisian (steamship), 174, 180
Parma, 37, 39, 67, 173
Parrington, Vernon L., 132
Parsons, T. W., translation of the *In-ferno,* 110 n.
Pattee, Fred Lewis, 132
Pedrocchi's Café, 32, 48
Pellico, Silvio, 116, 125, 125 n.
Pennell, Joseph, 185 n.
Perissenotti, Signorina (Howells's Ve-netian friend), 19-20
Perry, Bliss, 104 n.
Perry, Thomas Sergeant, 9 n., 178, 193
Petrarch, Francesco, 29, 32, 67, 99
Phelps, William Lyon, 183
Piatt, J. J., 4, 7 n., 13
"Pilgrimage to Petrarch's House at Arquà," 33
"Pilot's Story, The," 78, 80, 85, 86
Pisa, 45, 173, 176, 181, 196
Platt, Laura, 23
Po River, 70
Poe, Edgar Allan, "MS Found in a Bottle," 76, 77
Pole, William, 162 n.
Pompeii, 44, 68, 73, 195
Ponte Vecchio, 108, 183, 185
Pope, Charles R., 130, 130 n.
"Pordenone," 90-91
Possagno, 43, 43 n., 67, 159
Prati, Giovanni, 116, 125
"Proposed Purchase of Venetia, The," 97
Przemysl (Countess Capograssi), 35, 35 n.
Pulci, Luigi, 99, 99 n.; *Il Morgante,* 99
Putnam, G. P., 87, 88
Putnam's Magazine, 88 n.

Quality of Mercy, The, 187
Quebec City, 153, 174, 174 n.

Ragged Lady, 188-189
Raymond, Dr. John, 32

"Recent Italian Comedy," 37, 41, 79, 91-95, 136, 140-142
"Revival of Mosaic Painting in Ven-ice," 28
Richardson, Samuel, 141
Rise of Silas Lapham, The, 177, 183, 187 n.
Rockaway Beach, L. I., 190
Rome, 44, 68, 70, 187 n., 190, 192, 194, 195, 196
Roman Holidays and Others, 194, 195-196
Round Table, 60 n., 64 n., 109
"Roundabout to Boston," 41
Ruskin, John, 52, 63

Saguenay River, 153
"St. Christopher," 32, 83
St. Lawrence River, 174, 174 n.
St. Louis, Mo., 130
St. Mark's Library, 39, 96
Salviati, Antonio, 28
Salvini, Tommaso, 106, 129, 130, 131
Samson, see Sansone
San Lazzaro, 25, 157, 161
San Remo, 192, 193
Sansone, 126, 129-131
Sansovino, Jacopo, 90
Santa Maria Novella, Church of, 185
Savonarola, Girolamo, 183, 185
"Sawdust in the Arena," 36 n.
Scarbro, Elizabetta (Bettina), 34
Schiller, Johann C. F. von, 7
Scott, Sir Walter, 148, 148 n.
Scribner's Magazine, 168
Seward, F. W., 11 n., 13, 44 n., 46, 49
Seward, W. H., 47 n.
Shakespeare, William, 135, 144 n.
Shelley, Mary, 183
Siena, 173, 176, 181
"Sleep and a Forgetting, A," 193
Sleeping Car, The, 144
Smith, Roswell, 176, 191
Smith, S. M., 6 n.
Son of Royal Langbrith, The, 187 n.
Sordello, 96
Southey, Robert, 94 n.

"Spanish-Italian Amity," 97
Spectator, 58
Sprenger, J. J., 12
Stedman, E. C., 30, 31, 81, 84, 100, 102, 154, 155, 167
Stillman, W. J., 9, 10
"Stopping at Vicenza, Verona and Parma," 36
Storey, W. W., 167
Stuttgart, 6, 7
Suburban Sketches, 63, 153, 153 n.
"Sweet Clover," 81
Swinton, John, 33 n., 52 n.
Switzerland, 175-176, 177

Tasso, Torquato, 99 n., 125, 126; *Aminta*, 99
Tauchnitz editions, 66 n., 162, 168, 168 n.
Taylor, Bayard, 60-61, 62 n.
Teatro Apollo, 134
"Thanatopsis," 118
Their Silver Wedding Journey, 187
Their Wedding Journey, 153, 155, 175 n.
Through the Eye of the Needle, 147 n., 187 n.
Tiber River, 196
Ticknor & Fields, publishers, 56, 106
Ticknor, H. M., 7 n., 33, 81
Tintoretto, 90
Titian, 90
Tolstoy, Leo, 149
"Tonelli's Marriage," 19, 19 n., 83, 152, 163-165; compared with *Venetian Life*, 164
Torcello, 28
Tortorini, G. A., 14-15, 47, 179, 197
Trento, 173
Trieste, 11, 11 n., 15-16, 67, 74-78
Trollope, Anthony, 48
Trübner & Co., 25, 44, 47, 48, 54, 56, 57, 66 n., 85
Tubbs, Captain, 167, 167 n.
"Turning Point of My Life, The", 42, 88, 112
Tuscan Cities, 96, 101, 173-176, 177, 184, 186; plans for writing, 173, 173 n.; begins writing, 179; criti-

cism of, 180-183; reason for writing, 180-181; plan of work, 182; sources, 182-183; compared with *Venetian Life*, 181; compared with *Indian Summer*, 185

Unexpected Guests, The, 145, 146
Union College, 122
Unity of Italy, The, 199 n.

Vacation of the Kelwyns, The, 187 n.
Valentine, Edward, 26
Vasari, Giorgio, 182
Venetian Institute of Sciences, Letters, and Arts, 13, 27
Venetian Life, 20, 25, 26 n., 27, 29, 34, 39, 195; mosaic painting, 28; winter in Venice, 35; plans and arrangements for publishing, 44, 47, 48, 53, 54, 55; copies in print, 50; critical reception of, 50, 55, 56-61; earliest published part of, 51; plans for writing, 51, 52; "Some Islands of the Lagoons," 51; serial publication, 52, 53, 53 n.; rejected sketches, 52; "Churches and Pictures," 53-54, 91; "A Daybreak Ramble," 54; royalties on, 55-56, 56 n.; first English edition, 55-56; first American edition, 56; reprintings, 56 n.; second edition, 56; critique of, 61-63; Italian reception of, 62 n.; sources for, 63, 136-137; as preparation for novels, 63-64; publishing history of, 64-66, 66 n., 87; "Author to the Reader," 65; "Our Last Year in Venice," 65; "Venice Revisited," 65; "A Year in a Venetian Palace," 65, 158, 172 n.; revision of, 65 n.; compared with *Suburban Sketches*, 153; "Tonelli's Marriage," 163, 164; *The Lady of the Aroostook*, 166-167; "Venetian Dinners and Diners," 164
Venice, Howells's residence in, 3-49; as port, 11; Austrian occupation of, 19; Howells's sketches of, 50-66; poems about, 78-91; novels laid in, 151-171, 188-189; revisit to, 178-

180; proposed history of, 190-192; memoirs of, 196-198

Verga, Giovanni, *I Malavoglia (The House by the Medlar-Tree),* 149-150

Verona, 19, 36, 36 n., 39, 67, 173, 179, 180, 190

Vicenza, 36, 67, 173

Victor Emmanuel II, 29

Victor Emmanuel III, 194

Vienna, 7, 46

Vieusseux's Circulating Library, 185

Villari, Pasquale, *Life of Savonarola,* 183, 185

Volta, *Storia di Mantova,* 85

Ward, M. A., *Dante, and His Life and Works,* 109

Warner, Charles Dudley, 73, 190, 191

Wells, Thomas B., 197, 197 n., 198

Westminster Review, 57

Whipple, E. P., 64 n.

Winsor, Justin, 60 n.

Woman's Reason, A, 175

World of Chance, The, 187

Württemberg, 7

"Years of My Middle Life," 198

Years of My Youth, 24 n.

"Young Venetian Friend, A," 18, 18 n., 19, 197

Zeni-Foratti nuptials, poem for, 82-83, 163